M000272001

Troubleshooting SQL Server
A Guide for the Accidental DBA

By Jonathan Kehayias and Ted Krueger

First published by Simple Talk Publishing September 2011

Copyright Jonathan Kehayias and Ted Krueger 2011

ISBN 978-1-906434-78-6

The right of Jonathan Kehayias and Ted Krueger to be identified as the authors of this work has been asserted by them in accordance with the Copyright, Designs and Patents Act 1988.

All rights reserved. No part of this publication may be reproduced, stored or introduced into a retrieval system, or transmitted, in any form, or by any means (electronic, mechanical, photocopying, recording or otherwise) without the prior written consent of the publisher. Any person who does any unauthorized act in relation to this publication may be liable to criminal prosecution and civil claims for damages.

This book is sold subject to the condition that it shall not, by way of trade or otherwise, be lent, re-sold, hired out, or otherwise circulated without the publisher's prior consent in any form other than which it is published and without a similar condition including this condition being imposed on the subsequent publisher.

Edited by Tony Davis

Technical Review and Additional Material: Gail Shaw

Cover Image by Andy Martin

Typeset & Designed by Matthew Tye & Gower Associates

Table of Contents

Introduction **15**

Who is this book for? 16

Code Examples 17

Chapter 1: A Performance Troubleshooting Methodology..........**19**

Defining a Troubleshooting Methodology..................................20

Wait Statistics: the Basis for Troubleshooting 23

Virtual File Statistics 28

Performance Counters 30

Plan Cache Usage 38

Summary..40

Chapter 2: Disk I/O Configuration..**41**

Disk Configuration: Basic Considerations................................42

Disk size vs. disk throughput 43

Random versus sequential I/O 44

Choosing the Right RAID Level 45

A brief overview of RAID configurations 47

Disk size and throughput considerations 53

Workload considerations 56

Direct Attached Storage vs. Storage Area Networks..............60

Direct Attached Storage 60

Storage Area Networks 61

Diagnosing Disk I/O Issues 64

Common Disk I/O Problems...64

Sizing for capacity instead of I/O performance 65

Incorrect workload isolation 66

Incorrect partition alignment 67

Incorrect bandwidth using SAN configurations 69

Summary..70

Chapter 3: High CPU Utilization 73

Investigating CPU Pressure 74
  Performance Monitor 74
  SQL Trace 76
  Dynamic Management Views 77
Common Causes of High CPU Usage 85
  Missing indexes 86
  Outdated statistics 88
  Non-SARGable predicates..89
  Implicit conversions..93
  Parameter sniffing 95
  Ad hoc non-parameterized queries...103
  Inappropriate parallelism...108
  TokenAndPermUserStore 117
  Windows Server and BIOS power saving options.....................120
Summary...122
Additional Resources 122

Chapter 4: Memory Management..................................... 127

The Self-Tuning Database Engine 128
How SQL Server Allocates Memory...128
  32-bit Virtual Address Space limitations....................................132
  Using 64-bit SQL Server 141
  Memory configuration options with 64-bit SQL Server 144
Diagnosing Memory Pressure 150
  Memory-related counters 151
  Memory-related DMVs...155
Common Memory-Related Problems 156
  The SQL Server memory leak myth..156
  Paging problems 156
  OS instability due to Lock Pages in Memory plus unlimited max server memory 157
  App Domain is marked for unload due to memory pressure 158
  Error 701 and FAILED_VIRTUAL_RESERVE 159

Over-provisioned virtual machines...160

Memory settings for multiple instances...161

Summary...162

Chapter 5: Missing Indexes 165

Index Selection and Design 166

Index key column order 167

Use of included columns..171

Index width 174

Identifying Missing Indexes 174

Workload analysis with the Database Engine Tuning Advisor 175

Missing index feature 182

Missing indexes on foreign keys 190

Identifying Unused Indexes...191

Identifying Duplicate Indexes 193

Summary...194

Chapter 6: Blocking 195

Locks and Concurrency (a Brief Review)...196

Lock modes 196

Lock types..198

Lock escalation 199

Concurrency and the transaction isolation levels 200

Latches and latch contention...205

Monitoring Blocking...206

Using sysprocesses (SQL Server 2000 and later) 207

Cumulative wait statistics with DBCC SQLPERF (waitstats)..........................210

Dynamic Management Views 210

Performance Monitor 218

Automated Detection and Notification of Blocking 219

The sp_blocker_pss80 process..220

SQL Trace 220

Event notifications 225

Extended Events 228

Resolving Blocking 230
    Bad database design 231
    Inappropriate isolation level 231
    Poorly written queries 232
    Missing indexes 233
    Poor application design 233
    Outdated hardware 234
Hints, Trace Flags and Other Last Resorts 235
    Locking hints 235
Summary 238

Chapter 7: Handling Deadlocks 239

The Lock Monitor 240
Capturing Deadlock Graphs 240
    Trace Flag 1204 241
    Trace Flag 1222 243
    SQL Profiler XML Deadlock Graph event 243
    Service Broker event notifications 245
    WMI Provider for server events 247
    Extended Events 248
Reading Deadlock Graphs 251
    Interpreting Trace Flag 1204 deadlock graphs 251
    Interpreting Trace Flag 1222 deadlock graphs 256
    Interpreting XML deadlock graphs 259
Common types of deadlock and how to eliminate them 261
    Bookmark lookup deadlock.. 262
    Range scans caused by SERIALIZABLE isolation 264
    Cascading constraint deadlocks 266
    Intra-query parallelism deadlocks 267
    Accessing objects in different orders 268
Handling Deadlocks to Prevent Errors 269
    T-SQL TRY...CATCH blocks 270
    Handling ADO.NET SqlExceptions in .NET code 272

Controlling Deadlock Behavior with Deadlock Priority...................273

Summary...................274

Chapter 8: Large or Full Transaction Log 275

How the Transaction Log Works...................276

    How SQL Server writes to the transaction log 278

    Understanding log truncation 279

    Sizing and growing the log 280

Diagnosing a Runaway Transaction Log...................282

    Excessive logging: index maintenance operations 283

    Lack of log space reuse 287

    Other possible causes of log growth 297

Handling a "Transaction Log Full" Error...................301

Mismanagement or What Not To Do 304

    Detach database, delete log file...................304

    Forcing log file truncation 305

    Scheduled shrinking of the transaction log...................306

Proper Log Management 307

Summary...................309

Chapter 9: Truncated Tables, Dropped Objects and Other Accidents Waiting to Happen 311

Example Case: The Missing Sales Order Data...................312

Recovering Lost Data...................313

    Recovering from backup 313

    Recovering without a backup 323

Finding the Culprit 327

Prevention is Better than Cure 329

    Plan for recovery from all data losses...................330

    Implement a change control process...................332

    Implement an appropriate security model 333

    Access control measures 334

Summary...................341

Appendix: What to Do When All Else Fails........................343

Microsoft Customer Support Services......................................343

Online Resources 345

    Articles 346

    Blogs 346

    Forums 347

Hiring a Consultant 349

About the Authors

Jonathan Kehayias

Jonathan is currently employed as a Principal Consultant and Trainer for SQLskills, one of the best-known and most respected SQL Server training and consulting companies in the world. Jonathan is a SQL Server MVP and one of the few Microsoft Certified Masters for SQL Server 2008, outside of Microsoft. Jonathan frequently blogs about SQL Server, presents sessions at PASS Summit, SQLBits, SQL Connections and local SQL Saturday events, and has remained a top answerer of questions on the MSDN SQL Server Database Engine forum since 2007.

Jonathan is a performance tuning expert for both SQL Server and hardware, and has architected complex systems as a developer, business analyst, and DBA. He also has extensive development (T-SQL, C#, and ASP.Net), hardware and virtualization design expertise, Windows expertise, Active Directory experience, and IIS administration experience.

Outside of SQL Server, Jonathan is also a Drill Sergeant in the US Army Reserves and is married with two young children. On most nights he can be found at the playground, in a swimming pool, or at the beach with his kids.

Jonathan can be found online as **@SQLPoolBoy** on Twitter, or through his blog at HTTP://SQLSKILLS.COM/BLOGS/JONATHAN.

Ted Krueger

Ted is a Senior SQL Server consultant for a respected Microsoft Partner company. He is an MVP, author, blogger, speaker, volunteer, and mentor. Working with SQL Server for over a decade, Ted's areas of expertise are SSIS, high-availability, mirroring, and replication, as well as embracing all the other features that come along with this powerful database server. He works tirelessly to educate and help others in the community. He is a co-founder of the technical community at HTTP://LESSTHANDOT.COM. Ted can also be found answering forum questions, working as a PASS regional mentor, answering questions on Twitter, and fishing and golfing in his spare time.

Ted can be found online as **@onpnt** on Twitter, or through his blog at HTTP://BLOGS.LESSTHANDOT.COM.

Ted contributed Chapters 3 and 6 to this book.

About the Technical Reviewer

Gail Shaw

Gail is a Senior Consultant with Xpertease, based in Johannesburg, South Africa. She specializes in database performance tuning and database recovery, with a particular focus on topics such as indexing strategies, execution plans, and writing T-SQL code that performs well and scales gracefully.

Gail is a SQL Server MVP, and a frequent poster on both the SQL Server Central and SQLTeam forums. She writes articles for SQLServerCentral and Simple-Talk and blogs on all things relating to database performance on her blog at HTTP://SQLINTHEWILD.CO.ZA. She has spoken at TechEd Africa, several of the 24 Hours of PASS web events and, on multiple occasions, at the PASS Community summit. At the Pass Community Summit in 2009, her presentation on statistics was ranked 7th overall, for the event.

Gail is an Aikido Shodan (1st degree black belt) and an avid archer. In her copious spare time she is pursuing a Master's degree in Computer Science at the University of South Africa.

Gail also contributed additional material throughout the book, and particularly to Chapters 3, 5, and 6.

Acknowledgements

Jonathan Kehayias

Getting this book to print required more than just putting thoughts down as text, and a number of people contributed to it along the way. First and foremost, I'd like to acknowledge my wife, Sarah, and kids, Charlotte and Michael, and their ability and willingness to put up with the late hours I spent at night, locked in our home office, as well as the weekends spent sitting at my laptop when there were so many other things we could have been doing. Over the last year, even more than normal, Sarah spent many nights wondering if I was actually going to make it to bed or not, and provided distractions for Michael and Charlotte on a number of weekends, especially during the last few weeks before going to print. Without their support, I never would have made it through the first drafts let alone the repeated edits, as we worked towards final completion of the book.

Running a close second would be the technical editors associated with this book. The technical editor, Gail Shaw, contributed many ideas and topics to the book, as well as adding examples and text to enhance the content of many of the chapters. I knew, at the start of the book, that I wanted a leading member of the SQL Server forums as my technical editor, and though we primarily answer questions on different sites, Gail was at the top of a very short list of potential candidates. How Gail was able to find time to assist with this book defies understanding, but for her efforts I am forever indebted.

The chief editor of the book, Tony Davis, has to be one of the most patient people I have ever met. Through all the edits, delays, and then the final sprint to the end, Tony worked tirelessly to keep the book focused and progressing towards being printed. This book is as much their work as it is the authors'.

A final thank you goes to my friend, Amit Banerjee, a member of the Escalation Team in Microsoft Customer Support Services for SQL Server in Bangalore, India, who graciously reviewed Chapter 4 of the book for technical errors in the information on memory internals.

Additional recognition goes out to all of the mentors I've had over the years, the list of which is incredibly long. Without the commitment of SQL Server MVPs like Arnie Rowland, Paul Randal, Aaron Bertrand, Louis Davidson, Geoff Hiten, and countless others, I would never have remained committed to answering questions on the forums.

Ted Krueger

Being a contributor to this book was a great honor for me and I would not have been able to do it without the support of my loving wife, Michelle, and the patience and silliness of my sons, Ethan and Cameron. Family makes everything in a person, and the strength provided by my family was my motivating force throughout.

Special thanks to the technical reviewer, Gail Shaw, whose tireless efforts and knowledge helped make this the book it is. Thanks also to Jonathan Kehayias for his confidence and mentorship in allowing me to author Chapters 3 and 6. In all the years I've been working with SQL Server, no other person has taught and helped me more than Jonathan. He puts more time and energy into helping the community and understanding SQL Server, than any other person I've worked with, and does so in an unselfish manner.

Lastly, I'd like to thank the SQL Server Community for sharing their time and knowledge. I've been part of other development and engineering communities, but none could match the scale and energy of knowledge exchange that takes place every day in the SQL Server Community, via forums, articles, blogs and Twitter. I owe much of what I know to these people: Replication from Kendal Van Dyke, Execution Plans from Grant Fritchey, SQL Server Internals from Paul Randal, and many more.

Without their hard work, figuring out how to tame this complex database system would be a far more difficult task. I've tried my best, in turn, to share what I know with the community.

Introduction

I've spent much of the last six years of my working life trying to help people solve SQL Server-related performance problems, either hands-on, at client sites in my capacity as a consultant, or on various online community forums, answering people's questions.

Over that time I've been exposed to a few weird and wonderful SQL Server issues but, mainly, have seen the same problems, and the same confusions, crop up time and again. It was only a matter of time before I leapt to the foolhardy conclusion that I ought to write a book to explain what the most common problems were, why they occurred, and to offer sensible, practical solutions, aimed squarely at removing the root cause of the issue, rather than simply "papering over the cracks."

It turned out to be a much more daunting task than I imagined, for a number of reasons. Firstly, this is, by its very nature, a fairly broad-ranging book, covering topics stretching from CPU issues, to memory management, to missing indexes, and full transaction logs. Secondly, it is amazing how complex some of the simplest topics become when you try to put them down in text. Thirdly, technology changes rapidly, and the troubleshooter, and the advice he or she offers, must adapt accordingly. There were several cases in the writing of this book, where either a technology change meant I had to go back and adapt my original advice, or where my own opinion of the content and troubleshooting methodologies had evolved to the point where certain sections had to be completely rewritten.

Despite the occasionally bumpy road, what I hope I've achieved is a book that covers clearly and concisely the most common problems associated with the currently supported versions of SQL Server, namely SQL Server 2005, 2008, and 2008 R2. The first chapter explains my basic approach to performance troubleshooting, and the tools I use. It stresses, in particular, how rare it is that a problem can be diagnosed by looking at just a single data point.

The art of taming an unruly SQL Server is the art of gathering the various pieces of information that you need, and then assembling the "puzzle" so that you have a complete picture of what is going on inside of a server, and a true understanding of the real root cause of the problem.

The following eight chapters cover the areas in which I see problems arising with alarming regularity: disk I/O, high CPU, memory mismanagement, missing indexes, blocking and deadlocking, full transaction logs, and accidentally lost data.

In each case, I describe the most common problems, why they occur, how they can be diagnosed, using tools such as the Performance Monitor counters, Dynamic Management Views, server-side tracing, and so on, and how to fix them.

By applying the basic steps that I use daily to troubleshoot these performance problems, I hope that you, too, can begin to solve the performance problems in your environment, faster and more accurately.

Who is this book for?

The primary audience for this book is anyone who has found themselves in charge of SQL Server "by accident;" in other words, the accidental/involuntary DBAs and system administrators who have had guardianship of SQL Server databases added to their roles, because there is a SQL Server in their environment, and someone has got to look after it.

However, the troubleshooting concepts and methodologies covered in this book can be applied by anyone, including seasoned database administrators, to identify and resolve common problems and learn new tricks for managing and maintaining SQL Server. Anyone who has ever posted questions on one of the community forums will probably learn something new from this book.

Code Examples

Throughout this book are scripts demonstrating various ways to gather diagnostic data, and there are a few places where presentation of the full code was deferred, due to space restrictions. All the code you need to try out the examples in this book can be obtained from the following URL:

HTTP://WWW.SIMPLE-TALK.COM/REDGATEBOOKS/JONATHANKEHAYIAS/TROUBLESHOOTING-SQLSERVER_CODE.ZIP

All examples should run on all versions of SQL Server from SQL Server 2005 upwards, unless specified otherwise.

Chapter 1: A Performance Troubleshooting Methodology

Knowing where to start is the toughest part of solving a problem. As a Senior Database Administrator, I prided myself on being able to pinpoint the root cause of problems in my servers, and quickly restore services to normal working order. The ability to do this is partly down to a sound knowledge of your SQL Server environment, partly to having the right tools and scripts, and partly to what you learn to look out for, based on hard-earned lessons of the past.

Nailing down a specific methodology for troubleshooting problems with SQL Server is hard because, of course, the exact route taken to solve the problem will depend on the specific nature of the problem and the environment. One of the keys to accurate trouble-shooting is not only collecting and examining all of the relevant pieces of information, but also working out what they are telling you, collectively. There is a famous old proverb, recorded in John Heywood's *Dialogue Containing the Number in Effect of All the Proverbs in the English Tongue*, that sums this up very well: *I see, yet I cannot see the wood for the trees.*

If you collect and examine individually five separate pieces of performance data, it's possible that each could send you down a separate path. Viewed as a group, they will likely lead you down the sixth, and correct, path to resolving the issue. If there is one take-away from this chapter, as well as this book, it should be that focusing on a single piece of information alone can often lead to an incorrect diagnosis of a problem.

What I attempt to offer in this chapter is not a set of stone tablets, prescribing the exact steps to take to resolve all SQL Server problems, but rather a basic approach and set of tools that have served me well time and again in the six years I've spent working with SQL Server, troubleshooting performance problems. It covers a high-level description of my basic approach, followed by more detailed sections on each of my areas of focus, including wait statistics, virtual file statistics, SQL Server-related performance counters, and plan cache analysis.

Defining a Troubleshooting Methodology

As I noted in the introduction to this chapter, defining a troubleshooting methodology is hard, because the actual methodology that I apply depends entirely on the specific problem that I am trying to troubleshoot for a specific environment. However, my basic approach, and the tools I use, remain constant, regardless of whether the problem is users complaining of slow performance, or if I am just performing a standard server health check.

When I am examining a server for the first time, I need to establish a picture of its general health, and there are a number of items on which I'll focus in order to obtain this picture. For each piece of information I collect, I'll be examining it in relation to the previous data points, in order to validate or disprove any previous indicators as to the nature of the problem.

Fairly early on in any analysis, I'll take a look at the wait statistics, in the `sys.dm_os_wait_stats` Dynamic Management View (DMV), to identify any major resource waits in the system, at the operating system level. Let's say I identify very high `PAGEIOLATCH_SH` waits, which indicates that sessions are experiencing delays in obtaining a latch for a buffer page. This happens when lots of sessions, or maybe one session in particular, are requesting a lot of data pages that are not available in the buffer pool (and so physical I/O is needed to retrieve them). SQL Server must allocate a buffer page for each one, and place a latch on that page while it's retrieved from disk. The bottleneck here is disk I/O; the disk subsystem simply can't return pages quickly enough to satisfy all of the page requests, and so sessions are waiting for latches, and performance is suffering. However, this does not necessarily mean that a slow disk subsystem is the cause of the bottleneck; it may simply be the victim of excessive I/O caused by a problem elsewhere in the system.

At this point, I'll want to validate this information by examining the virtual file stats, in `sys.dm_io_virtual_file_stats`. Specifically, I'll be looking for evidence of high latency associated with the read and write operations being performed by SQL Server. At the same time, I'll be drilling deeper into the problem, since the virtual file stats will tell me how much I/O activity is being performed by SQL Server, and how the I/O load is distributed across files and databases on the SQL Server instance. To corroborate this data further, I may also check the values of the `Physical Disk\Avg. Disk Reads/sec` and `Physical Disk\Avg. Disk Writes/sec` PerfMon counters. So, at this stage, let's say I've confirmed high latency associated with read and write operations, and found that a particular database is experiencing a very high level of mainly read-based I/O.

My next step will be to investigate the execution statistics for queries against this database, which are maintained in `sys.dm_exec_query_stats` for the execution plans that are in the plan cache. I'll identify the queries that have the highest accumulated physical reads, and then review their associated execution plans, looking for any performance tuning opportunities, either by adding missing indexes (see *Chapter 5*) to the database, or making changes to the SQL code, in order to optimize the way the database engine accesses the data.

It may be that the code is optimized as far as it can be, but a commonly executed reporting query simply needs to read 6 GB of data from the database, for aggregation, as a part of its execution. If most of this data isn't found in the buffer cache, it will cause high physical I/O, and will account for the high `PAGEIOLATCH_SH` waits. At this point, we may need to look at our hardware configuration and see if the actual root of our problem is a lack of memory installed in the server. In order to verify this, I'll examine the PerfMon memory counters (see *Chapter 4*). If I see that the `Page Life Expectancy` is consistently fluctuating, and the system is experiencing non-zero values for `Free List Stalls/sec`, and high `Lazy Writes/sec`, then I can be fairly certain that the buffer pool for the instance is inadequately sized for the amount of data that is being used by the workload. This does not necessarily mean the server needs more memory; it may be that the queries are inefficient and are reading far more data than necessary. To identify the appropriate fix will require further and deeper analysis. This is just one of many possible examples, but it is a real-world example that I have encountered on many occasions while trouble-shooting performance problems with SQL Server.

There are a number of points in this troubleshooting process where it would have been very easy to jump to the wrong conclusion regarding the nature of the problem. For example, after reviewing the virtual file statistics and the performance counters for the Physical Disks in the server, it would be easy to conclude that the disk I/O subsystem for the server was inappropriately sized for the amount of work being done, and that additional disks needed to be purchased to handle the disk I/O demands for the server. Unfortunately, scaling up a disk I/O subsystem can be an extremely expensive solution if the problem happens to be a missing index related to a commonly executed query, or buffer pool memory pressure. It is possible that buying a large enough disk configuration will temporarily mask the problem, but since the underlying root cause has not been resolved, you can be sure that the same problem will recur later, as the system continues to grow.

Having provided an overview of my basic approach, the following sections will drill a little deeper into the specific areas of focus, such as wait statistics, virtual file statistics, performance counters, and plan cache usage. I'll explain the information they offer individually, and how all of this information interrelates, to help you assemble a complete understanding of what is going on inside of a server.

Don't forget the obvious

*Just a gentle reminder: before you get yourself all giddy collecting diagnostic data, make sure you've checked for obvious problems. If a user reports that their application is "not working properly," the first thing you should probably do is to ensure that the SQL Server services are actually running on your server. If you open **SQL Server Configuration Manager (SSCM)** and find that the status of the **Database Engine** service, which has a **Service Type** of SQL Server, is **Stopped** then this is very likely the cause of the problem, unless the instance is running in a failover cluster, at which point you need to look at the **Failover Cluster Manager** to identify if the service and its dependent resources are online, and begin troubleshooting why the service fails to start, based on what you find!*

Wait Statistics: the Basis for Troubleshooting

One of the first items that I check, when troubleshooting performance problems on a SQL Server, is the wait statistics, which are tracked by the SQLOS during normal operations of any SQL Server.

The SQLOS is a pseudo-operating system that runs as a part of the SQL Server database engine and provides thread scheduling, memory management, and other functions to SQL Server. Normally, such services would, for any processes running inside the operating system, be provided by the operating system. The reason that SQL Server provides its own pseudo-operating system environment is that SQL Server knows how to schedule its tasks better than the Windows operating system does, and the cooperative scheduling that is implemented by the SQLOS allows for higher levels of concurrency than the preemptive scheduling provided by the Windows operating system.

As an example of this, any time that SQL Server has to wait while executing an operation or statement, the time spent waiting is tracked by the SQLOS, as **wait time**. This data is exposed, for each instance of SQL Server installed on a server, in the `sys.dm_os_wait_stats` DMV. The cause and length of the various waits that SQL Server is experiencing can provide significant insight into the cause of the performance problems, as long as you understand exactly what the wait statistics are telling you, and know how to correlate the wait information with the additional troubleshooting information such as the PerfMon counters, and other DMVs.

One of the reasons that wait statistics is such a good place to begin troubleshooting SQL Server performance problems is that, often times, the specifics of the problem are not well defined by the users, when reporting the problem. More often than not, the description of the problem is limited to, "x, y, or z process is slower than normal, can you fix it?" One of the easiest ways to troubleshoot an unknown problem with performance is to look at where and why SQL Server actually had to wait to continue execution of its various tasks.

Usually, Windows Server and SQL Server patches will have been regularly applied to the server, so you'll know how long ago the server was restarted, and therefore over what period the statistics have accumulated (unless someone manually cleared them out – see later). Ideally, you'll want this period to be longer than around two weeks (in order to ensure the stats cover the entire workload), but not so long that the data becomes hard to analyze. In the latter case, you might also consider capturing the values, waiting a period, capturing again and comparing the two.

Diagnosing wait statistics for a single instance of SQL Server is no small task. Often times, the information provided by the wait statistics is only a symptom of the actual problem. To use this wait information effectively, you need to understand the difference between resource (i.e. traceable to a hardware resource) and non-resource waits in the system, and the other outputs provided by SQL Server, in relation to the wait information that is being tracked by the SQL Server instance overall.

As a part of the normal operations of SQL Server, a number of wait conditions exist which are non-problematic in nature and generally expected on the server. These wait conditions can generally be queried from the **sys.dm_os_waiting_tasks** DMV for the system sessions, as shown in Listing 1.1.

```
SELECT DISTINCT
        wt.wait_type
FROM    sys.dm_os_waiting_tasks AS wt
        JOIN sys.dm_exec_sessions AS s ON wt.session_id = s.session_id
WHERE   s.is_user_process = 0
```

Listing 1.1:   Discovering system session waits.

When looking at the wait statistics being tracked by SQL Server, it's important that these wait types are eliminated from the analysis, allowing the more problematic waits in the system to be identified. One of the things I do as a part of tracking wait information is to maintain a script that filters out the non-problematic wait types, as shown in Listing 1.2.

```sql
SELECT TOP 10
        wait_type ,
        max_wait_time_ms wait_time_ms ,
        signal_wait_time_ms ,
        wait_time_ms - signal_wait_time_ms AS resource_wait_time_ms ,
        100.0 * wait_time_ms / SUM(wait_time_ms) OVER ( )
                                AS percent_total_waits ,
        100.0 * signal_wait_time_ms / SUM(signal_wait_time_ms) OVER ( )
                                AS percent_total_signal_waits ,
        100.0 * ( wait_time_ms - signal_wait_time_ms )
        / SUM(wait_time_ms) OVER ( ) AS percent_total_resource_waits
FROM    sys.dm_os_wait_stats
WHERE   wait_time_ms > 0 -- remove zero wait_time
        AND wait_type NOT IN -- filter out additional irrelevant waits
( 'SLEEP_TASK', 'BROKER_TASK_STOP', 'BROKER_TO_FLUSH',
  'SQLTRACE_BUFFER_FLUSH','CLR_AUTO_EVENT', 'CLR_MANUAL_EVENT',
  'LAZYWRITER_SLEEP', 'SLEEP_SYSTEMTASK', 'SLEEP_BPOOL_FLUSH',
  'BROKER_EVENTHANDLER', 'XE_DISPATCHER_WAIT', 'FT_IFTSHC_MUTEX',
  'CHECKPOINT_QUEUE', 'FT_IFTS_SCHEDULER_IDLE_WAIT',
  'BROKER_TRANSMITTER', 'FT_IFTSHC_MUTEX', 'KSOURCE_WAKEUP',
  'LAZYWRITER_SLEEP', 'LOGMGR_QUEUE', 'ONDEMAND_TASK_QUEUE',
  'REQUEST_FOR_DEADLOCK_SEARCH', 'XE_TIMER_EVENT', 'BAD_PAGE_PROCESS',
  'DBMIRROR_EVENTS_QUEUE', 'BROKER_RECEIVE_WAITFOR',
  'PREEMPTIVE_OS_GETPROCADDRESS', 'PREEMPTIVE_OS_AUTHENTICATIONOPS',
  'WAITFOR', 'DISPATCHER_QUEUE_SEMAPHORE', 'XE_DISPATCHER_JOIN',
  'RESOURCE_QUEUE' )
ORDER BY wait_time_ms DESC
```

Listing 1.2: Finding the top ten cumulative wait events.

In general, when examining wait statistics, I focus on the top waits, according to wait_time_ms, and look out for high wait times associated with the following specific wait types, each of these are covered in more detail in the appropriate chapters of this book:

- **CXPACKET**

  - Often indicates nothing more than that certain queries are executing with parallelism; CXPACKET waits in the server are not an immediate sign of problems, although they may be the symptom of another problem, associated with one of the other high value wait types in the instance, as covered in *Chapter 3*.

- **SOS_SCHEDULER_YIELD**

  - The tasks executing in the system are yielding the scheduler, having exceeded their quantum, and are having to wait in the runnable queue for other tasks to execute. This may indicate that the server is under CPU pressure. See *Chapter 3* for more information on this.

- **THREADPOOL**

  - A task had to wait to have a worker bound to it, in order to execute. This could be a sign of worker thread starvation, requiring an increase in the number of CPUs in the server, to handle a highly concurrent workload, or it can be a sign of blocking, resulting in a large number of parallel tasks consuming the worker threads for long periods.

- **LCK_***

  - These wait types signify that blocking is occurring in the system and that sessions have had to wait to acquire a lock of a specific type, which was being held by another database session. This problem can be investigated further using the information in the `sys.dm_db_index_operational_stats` and techniques described in *Chapter 6* of this book.

- **PAGEIOLATCH_***, **IO_COMPLETION**, **WRITELOG**

  - These waits are commonly associated with disk I/O bottlenecks, though the root cause of the problem may be, and commonly is, a poorly performing query that is consuming excessive amounts of memory in the server. `PAGEIOLATCH_*` waits are specifically associated with delays in being able to read or write data from the database files. `WRITELOG` waits are related to issues with writing to log files. These waits should be evaluated in conjunction with the virtual file statistics as well as Physical Disk performance counters, to determine if the problem is specific to a single database, file, or disk, or is instance wide.

- **PAGELATCH_***

  - Non-l/O waits for latches on data pages in the buffer pool. A lot of times PAGELATCH_* waits are associated with allocation contention issues. One of the best-known allocations issues associated with PAGELATCH_* waits occurs in tempdb when the a large number of objects are being created and destroyed in tempdb and the system experiences contention on the Shared Global Allocation Map (SGAM), Global Allocation Map (GAM), and Page Free Space (PFS) pages in the tempdb database.

- **LATCH_***

  - These waits are associated with lightweight short-term synchronization objects that are used to protect access to internal caches, but not the buffer cache. These waits can indicate a range of problems, depending on the latch type. Determining the specific latch class that has the most accumulated wait time associated with it can be found by querying the **sys.dm_os_latch_stats** DMV.

- **ASYNC_NETWORK_IO**

  - This wait is often incorrectly attributed to a network bottleneck. In fact, the most common cause of this wait is a client application that is performing row-by-row processing of the data being streamed from SQL Server as a result set (client accepts one row, processes, accepts next row, and so on). Correcting this wait type generally requires changing the client-side code so that it reads the result set as fast as possible, and then performs processing.

These basic explanations of each of the major wait types won't make you an expert on wait type analysis, but the appearance of any of these wait types high up in the output of Listing 1.2 will certainly help direct your subsequent investigations. For example, if you see PAGEIOLATCH_* waits you will probably want to make your next focus the virtual file stats, as explained in the previous example.

Conversely, if the primary wait types in the system are LCK_* waits, then you won't want to waste time looking at the disk I/O configuration, but instead focus on discovering what might be causing blocking inside the databases on the server. When LCK_* wait types crop up, I tend to jump immediately into more advanced troubleshooting of that specific problem, and begin looking at blocking in the system using the sys.dm_exec_requests DMV and other methods as described in *Chapter 6*, rather than strictly adhering to my normal methodology. However I may, depending on what I find, double back to see what other problems are in the system.

After fixing any problem in the server, in order to validate that the problem has indeed been fixed, the wait statistics being tracked by the server can be reset using the code in Listing 1.3.

```
DBCC SQLPERF('sys.dm_os_wait_stats', clear)
```

Listing 1.3: Clearing the wait statistics on a server.

- One of the caveats associated with clearing the wait statistics on the server, is that it will take a period of time for the wait statistics to accumulate to the point that you know whether or not a specific problem has been addressed.

Virtual File Statistics

A common trap in my experience, when using wait statistics as a primary source of troubleshooting data, is that most SQL Servers will demonstrate signs of what looks like a disk I/O bottleneck. Unfortunately, the wait statistics don't tell you what is causing the I/O to occur, and it's easy to misdiagnose the root cause.

This is why an examination of the virtual file statistics, alongside the wait statistics, is almost always recommended. The virtual file statistics are exposed through the sys.dm_io_virtual_file_stats function which, when passed a file_id (and possibly database_id), will provide cumulative physical I/O statistics, the number of reads and writes on each data file, and the number of reads and writes on each log file, for the various databases in the instance, from which can be calculated the ratio of reads to writes. This also shows the number of I/O stalls and the stall time associated with the requests, which is the total amount of time sessions have waited for I/O to be completed on the file.

```sql
SELECT   DB_NAME(vfs.database_id) AS database_name ,
         vfs.database_id ,
         vfs.file_id ,
         io_stall_read_ms / NULLIF(num_of_reads, 0) AS avg_read_latency ,
         io_stall_write_ms / NULLIF(num_of_writes, 0)
                                       AS avg_write_latency ,
         io_stall_write_ms / NULLIF(num_of_writes + num_of_writes, 0)
                                       AS avg_total_latency ,
         num_of_bytes_read / NULLIF(num_of_reads, 0)
                                       AS avg_bytes_per_read ,
         num_of_bytes_written / NULLIF(num_of_writes, 0)
                                       AS avg_bytes_per_write ,
         vfs.io_stall ,
         vfs.num_of_reads ,
         vfs.num_of_bytes_read ,
         vfs.io_stall_read_ms ,
         vfs.num_of_writes ,
         vfs.num_of_bytes_written ,
         vfs.io_stall_write_ms ,
         size_on_disk_bytes / 1024 / 1024. AS size_on_disk_mbytes ,
         physical_name
FROM     sys.dm_io_virtual_file_stats(NULL, NULL) AS vfs
         JOIN sys.master_files AS mf ON vfs.database_id = mf.database_id
                                   AND vfs.file_id = mf.file_id
ORDER BY avg_total_latency DESC
```

Listing 1.4:   Virtual file statistics.

What I'm primarily looking at in the results is patterns of activity on the file, whether heavy-read or heavy-write, and at the average latency associated with the I/O, as this will direct further investigation and possible solutions.

If the data and log files are on a shared disk array in the server, and the calculated avg_total_latency is the same across all of the databases, and higher than what is acceptable for the specific workload, then the problem may be that the workload has outgrown the disk I/O subsystem.

However, if the server hosts a database that is used for archiving data to slower storage, for year-on-year reporting, then it may be that having `PAGEIOLATCH_*` waits in the database is entirely normal, and the `io_stall` information for the specific database files may lead us to determine that the waits are most likely attributable to the archiving process. This highlights the fact that it helps to have a sound knowledge of the underlying configuration and type of workload for the server, while you're troubleshooting the problem.

If a particular file is subject to very heavy read activity (for example a ratio of 10:1, or higher, for the read:write ratio), and is showing high average latency, then I may recommend a RAID change for the disk array, for example from RAID 10 to RAID 5, offering more spindles to share the read I/O.

Hopefully, this discussion has highlighted the key element of effective troubleshooting, which is that you need to examine many "data points" together, in order to arrive at a true diagnosis. The discovery of I/O pressure, revealed by high I/O-related waits, could be caused by inadequate capacity or configuration of the disk subsystem, but its root cause is actually more likely to lie elsewhere, such as in a memory bottleneck in the buffer pool, or excessive index and/or table scans due to poorly written queries (see the *Plan Cache Usage* section of this chapter) and a lack of indexing.

Performance Counters

Many articles, white papers, and blog posts on the Internet attempt to provide detailed lists of the important performance counters that should be monitored for SQL Server instances, along with general guidelines for acceptable values for these counters. However, if you try to collect and analyze the values for all of the available counters, you'll quickly find it an overwhelming task.

Personally, at least in the initial stages of my investigation, I rely on a small subset of counters, directly related to SQL Server. At a more advanced stage in the troubleshooting process, I may also begin collecting Windows counters, in order to verify the information that I already have, or to help isolate an edge case problem to a specific cause.

One of my favorite tools, when I get to the point that I need to collect a larger subset of counters, collecting information from Windows as well as SQL Server, is the **Performance Analysis of Logs** (PAL) tool, which has been made available by Microsoft for free on HTTP://PAL.CODEPLEX.COM.

The tool provides built-in templates that can be exported to create a **Performance Collector Set** in Windows, each set containing the key counters for a specific product. It includes a template for SQL Server 2005 and 2008. The greatest benefit of this tool is that it also has built-in threshold templates that can be used to process the performance counter data after it has been collected. These can be used to produce a detailed report, breaking down the data into time slices and so automating the analysis of the data into periods of time and activity. If you want to know more about all of the counters related to SQL Server performance, what they mean, and what Microsoft currently says the threshold values for those counters are, I would recommend downloading the tool and taking a look at all the information contained in the SQL Server threshold file.

Nevertheless, the counters I investigate initially are limited to those related to specific areas of SQL Server, and are ones that have proven themselves over the years to provide information critical to determining how to continue with the troubleshooting process. The counters are all available from within SQL Server through the `sys.dm_os_performance_counters` DMV and can be queried using T-SQL alone.

One of the challenges with querying the raw performance counter data directly is that some of the performance counters are cumulative ones, increasing in value as time progresses, and analysis of the data requires capturing two snapshots of the data and then calculating the difference between the snapshots. The query in Listing 1.5 performs the snapshots and calculations automatically, allowing the output to be analyzed directly.

There are other performance counters, not considered in Listing 1.5, which have a secondary, associated base counter by which the main counter has to be divided to arrive at its actual value.

```sql
-- Capture the first counter set
SELECT   CAST(1 AS INT) AS collection_instance ,
         object_name ,
         counter_name ,
         instance_name ,
         cntr_value ,
         cntr_type ,
         CURRENT_TIMESTAMP AS collection_time
INTO     #perf_counters_init
FROM     sys.dm_os_performance_counters
WHERE    ( object_name = 'SQLServer:Access Methods'
           AND counter_name = 'Full Scans/sec'
         )
         OR ( object_name = 'SQLServer:Access Methods'
              AND counter_name = 'Index Searches/sec'
            )
         OR ( object_name = 'SQLServer:Buffer Manager'
              AND counter_name = 'Lazy Writes/sec'
            )
         OR ( object_name = 'SQLServer:Buffer Manager'
              AND counter_name = 'Page life expectancy'
            )
         OR ( object_name = 'SQLServer:General Statistics'
              AND counter_name = 'Processes Blocked'
            )
         OR ( object_name = 'SQLServer:General Statistics'
              AND counter_name = 'User Connections'
            )
         OR ( object_name = 'SQLServer:Locks'
              AND counter_name = 'Lock Waits/sec'
            )
         OR ( object_name = 'SQLServer:Locks'
              AND counter_name = 'Lock Wait Time (ms)'
            )
         OR ( object_name = 'SQLServer:SQL Statistics'
              AND counter_name = 'SQL Re-Compilations/sec'
            )
         OR ( object_name = 'SQLServer:Memory Manager'
```

```
                AND counter_name = 'Memory Grants Pending'
            )
        OR ( object_name = 'SQLServer:SQL Statistics'
            AND counter_name = 'Batch Requests/sec'
            )
        OR ( object_name = 'SQLServer:SQL Statistics'
            AND counter_name = 'SQL Compilations/sec'
            )

-- Wait on Second between data collection
WAITFOR DELAY '00:00:01'

-- Capture the second counter set
SELECT  CAST(2 AS INT) AS collection_instance ,
        object_name ,
        counter_name ,
        instance_name ,
        cntr_value ,
        cntr_type ,
        CURRENT_TIMESTAMP AS collection_time
INTO    #perf_counters_second
FROM    sys.dm_os_performance_counters
WHERE   ( object_name = 'SQLServer:Access Methods'
          AND counter_name = 'Full Scans/sec'
        )
        OR ( object_name = 'SQLServer:Access Methods'
            AND counter_name = 'Index Searches/sec'
            )
        OR ( object_name = 'SQLServer:Buffer Manager'
            AND counter_name = 'Lazy Writes/sec'
            )
        OR ( object_name = 'SQLServer:Buffer Manager'
            AND counter_name = 'Page life expectancy'
            )
        OR ( object_name = 'SQLServer:General Statistics'
            AND counter_name = 'Processes Blocked'
            )
        OR ( object_name = 'SQLServer:General Statistics'
            AND counter_name = 'User Connections'
            )
        OR ( object_name = 'SQLServer:Locks'
            AND counter_name = 'Lock Waits/sec'
            )
        OR ( object_name = 'SQLServer:Locks'
```

```
                AND counter_name = 'Lock Wait Time (ms)'
            )
        OR ( object_name = 'SQLServer:SQL Statistics'
             AND counter_name = 'SQL Re-Compilations/sec'
            )
        OR ( object_name = 'SQLServer:Memory Manager'
             AND counter_name = 'Memory Grants Pending'
            )
        OR ( object_name = 'SQLServer:SQL Statistics'
             AND counter_name = 'Batch Requests/sec'
            )
        OR ( object_name = 'SQLServer:SQL Statistics'
             AND counter_name = 'SQL Compilations/sec'
            )

-- Calculate the cumulative counter values
SELECT   i.object_name ,
         i.counter_name ,
         i.instance_name ,
         CASE WHEN i.cntr_type = 272696576
                   THEN s.cntr_value - i.cntr_value
              WHEN i.cntr_type = 65792 THEN s.cntr_value
         END AS cntr_value
FROM     #perf_counters_init AS i
         JOIN #perf_counters_second AS s
             ON i.collection_instance + 1 = s.collection_instance
                AND i.object_name = s.object_name
                AND i.counter_name = s.counter_name
                AND i.instance_name = s.instance_name
ORDER BY object_name

-- Cleanup tables
DROP TABLE #perf_counters_init
DROP TABLE #perf_counters_second
```

Listing 1.5: SQL Server performance counters.

The performance counters collected by this script are:

- `SQLServer:Access Methods\Full Scans/sec`

- `SQLServer:Access Methods\Index Searches/sec`

- `SQLServer:Buffer Manager\Lazy Writes/sec`

- `SQLServer:Buffer Manager\Page life expectancy`

- `SQLServer:Buffer Manager\Free list stalls/sec`

- `SQLServer:General Statistics\Processes Blocked`

- `SQLServer:General Statistics\User Connections`

- `SQLServer:Locks\Lock Waits/sec`

- `SQLServer:Locks\Lock Wait Time (ms)`

- `SQLServer:Memory Manager\Memory Grants Pending`

- `SQLServer:SQL Statistics\Batch Requests/sec`

- `SQLServer:SQL Statistics\SQL Compilations/sec`

- `SQLServer:SQL Statistics\SQL Re-Compilations/sec`

The two **Access Methods** counters provide information about the ways that tables are being accessed in the database. The most important one is the `Full Scans/sec` counter, which can give us an idea of the number of index and table scans that are occurring in the system.

If the disk I/O subsystem is the bottleneck (which, remember, is most often caused by pressure placed on it by a problem elsewhere) and this counter is showing that there are scans occurring, it may be a sign that there are missing indexes, or inefficient code in the database. How many scans are problematic? It depends entirely on the size of the objects being scanned and the type of workload being run. In general, I want the number of `Index Searches/sec` to be higher than the number of `Full Scans/sec` by a factor of 800–1000. If the number of Full Scans/sec is too high, refer to *Chapter 5, Missing Indexes* to determine if there are missing indexes in the database, resulting in excess I/O operations.

The **Buffer Manager** and **Memory Manager** counters can be used, as a group, to identify if SQL Server is experiencing memory pressure. The values of the Page Life Expectancy, Free List Stalls/sec, and Lazy Writes/sec counters, when correlated, will validate or disprove the theory that the buffer cache is under memory pressure.

A lot of online references will tell you that if the Page Life Expectancy (PLE) performance counter drops lower than 300, which is the number of seconds a page will remain in the data cache, then you have memory pressure. However, this guideline value for the PLE counter was set at a time when most SQL Servers only had 4 GB of RAM, and the data cache portion of the buffer pool was generally 1.6 GB. In modern servers, where it is common for SQL Servers to have 32 GB or more of installed RAM, and a significantly larger data cache, having 1.6 GB of data churn through that cache every 5 minutes is not necessarily a significant event.

In short, the appropriate value for this counter depends on the size of the SQL Server data cache, and a fixed value of 300 no longer applies. Instead, I evaluate the value for the PLE counter based on the installed memory in the server. To do this, I take the base counter value of 300 presented by most resources, and then determine a multiple of this value based on the configured buffer cache size, which is the 'max server memory' sp_configure option in SQL Server, divided by 4 GB. So, for a server with 32 GB allocated to the buffer pool, the PLE value should be at least (32/4)*300 = 2400. See *Chapter 4, Memory Management* for a more thorough discussion of memory configuration and considerations.

If the PLE is consistently below this value, and the server is experiencing high Lazy Writes/sec, which are page flushes from the buffer cache outside of the normal CHECKPOINT process, then the server is most likely experiencing data cache memory pressure, which will also increase the disk I/O being performed by the SQL Server. At this point, the `Access Methods` counters should be investigated to determine if excessive table or index scans are being performed on the SQL Server.

The `General Statistics\Processes Blocked`, `Locks\Lock Waits/sec`, and `Locks\Lock Wait Time (ms)` counters provide information about blocking in the SQL Server instance, at the time of the data collection. If these counters return a value other than zero, over repeated collections of the data, then blocking is actively occurring in one of the databases and the information contained in *Chapter 6, Blocking* should be used to troubleshoot the problems further.

The three `SQL Statistics` counters provide information about how frequently SQL Server is compiling or recompiling an execution plan, in relation to the number of batches being executed against the server. The higher the number of `SQL Compilations/sec` in relation to the `Batch Requests/sec`, the more likely the SQL Server is experiencing an ad hoc workload that is not making optimal using of plan caching. The higher the number of `SQL Re-Compilations/sec` in relation to the `Batch Requests/sec`, the more likely it is that there is an inefficiency in the code design that is forcing a recompile of the code being executed in the SQL Server. In either case, investigation of the Plan Cache, as detailed in the next section, should identify why the server has to consistently compile execution plans for the workload.

The `Memory Manager\Memory Grants Pending` performance counter provides information about the number of processes waiting on a workspace memory grant in the instance. If this counter has a high value, SQL Server may benefit from additional memory, but there may be query inefficiencies in the instance that are causing excessive memory grant requirements, for example, large sorts or hashes that can be resolved by tuning the indexing or queries being executed.

Plan Cache Usage

In my experience, the Plan Cache in SQL Server 2005 and 2008 is one of the most underused assets for troubleshooting performance problems in SQL Server. As a part of the normal execution of batches and queries, SQL Server tracks the accumulated execution information for each of the plans that is stored inside of the plan cache, up to the point where the plan is flushed from the cache as a result of DDL operations, memory pressure, or general cache maintenance. The execution information stored inside of the plan cache can be found in the **sys.dm_exec_query_stats** DMV as shown in the example query in Listing 1.6. This query will list the top ten statements based on the average number of physical reads that the statements performed as a part of their execution.

```
SELECT TOP 10
        execution_count ,
        statement_start_offset AS stmt_start_offset ,
        sql_handle ,
        plan_handle ,
        total_logical_reads / execution_count AS avg_logical_reads ,
        total_logical_writes / execution_count AS avg_logical_writes ,
        total_physical_reads / execution_count AS avg_physical_reads ,
        t.text
FROM    sys.dm_exec_query_stats AS s
        CROSS APPLY sys.dm_exec_sql_text(s.sql_handle) AS t
ORDER BY avg_physical_reads DESC
```

Listing 1.6: SQL Server execution statistics.

The information stored in the plan cache can be used to identify the most expensive queries based on physical I/O operations for reads and for writes, or based on different criteria, depending on the most problematic type of I/O for the instance, discovered as a result of previous analysis of the wait statistics and virtual file statistics.

Additionally, the `sys.dm_exec_query_plan()` function can be cross-applied using the `plan_handle` column from the `sys.dm_exec_query_stats` DMV to get the execution plan that is stored in the plan cache. By analyzing these plans, we can identify problematic operations that are candidates for performance tuning.

Query performance tuning

A full discussion of query performance tuning is beyond the scope of this book. In fact, several notable books have been written on this topic alone, including "SQL Server 2008 Query Performance Tuning Distilled" (HTTP://WWW.AMAZON.COM/SERVER-PERFORMANCE-TUNING-DISTILLED-EXPERTS/DP/1430219025) *and "Inside Microsoft SQL Server 2008: T-SQL Querying"* (HTTP://WWW.AMAZON.COM/INSIDE-MICROSOFT®-SQL-SERVER®-2008/DP/0735626030).

The information in the `sys.dm_exec_query_stats` DMV can also be used to identify the statements that have taken the most CPU time, the longest execution time, or that have been executed the most frequently.

In SQL Server 2008, two additional columns, `query_hash` and `query_plan_hash`, were added to the `sys.dm_exec_query_stats` DMV. The `query_hash` is a hash over the statement text to allow similar statements to be aggregated together. The `query_plan_hash` is a hash of the query plan shape that allows queries with similar execution plans to be aggregated together. Together, they allow the information contained in this DMV to be aggregated for ad hoc workloads, in order to determine the total impact of similar statements that have different compiled literal values.

Summary

This chapter has outlined my basic approach to investigating performance problems in SQL Server. This approach is more or less the same, regardless of whether it is a server I know well, or one I'm investigating for the first time, with no prior knowledge of the health and configuration of the SQL Server instance it houses. Based on the information gathered using this methodology, more advanced diagnosis of the identified problem areas can be performed, using information contained in the subsequent chapters in this book.

The most important point that I want to stress in this opening chapter is that no single piece of information in SQL Server should be used to pinpoint any specific problem. The art of taming an unruly SQL Server is the art of assembling the various pieces of the puzzle so that you have a complete understanding of what is going on inside of a server. If you focus only on what is immediately in front of you, you will, in most cases, miss the most important item, which is the true root cause of a particular problem in SQL Server.

Chapter 2: Disk I/O Configuration

Improper hardware configuration is a common cause of SQL Server performance and scalability problems. If you try to run SQL Server on workstation-grade hardware, you will run into problems, but even on server-grade hardware, performance problems can and will occur if one or more of the hardware components have been improperly sized and configured for the SQL Server workload.

SQL Server is very different from other applications in terms of its disk usage characteristics and storage requirements, and the disk subsystem is one of the most commonly undersized and poorly-configured hardware components for SQL Server. Often the I/O workload can be substantially reduced by measures such as appropriate use of indexing, or ensuring queries don't read more data than strictly necessary. However, if I/O problems persist as indicated, for example, by high latency values for the `Physical Disk\Disk Reads/sec` and `Physical Disk\Disk Writes/sec` PerfMon counters, or specific I/O-related wait types in the DMVs, then you'll need to troubleshoot your disk I/O system. This task may be relatively straightforward, or grievously complex, depending on whether you're using simple, directly attached storage, or a vast and complex, enterprise-wide Storage Area Network (SAN).

This chapter discusses the basics of disk I/O subsystem configuration for SQL Server, and the most common problems associated with the incorrectly sized or incorrectly designed disk configurations, covering topics such as:

- **Appropriate choice of hardware RAID level** – there are many possible configurations, and the right one will depend largely on the nature of the SQL Server workload.

- **Storage capacity versus throughput** – 1 TB of database storage can be satisfied with a single 1 TB disk drive, but the I/O throughput and performance are likely to be poor.

- **Workload type and distribution** – specific considerations for data, log, and `tempdb` files.

- **Common disk I/O problems** – such as disk partition misalignment and network bandwidth issues in SANs.

By far the best way to deal with disk I/O issues is to work as hard as you can during the system design phase to prevent them from occurring. The only way to be sure that your disk I/O subsystem will meet your I/O performance and throughput requirements is to understand what those requirements are, and test the performance of your disk subsystem under realistic loads, using a tool such as SQLIO or IOmeter.

Disk Configuration: Basic Considerations

Memory scalability has improved substantially over recent years. It is now relatively inexpensive to over-provision RAM capacity for SQL Server, to help minimize disk I/O. Likewise, as powerful processors with eight, or even twelve, physical cores emerge onto the market, many modern servers often have spare CPU capacity which, again, can be used to help reduce pressure on the disk I/O system.

The common theme here seems to be that the disk subsystem needs as much help as it can get. It's certainly true that, over a similar time period, performance improvements of the traditional magnetic disk drives which still underpin the vast majority of SQL Server installations have been relatively modest by comparison with improvements in memory and CPU. As such, great care needs to be taken when provisioning and configuring the disk subsystem hardware for SQL Server installations, in order to ensure that it meets the I/O workload requirements of the SQL Server database that runs on it.

This section will briefly review some of the major considerations when sizing and configuring the disk subsystem, and we'll drill into each of these issues as we progress through the chapter.

Disk size vs. disk throughput

One of the most common mistakes made when planning and building a disk I/O subsystem for SQL Server is to think purely in terms of how much disk space is required, rather than the disk throughput required to support the transaction workload on the database.

For conventional hard drives that have a rotating platter then, purely in terms of the disk mechanics, the limiting factors for performance and throughput, stated in IOPS and MB/sec, are:

- **rotations per minute** – how quickly the platter spins to read data off of the disk

- **seek time in ms** – the time it takes to reposition the drive head to locate data on the disk.

If you need 1 TB of storage for a database then you can satisfy that with a single, 1 TB disk drive, but you'll find that both the rotational latency and disk head latency will be high, and the I/O performance and throughput correspondingly low. Such a single-disk set up would be inadvisable, regardless of the supported workload type, but would be especially problematic when the workload generated a large number of random read/write operations (such as would be typical for an OLTP workload), resulting in severe disk head latency issues.

The way to mitigate disk latency issues, and vastly improve disk I/O performance and throughput, is to stripe the data across a large number of smaller disks, configured in one of the various available RAID configurations (discussed later), which can then be presented to Windows as a single hardware device.

Of course, this can lead to a substantial increase in the complexity of the storage system, and means that the ultimate disk I/O throughput and performance is affected, not just by the physical disk characteristics, but also by issues such as the chosen RAID configuration, the architecture of the storage array (DAS or SAN, as discussed later), and the

43

performance of other components of the storage array, such as Host Bus Adapters or RAID controllers, and so on.

Solid state drives

Modern solid state disks contain no moving parts, so they are not subject to the same throughput limitations as conventional disks, and they are gradually pushing the IOPS potential beyond the capabilities of most large, conventional disk arrays, in a single hardware device. They are still relatively new technology, and not currently in heavy use for transactional database systems, due to lifespan and cost considerations, and are not covered further in this chapter. However, they may redefine the storage space in the near future.

Random versus sequential I/O

The basic building block in SQL Server is known as a page, which is 8 KB in size. To minimize the number of I/O requests when reading data from disk, SQL Server employs a read-ahead mechanism that can read a number of contiguous pages, up to 128 pages on Standard Edition and 1,024 pages on Enterprise Edition, in a single I/O operation.

At the same time, rather than continuously writing any data modifications to disk, the changes are made to data pages in the buffer pool, which are collected into contiguous blocks and written to disk in a single I/O operation, at CHECKPOINT, after the descriptions of the changes have been hardened to the transaction log.

SQL Server databases perform a mix of random and sequential I/O operations depending on the activities being performed. **Sequential I/O** is any operation where the blocks can be read from, or written to, disk without having to reposition the disk head on the drive. Sequential I/O is used by SQL Server for read-ahead operations, and for all transaction log operations, and is the fastest type of I/O that can be performed using conventional disks. **Random I/O** is any operation where the disk head on the drive has to change positions on the platter, incurring seek latency as a part of the operation, which reduces the performance and number of operations in comparison to sequential I/O. Read operations in general, especially in OLTP systems, are random I/O operations, reading relatively small blocks of pages sequentially as a part of larger random I/O requests.

For this reason, the chosen disk configuration should be heavily influenced by the type of file being stored on the disks, and the type of I/O activity to which it is subjected. In short, for optimum performance, the disk I/O subsystem for the log files should be configured differently than the disk I/O subsystem for the data files.

The disk configuration for the database data files should be optimized for 64 KB random read I/O, and performance benchmarked for I/O sizes of 8 KB, 64 KB, 128 KB, and 256 KB to determine the potential performance and throughput capacity of the configuration. If the server is being used primarily for a large data warehouse or decision support system (DSS) database, the I/O subsystem should be benchmarked for larger I/O sizes up to 1024 KB for read-ahead operations, depending on the database design, and how it is being used. However, the **transaction log** in SQL Server primarily performs sequential write operations in random sizes up to 60 KB.

Choosing the Right RAID Level

RAID, an acronym for Redundant Array of Independent Disks, is the technology used to achieve the following objectives:

- **increase levels of I/O performance**, measured in Input/Output Operations Per Second (IOPS), which is roughly (`MB/sec /IO size in KB`)*1024

- **increase levels of I/O throughput**, measured in Megabytes Per Second (MB/sec) which is roughly (`IOPS*IO size in KB`)/1024

- **increase storage capacity available in a single logical device** – you can't purchase a single 5 TB disk yet, but you can have a 5 TB disk in Windows, for example, by using RAID to stripe six 1 TB drives in a RAID5 array

- **gain data redundancy** through storing parity information across multiple disks, or using mirroring of the physical disks in the array.

The choice of RAID level is heavily dependent on the nature of the workload that the disk array must support. For example, as discussed earlier, the difference in the nature of the I/O workloads for data and for log files means that different RAID configurations may be applicable in each case.

Data files are subject primarily to random read activity and, due to the way that SQL Server batches write operations to disk with CHECKPOINT, this allows the use of RAID levels that trade-off write performance for higher read performance and better usage of the available disk storage capacity. The sequential activity for the log files is primarily for write activities during log buffer flushes, making write performance much more critical a consideration than it may be for the data files.

Choosing the appropriate RAID level is often a difficult task and, unless money is no object, often involves some sort of compromise between factors such as the overall cost of the solution, storage capacity, disk throughput, and the degree of "protection" in case of a failure of one of the disks in the array.

There are a number of RAID levels currently available on the market, each of which has its own associated costs and benefits. Over the following sections, we'll examine the most common standard RAID levels (0, 1, 5 and 6) as well as nested RAID levels, such as RAID 0+1 or 1+0, whereby one RAID array is used inside of a secondary RAID array. We'll explain, briefly, how each level works, and its relative merits and drawbacks for SQL Server systems.

A brief overview of RAID configurations

The most common RAID levels used with SQL Server are RAID 1, 5, 6 and 1+0, since these ensure that the data stored on the array will not be lost or damaged/corrupted if one of the disks in the array fails catastrophically. The protection of the data stored inside SQL Server should be considered as the most important factor in RAID level selection, followed closely by the desired performance characteristic for the disk array. The fastest disk array in the world won't be useful if it loses all your organization's information in a single failure.

RAID 0

RAID 0, most commonly known as **striping**, provides improved I/O rates (in terms of **IOPS**) by striping the data across multiple drives, allowing the read and write operations to be shared amongst the drives inside the array. Figure 2.1 shows a RAID 0 implementation where A1, A2, and so on, represent logically sequential segments of data. We can see that, although A2 comes sequentially after A1, it is stored on a separate drive, allowing multiple segments to be accessed simultaneously.

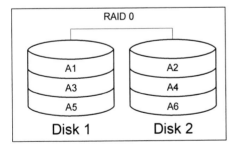

Figure 2.1:   RAID 0.

This level of RAID provides the best performance for both read and write operations, but provides no redundancy or protection against data loss. In the event of a single disk failure in the array, all of the data is lost. As such, this RAID level is not appropriate for SQL Server implementations.

RAID 1

RAID 1, most commonly known as mirroring, provides protection against the loss of data from a single disk by mirroring the writes to a second disk, as shown in Figure 2.2. A RAID 1 configuration provides redundancy, but doesn't provide added write performance to the system, since the maximum throughput for the array is limited to the I/O capacity of a single disk. If you have a duplexing setup (an extension of mirroring where both disks in the mirror can be read simultaneously) then it's possible, in theory, to get a read performance benefit. In practice, however, the improvements are highly variable, though generally small, and dependent on the hardware implementation.

While RAID 1 provides data redundancy, protecting it from a single disk loss, it effectively doubles the cost of storage.

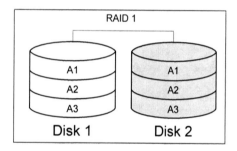

Figure 2.2: RAID 1 implementation.

For low I/O demands, RAID 1 can provide acceptable performance for SQL Server data files, but it generally doesn't meet the IOPS requirements associated with heavy, random-read operations, even on moderately-sized databases. In most cases, however, RAID 1 can be used for storing a *single* transaction log. The sequential nature of the transaction log activity means that the read/write head of each drive is relatively static, and moves in a progressive sweep across the disk head as writes occur. This minimizes I/O latency and allows for significantly higher IOPS than is possible for random I/O operations.

If multiple transaction log files are placed on a single RAID 1 array, the net effect of the combined sequential I/O activity for each file will be random I/O at the physical level, and higher latency will result from the movement of the disk head to perform operations against each of the files being written to sequentially.

RAID 5 (and 6)

RAID 5 is commonly known as "striping with parity;" the data is striped across multiples disks, as per RAID 0, but parity data is stored in order to provide protection from single disk failure. The minimum number of disks required for a RAID 5 array is three. The parity blocks containing the parity data are staggered across the stripes inside the array, as shown in Figure 2.3. So, for example, the **Ap** segment stores parity data arising from the comparison of data in segments **A1** and **A2**. If Disk 2 were to fail, then the data in the **A2** segment could be reconstructed, by a comparison of the data in **A1** with the parity data.

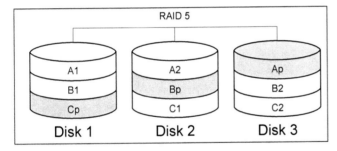

Figure 2.3: RAID 5 implementation.

Note that the total storage capacity for a RAID 5 array is $(n-1)*$disk size, where n is the number of disks. So for a RAID 5 array of (say) 3 x 100 GB disks, we'd have 200 GB for data storage. For a 5-disk array, we'd have 400 GB for data storage, and so on.

In this manner, RAID 5 provides redundancy with minimal reduction in storage capacity, which is one of the major reasons for its popularity. Striping the data across multiple disks improves read performance, but the need to maintain parity data incurs a performance penalty for writes; for example, each time data is updated in segment **A1**, the parity data must be recalculated and rewritten. Additionally, if one of the disks in a RAID 5 array fails physically, the array performance becomes degraded by the parity comparisons that have to be performed to read the data stored on the array. The level of degradation depends on the number of disks configured in the array; as the number of disks increases, the number of comparisons increases, reducing the performance further.

For heavy read but low write databases, RAID 5 can be optimal for the data files. However, in circumstances where that database incurs heavy write activity, the cost of the parity calculations can reduce the performance of the system. For this same reason, RAID 5 is not recommended for the database transaction log files, which primarily perform sequential writes and require the lowest write latency possible.

RAID 6, is an extension of RAID 5 but, instead of a single distributed parity bit, it uses double-distributed parity bits, where the calculated parity data is stored on two separate disks in the array, allowing for a double disk failure in the array, while still protecting the data. So, for example, in Figure 2.4, parity data arising from the comparison of data in the **A1** and **A2** segments is stored in both the **Aq** and **Ap** parity data segments.

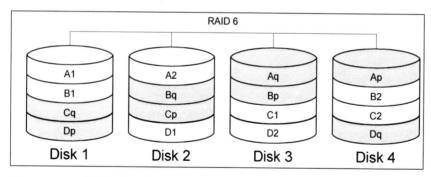

Figure 2.4:   RAID 6 implementation for a 4-disk array.

In RAID 6, the total storage capacity is $(n-2)$*disk size so, for this 4-disk array, we lose half the disk space for parity data storage. Also, the performance impact of the parity calculations will be relatively high. For these reasons, RAID 10 is a better RAID configuration to support double disk loss, when only four disks are in the array.

Figure 2.5 shows a more typical RAID 6 implementation, involving a 7-disk array.

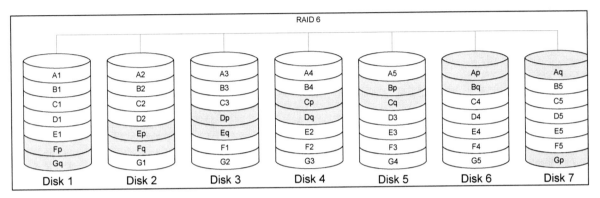

Figure 2.5:   RAID 6 implementation for a 7-disk array.

RAID 6 is common for Storage Area Network (SAN) applications where the number of disks in a single array is higher than for most Direct Attached Storage (DAS) applications, increasing the possibility of multiple disk failures during the period of time when a single disk may be offline. RAID 6 has a performance penalty similar to RAID 5 for write operations, since the parity bit calculation impacts performance.

RAID 10

RAID 10, or RAID 1+0, is a nested RAID level known as a "striped pair of mirrors." It provides redundancy by first mirroring each disk, using RAID 1, and then striping those mirrored disks, with RAID 0, to improve performance. There is a significant monetary cost increase associated with this configuration since only half of the disk space is available for use. However, this configuration offers the best configuration for redundancy since, potentially, it allows for multiple disk failures while still leaving the system operational, and without degrading system performance.

In the configuration shown in Figure 2.6, each of the RAID 1 mirrored pairs could sustain a single disk failure and the array would continue to remain operational. However, if both of the disks in a single RAID 1 mirrored pair were to fail at the same time, the system would no longer be operational.

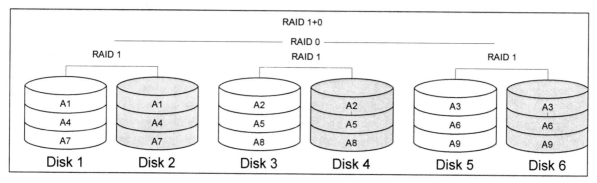

Figure 2.6: RAID 1+0 implementation.

Since no parity calculations must occur, RAID 1+0 is the fastest RAID configuration for writes that also provides redundancy, offering performance near to, or matching, the performance of a RAID 0 configuration. However, for the number of spindles that comprise the array, read performance will generally be lower than a RAID 5 array configured with the same number of physical disks.

RAID 01

RAID 01 or RAID 0+1, is a nested RAID level also known as "mirrored pairs of striped disks." In a RAID 0+1 configuration, the nested levels are the opposite of the RAID 1+0, with the disks first being striped in a RAID 0 and then mirrored using RAID 1. However, this type of configuration only allows for a single disk loss from one side of the array, since a single disk failure in a RAID 0 array causes that array to fail. A loss of a single disk in both of the RAID 0 striped arrays would result in total data loss. The higher risk of data loss in RAID 01 means that, in most circumstances, RAID 1+0 is preferable for SQL Server installations.

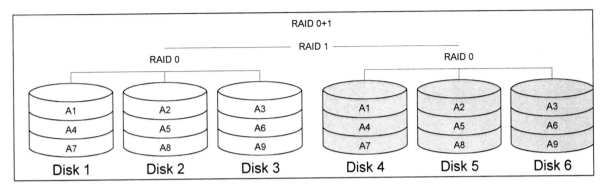

Figure 2.7: RAID 0+1 implementation.

Disk size and throughput considerations

Modern hard disks are much larger in size than previously available, making larger capacities possible with fewer disks. However, as discussed earlier, purchasing a small number of large disks may not be the best option in terms of I/O performance and throughput. For example, consider a database that is 400 GB in size and performs a balanced mix of random read and write operations. The number of possible RAID and disk configurations for this database exceeds the space available for this entire book. However, a few potential configurations are as follows:

1. RAID 1 using 2 x 600 GB 15 K RPM disks

2. RAID 5 using 3 x 300 GB 15 K RPM disks

3. RAID 5 using 5 x 146 GB 15 K RPM disks

4. RAID 10 using 8 x 146 GB 15 K RPM disks

5. RAID 10 using 14 x 73 GB 15 K RPM disks.

Based on the above RAID configurations, the following I/O throughput rates would be theoretically possible based on a 64 K random I/O workload for SQL Server:

1. 185 IOPS at 11.5 MB/sec

2. 222 IOPS at 14 MB/sec

3. 345 IOPS at 22 MB/sec

4. 816 IOPS at 51 MB/sec

5. 1609 IOPS at 101 MB/sec.

Hopefully, the message is clear: the number of disk heads, and the RAID configuration, will have a direct and dramatic impact on the potential I/O capacity of the RAID array.

Remember, though, that these numbers are theoretical, meaning that they are solely based on the potential I/O capacity of the disks in a given configuration. They take no account of other factors that can and will have an impact on overall throughput, including:

- **RAID controller cache size and configuration** for read and write caching, which can improve read-ahead pre-fetch if more cache is dedicated to reads, or absorb heavy bursts of write activity if more cache is dedicated to writes.

- **RAID stripe size**, which determines the amount of data that is written to, or read from, a single disk in a stripe before advancing to the next disk in the stripe.

- **Partition alignment**, which ensures that the starting offset of a disk partition is aligned with the RAID stripe size and sector offset for the disk, so that read and write operations don't cross sector boundaries, incurring an additional I/O operation to complete. See *Incorrect partition alignment*, later in this chapter, for further details.

- **NTFS format allocation unit sizes**; the 4 K default for NTFS is good for file servers and the operating system drives, but not database data files which perform better using a 64 K allocation unit.

The only way to be sure that your selected disk configuration will cope gracefully with the workload placed on it by your databases is to perform proper benchmarking of the I/O subsystem, prior to usage. Never rely on theoretical calculations for your values of either IOPS or MB/s throughput. You need to simulate a realistic I/O workload, using multiple workers, and get the actual numbers.

A number of tools exist for measuring the I/O throughput of a given configuration, but the two most common tools used for benchmarking storage configurations for SQL Server are **SQLIO** and **IOmeter.**

SQLIO has to be one of the worst-named tools in the world, since it leads to the common misconception that it simulates the I/O workload of SQL Server. The truth is that the tool has absolutely nothing to do with SQL Server; it is simply an I/O stress tool that generates I/O based on the command-like parameters that are passed to the tool. IOmeter is also an I/O stress testing tool, originally developed by Intel and later released as an open source project. Of the two, IOmeter is the most flexible, and can generate mixed I/O workloads that more closely reflect what might be generated by SQL Server. IOmeter also has a graphical user interface that is used for configuring the tests and monitoring their progress.

Downloading SQLIO or IOmeter

SQLIO can be downloaded for free from Microsoft's website at HTTP://WWW.MICROSOFT.COM/DOWN-LOAD/EN/DETAILS.ASPX?ID=20163.

IOmeter can be downloaded for free from HTTP://WWW.IOMETER.ORG/.

Microsoft provides a separate tool for testing the reliability and integrity of a disk configuration, named **SQLIOSim.** This tool tests the storage using the same disk operations that SQL Server would perform for reads, writes, checkpoints, backups, and read-ahead operations, to ensure that the storage meets the reliability requirements for SQL Server. Unlike SQLIO and IOmeter, SQLIOSim uses separate data and log files to simulate the reading and writing activity of SQL Server, using the same types of I/O patterns for each file that would occur under normal operations. This tool should be used to validate that the I/O subsystem functions correctly under heavy loads, but it should not be used for performance benchmarking the configuration.

Downloading SQLIOSim

SQLIOSim can be downloaded from Microsoft's website at HTTP://SUPPORT.MICROSOFT.COM/ KB/231619/EN-US.

Workload considerations

As discussed previously, there are many factors that will influence the choices you make for your disk I/O subsystem, and especially the RAID level, such as how often the data is written compared to read, and whether the I/O is largely sequential or random in nature. Also important is the need to correctly distribute your workload across the hardware resources, by placing data and log files on separate, dedicated disks, and making special consideration for the `tempdb` database.

Data files

The appropriate disk configuration for the data files of a database depends heavily on the read-to-write ratio for the database. SQL Server tracks the I/O usage of the database files for an instance and makes this information available in the `sys.dm_io_virtual_file_stats` Dynamic Management Function. While this information can be used to determine if your overall workload is heavier for reads vs. writes, the information contained in the output is based on the operations that have occurred since the last time the SQL Server instance started up, so it is important to ensure that your normal representative workload for the server has occurred, before using this information to determine your workload division.

For a database that is primarily read-only, RAID 5 or RAID 6 can offer good read performance, while also maximizing the available storage. RAID 5 or 6 arrays are commonly used for data warehouses, or for storing data where write latency doesn't impact overall system performance.

However, for highly transactional databases where the number of writes is comparable to the number of reads, using a RAID 5 or RAID 6 configuration for the data files disks can cause a bottleneck during checkpoint operations, when "dirty pages" in the buffer cache are written to the data file.

For OLTP implementations of heavy-write databases, RAID 1+0 provides the best performance since it doesn't perform parity calculations during write operations. Of course, RAID 1+0 arrays bring a much higher implementation cost, since the available storage is exactly half of the configured disks in the array.

Log files

For databases that are subject to a substantial amount of write activity, the sizing and configuration of the disks for the transaction log file, and hence the performance of log writes, can be critical to the overall performance of the system. This is because all data changes must first be hardened in the log file before a transaction commit (either implicit or explicit) can be considered complete, and before the data pages can be written to disk (in the case where CHECKPOINT or LAZY WRITER write a dirty data page to disk before the transaction commits).

Since the transaction log is written to sequentially, RAID 1 can be used in most situations. For highly transactional databases, the transaction log for each database should be located on dedicated physical disks. Having the log files for multiple highly transactional databases on the same physical disks can result in write I/O bottlenecks, often shown by high WRITELOG waits in sys.dm_os_wait_stats, and by high io_write_stall_ms values in sys.dm_io_virtual_file_stats() for the transaction log file. These waits are caused by the disk head having to be repositioned across the disk platters to perform the writes, and can be worse when multiple transaction log files are physically interleaved, or physically fragmented on disk.

Special considerations for tempdb

The `tempdb` database in SQL Server is a special database that is used by the database engine during the execution of user requests, for performing sorts that exceed the memory allocated to the sort, hash operations, and to store data for temporary tables and table variables. In SQL Server 2005 and 2008, it is also used to maintain version store information, for trigger execution, online index operations, when using the `SNAPSHOT` and `READ COMMITTED SNAPSHOT` Isolation levels (a.k.a. row versioning), and in SQL Server 2008 for maintaining Change Tracking information. In addition to the general usage of `tempdb`, some maintenance operations, such as `DBCC CHECKDB` and index rebuilds performed `ONLINE` or using the `SORT_IN_TEMPDB` option, can make heavy use of `tempdb`.

The `tempdb` database is a global resource, used in the manner described above by all sessions connected to a SQL Server instance. One of the best descriptions of `tempdb` was made by SQL Server MVP Brent Ozar, who described it as being "like a public toilet, anyone can abuse it with all sorts of horrific things you probably wouldn't approve of." As such, special consideration is needed with regard to disk configuration, in order to avoid contention on this resource.

As a general rule, the `tempdb` database files should be physically separate from the user data files and transaction log files, on a dedicated disk array. Since `tempdb` is a write-heavy database, RAID 1 or RAID 1+0 are usually the configurations best able to support the concurrent workload of `tempdb`.

However, since `tempdb` is used for temporary storage only, Solid State Disks and even RamDisks (disks created by software drivers using RAM from the server, or from specialized hardware devices) can be used to significantly improve the I/O characteristics of the `tempdb` database, removing the rotating media and disk head from the configuration, and so reducing the seek latency for both reads and writes.

The `tempdb` database is subject to specific problems that generally don't affect standard user databases, specifically **PFS**, **GAM**, and **SGAM** contention, associated with the consistent creation and destruction of temporary objects (see HTTP://BLOGS.MSDN.COM/ SQLSERVERSTORAGEENGINE/ARCHIVE/2009/01/04/WHAT-IS-ALLOCATION-BOTTLENECK.ASPX for more details). To minimize the impact of this problem and, in most cases, to eliminate it, multiple data files can be created for the `tempdb` database that are the same size, and are configured with the same AutoGrowth settings. When a database has multiple files in the same filegroup, allocations are made from each file, using a proportionate fill factor, which causes the files to be used equally in proportion to their size and available free space. Since each file has its own **PFS**, **GAM** and **SGAM** pages, creating multiple files for `tempdb` will reduce contention on these pages when allocations are made.

Tip: configuring a single file per processor, or not!

SQL Server MVP Paul Randal provides guidance on the **PFS**, **GAM**, **SGAM** *problem with* `tempdb` *and the appropriate number of files to configure based on the number of processors on his blog posts: "Search Engine Q&A #12: Should you create multiple files for a user DB on a multi-core box?"* (HTTP://WWW.SQLSKILLS.COM/BLOGS/PAUL/POST/SEARCH-ENGINE-QA-12-SHOULD-YOU-CREATE-MUL-TIPLE-FILES-FOR-A-USER-DB-ON-A-MULTI-CORE-BOX.ASPX) *and "A SQL Server DBA myth a day: (12/30) tempdb should always have one data file per processor core"* (HTTP://SQLSKILLS.COM/BLOGS/PAUL/POST/A-SQL-SERVER-DBA-MYTH-A-DAY-(1230)-TEMPDB-SHOULD-ALWAYS-HAVE-ONE-DATA-FILE-PER-PROCESSOR-CORE.ASPX).

Direct Attached Storage vs. Storage Area Networks

The two most common configurations used for SQL Server storage are Direct Attached Storage (DAS) and Storage Area Networks (SAN), and each has its own pros and cons that must be understood in order to arrive at an appropriate implementation for SQL Server.

Direct Attached Storage

DAS is the traditional method of providing storage for servers, where the disks used by the server are directly attached to the server. The disks are either built into the server chassis, or are housed in external expansion bays that are plugged in to the server using a RAID controller.

DAS implementations are cheap to build, provide predictable performance characteristics, since the disks are dedicated to a single server, and require the least amount of experience and knowledge to implement properly. However, depending on the specific implementation, DAS solutions will not have the advanced feature set that may be available when using a SAN, such as support for failover clustering, disk array snapshots, and cross-data center, array-based replication (a redundancy feature, which allows data written to the array to be replicated to a second SAN).

With DAS solutions, performance troubleshooting is greatly simplified, since the number of components is reduced, and there is only a single system utilizing the I/O subsystem.

Storage Area Networks

SAN implementations are a more advanced configuration for enterprise-wide storage requirements. The storage is centrally managed in a shared environment, allowing for higher usage density of the available storage. In other words, SANs are designed to optimize storage usage, not necessarily optimize storage performance. However, SANs do offer a significantly more advanced feature set than is generally available through DAS. A basic example of a typical SAN environment is shown in Figure 2.8.

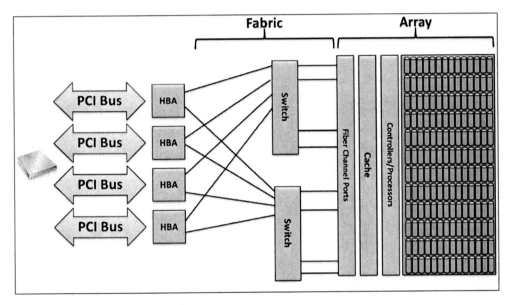

Figure 2.8: Typical SAN implementation.

However, the shared storage implementation also adds to the complexity of trouble-shooting performance problems. Depending on the specific implementation, storage can be optimized for I/O performance, and/or it can be optimized solely for capacity, or it can be entirely proprietary to the SAN vendor, in which case little control exists for the physical implementation of the environment.

One of the biggest problems with SAN-based storage arrays, for many SQL Server DBAs, is the manner in which the physical implementation of the storage array is "abstracted." When accessing data in a SAN array, all Windows sees is a "single physical disk," presented as a Logical Unit Number (LUN). However, a SAN might be using 50 LUNs from a shared pool of disks that are also being used by the rest of the enterprise. This can have performance ramifications for SQL Server. Unless a DBA has worked directly with a SAN administrator to plan out the I/O configuration of the LUNs being used by a SQL Server, the DBA has no idea how the physical hardware is actually being used.

Depending on the vendor, the SAN implementation, and the workload requirements, sharing storage at the physical level can result in acceptable performance but can become a nightmare for troubleshooting when problem arise, where one team points the finger at the other and vice versa.

As a general recommendation, when using SAN-based storage for SQL Server, the same I/O considerations must be made that would be made when using a DAS implementation. The underlying storage for the data files should be optimized for random I/O and segregated physically from the underlying storage for the transaction log files, which should be optimized for sequential I/O. The I/O throughput must be able to sustain the workload requirements, and any bottlenecks in the system must be fully understood before actually implementing the configuration for production usage.

For SAN implementations, the "SAN fabric" is the network that is configured to provide access from the server to the physical disks which back the LUNs being presented to the server. This SAN fabric consists of multiple switched interconnections that provide redundancy to the configuration. There are multiple components, such as Host Bus Adapters (HBAs), storage controllers, and network switches, in the connection between the server and the SAN, any of which could become a potential bottleneck to your overall I/O capacity.

SAN-based implementations make use of HBAs, which are purpose-built network cards that provide access to the storage network (Fabric + Array, in Figure 2.8), via fiber optic cables (FC), standard network Ethernet (iSCSI), or a hybrid mix of the two known as

Fiber Channel over Ethernet (FCOE). Depending on the specific implementation being used, and whether or not multi-path I/O has been configured appropriately for the environment, the I/O performance and throughput may be limited to the port speed of a single HBA in server.

Multi-path I/O

Multi-path I/O (MPIO) provides multiple, redundant paths from a single server to the SAN implementation. Depending on the configuration of the MPIO, one of the benefits can also be load balancing across the connections, which can result in performance improvements compared to using a single connection. Different MPIO implementations have different characteristics, and it is best to work with your specific hardware vendor to configure MPIO in your environment.

The HBAs of the servers connect to network switches that, in turn, connect to the storage controllers on the SAN. The storage controllers manage the physical disks which comprise the actual storage available to the SAN implementation. Each of the storage controllers can have one or more connections into the network, and each one maintains its own cache for frequently read data, and/or to handle writes immediately, allowing deferred flushes to the physical disks, which can be slower than writing directly to cache. These caches can be mirrored to other controllers over high-speed connections, to allow failure to occur with minimal to no impact on the environment. In this way, multiple storage controllers work together as a sort of "failover cluster" for the SAN, providing high availability.

When using SAN-based storage implementations, the slowest point in the overall configuration will be the bottleneck for the system. For example, consider a SAN using a 4 Gb/sec HBA and connecting to a 4 Gb/sec switch that connects to a 2 Gb/sec storage controller port. Even if the physical disks in the array are capable of 8 Gb/sec of I/O, the 2 Gb/sec storage controller port will be the bottleneck in the implementation.

This is the reason that troubleshooting SAN-based implementations for SQL Server can be incredibly difficult. Any time a SAN is being used with SQL Server, troubleshooting the performance problems in the environment requires additional support from the SAN administrator.

Diagnosing Disk I/O Issues

My primary tool for investigating disk I/O issues is PerfMon and specifically the `Physical Disk\Disk Reads/sec` and `Physical Disk\Disk Writes/sec` counters. The key for performance is having the lowest latency possible and my guideline latency values for each of these counters are as follows:

- Less than 10 ms = good performance

- Between 10 ms and 20 ms = slow performance

- Between 20 ms and 50 ms = poor performance

- Greater than 50 ms = significant performance problem.

In addition to the performance counters, high wait times for `PAGEIOLATCH_*`, `ASYNC_IO_COMPLETION`, `IO_COMPLETION`, or `WRITELOG` waits can be signs of disk I/O bottlenecks on the server. The query to retrieve the wait statistics for an instance of SQL Server is included in the *Wait Statistics: the Basis for Troubleshooting* section of *Chapter 1*.

Common Disk I/O Problems

As with many of the problems covered throughout this book, the first port of call when attempting to resolve I/O issues is to ensure that a lack of indexing (*Chapter 5*), or poorly written queries, isn't causing a needlessly excessive amount of I/O. If your database design and query workload are as tuned as they can be, and the I/O problem persists, then you're probably suffering from a disk misconfiguration issue. Based on the questions I see in online technical forums, and on my experience as a consultant, the following misconfigurations are at the heart of many of the disk I/O issues that I see:

- sizing for capacity instead of I/O performance

- incorrect workload isolation

- incorrect partition alignment

- incorrect bandwidth using SAN configurations.

Each of these problems and the steps necessary to troubleshoot them will be covered in the remaining sections of this chapter.

Sizing for capacity instead of I/O performance

As previously covered in this chapter, proper sizing of the disk subsystem for SQL Server is primarily a matter of performance, and not actual storage capacity. Often, unless an experienced DBA is involved in the purchasing decisions, the key factor used in provisioning hardware is the size of the database, and not the workload I/O performance requirements.

A 800 GB database can be stored on a single 1TB drive, but the chances of a single 1TB drive being able to supply the I/O capacity that will deliver satisfactory performance under concurrent user access, are slim at best. The key to high-performance disk configurations is having lots of physical disks working together, using RAID, to provide both the required I/O capacity and the necessary storage space.

With SAN implementations, it is more likely that you will get the number of disks necessary to handle the I/O performance requirements. However, since most SAN implementations are not dedicated to SQL Server alone, you also have to account for the shared I/O performance requirements of the other servers, using the same physical disks, and the potential impact that this shared I/O will have on SQL Server performance.

Troubleshooting problems with I/O performance requires monitoring the performance counters for the disk I/O subsystem, as well as monitoring the virtual file and wait stats for the database instance, to determine the impact the I/O subsystem may be having on SQL Server performance.

Incorrect workload isolation

Workload isolation is critical for SQL Server storage planning. As discussed earlier, the I/O characteristics of the transaction log files and data files are significantly different, and segregating the I/O for the two files is critical to overall system performance. For high-write workloads, in particular, where the transaction log files are constantly written to, the need to isolate the transaction log files on separate physical disk arrays is paramount.

In SAN-based implementations, where there are no dedicated spindles configured specifically for SQL Server, workload isolation also has to take into account the other systems that are sharing the physical spindles, and the impact that they will have on the performance of SQL Server.

As discussed in the SAN section, earlier, it is very common in small and medium business infrastructures to have SANs that allocate storage to SQL Server from a disk pool that is shared by the whole enterprise, and so is being used by all manner of other applications. My advice is to consider this sort of configuration inappropriate for use with SQL Server, unless appropriate testing proves otherwise, or the pool of disks is large enough to support the required I/O throughput for the shared demand.

If a shared pool of disks is being used, it is important to have the right monitoring tools in place for the configuration. Having a SQL Server database, Oracle database, and busy Exchange mailbox database sharing a small disk pool is likely to be problematic for all three in terms of performance, due to the competing high I/O workloads.

Incorrect partition alignment

At PASS Summit 2008, Jimmy May, a member of the SQLCAT team, presented a session on *Disk Partition Alignment Best Practices for SQL* Server, which was later turned into a white paper of the same name (HTTP://MSDN.MICROSOFT.COM/EN-US/LIBRARY/DD758814%28V=SQL.100%29.ASPX). At that time, few people had ever heard of partition alignment, let alone realized that it had long been a silent performance killer for disk storage arrays, often reducing performance by as much as 20–30% overall.

The crux of the problem is that disk hardware reports 63 hidden sectors at the beginning of the drive, which are used for the master boot record (MBR) and Windows reserves the space required for the MBR when creating a partition on the disk. This offset of 63 sectors results in a 31.5 KB offset of the disk, which is misaligned with the standard stripe unit sizes used by RAID controllers, which range from 4 KB to 512 KB based on the specific controller and configuration being used to control the size of each stripe element written to, or read from, each disk in the stripe.

Most disks commonly used today have a 512-byte sector size, but newer disks and SSDs may use a 4 KB sector size. The recommended allocation unit size for SQL Server is 64 KB, instead of the default 4 KB on NTFS and, based on the recommended allocation unit size for a 512-byte sector, a 64 KB block of data will use 128 sectors.

When this is offset by 63 sectors, the result is a split I/O, where one disk in the array incurs an I/O operation to read 65 sectors of information and a second I/O request occurs to the next disk in the array to read the remaining 63 sectors of data for the 64 KB block of data.

To prevent this problem from continuing in the future, Microsoft changed Windows Server 2008 to offset the starting partition at a 1 MB boundary, which is compatible with all existing stripe unit sizes for RAID, and results in appropriate alignment of the disk. The problem is that moving a disk to Windows Server 2008 doesn't fix the problem, and any disk that was partitioned on Windows Server 2000 or 2003 will be misaligned unless it was explicitly aligned using `diskpar` (Windows Server 2000) or `diskpart` (Windows Server 2003) from the command line.

The only way to find out if you have this problem is to run the WMIC command shown in Listing 2.1, from the command line, to retrieve the current partition offset information from Windows, and determine if any of the partitions are misaligned.

```
wmic partition get BlockSize, StartingOffset, Name, Index
```

Listing 2.1: Using WMI query to investigate possible disk partition misalignment.

If the `StartingOffset` value is not evenly divisible without a remainder, or decimal result, by the stripe unit size being used by the RAID controller, then the disk is misaligned.

The good news is that fixing a misaligned partition is very easy to do, but the bad news is that, to fix the problem, you have to delete the existing partitions and data from the disks and start over. The `diskpart` tool in Windows Server 2003, 2008, and 2008 R2 can be used to create a partition on a disk that is aligned to a specified size in KB. The following `diskpart` command will create a partition that is aligned at 64 KB.

```
create partition primary align=64
```

Listing 2.2: Creating a 64 KB aligned partition.

Once the partition is aligned it can be assigned a letter and formatted, using the recommended 64 KB allocation unit size, then put back into service as a host for database files, without the costly performance impact associated with misalignment.

Incorrect bandwidth using SAN configurations

In SAN environments, where the storage is attached through a network connection, one of the biggest limiting factors to storage performance is the bandwidth available for the connection. This is true regardless of whether the connection is Fiber Channel, or iSCSI, using traditional Ethernet for the connectivity.

When I first started working with SAN environments for SQL Server the prevailing technology in use was Fiber Channel, and the standard port speed was 2 Gb/sec for a single path. At the time, newer hardware that supported 4 Gb/sec connections for a single path was just being implemented in environments. Soon thereafter, 1 Gb/sec iSCSI began to appear in small-to-medium business environments, as a lower-cost implementation of shared storage for the enterprise.

For me, one of the hardest things to understand, when working with SANs, was the impact that the paths to the SAN had on storage performance, especially in multi-path environments where the expectation was that multiple paths to the SAN would improve the overall performance of the storage connections.

When using SAN multi-path technologies, the initial benchmarking and validation of the storage configuration is incredibly important. You need to verify whether or not the multiple paths to the SAN really *are* being used in conjunction with each other to improve the performance.

Typically, a 1 Gb/sec connection to a SAN will be capable of a maximum throughput of 90–95 MB/sec, assuming the underlying storage configuration will support this level of throughput. So, theoretically, two 1 Gb/sec connections should provide 180–190 Mb/sec of throughput. However, depending on the exact multi-path configuration, this may not be an accurate expectation.

A full discussion of multi-path configurations of SANs is beyond our remit, but the key point in determining the available bandwidth is **appropriate benchmarking of the storage subsystem** using tools like SQLIO or IOmeter. If the storage performance is not meeting the expectations for the configuration, you will have to determine where exactly the bottleneck in the configuration lies, and continue troubleshooting from there. It could be that the number of disks underlying the storage array cannot support the throughput requirements, or that the SAN caching is the bottleneck, or that the multi-path configuration is not functioning as expected and you are only getting an actual single path to the SAN for I/O.

Summary

Proper configuration of the hardware, as well as the SQL Server database engine, is critical to the optimum performance of the overall system. Incorrect hardware configurations, generally in the disk I/O subsystem, often result in a system that fails to meet performance expectations.

The best strategy with regard to disk I/O configuration problems could be summarized as "avoid them as far as possible, through appropriate planning and testing."

- Don't consider only storage capacity when provisioning the disk subsystem; I/O performance and throughput are critical.

- Make sure your files are separated according to the type of I/O workload. Data files, log files, and tempdb files should all be on separate disks, and configured appropriately for the given workload type.

- Test the performance of your disk subsystem under realistic loads; it's the only way to be sure will meet your I/O performance and throughput requirements.

If your system does suffer from disk I/O issues, there are very few quick fixes. First, you need to ensure that you're not wasting I/O cycles, either through poorly designed queries, lack of indexing, or through hardware-related "bugs" such as disk partition misalignment.

Beyond that, you probably need to add I/O capacity, or work out what component is causing the I/O bottleneck. If you are using DAS, this may be relatively straightforward. If you're using a SAN, it helps if you are friendly with your SAN administrator.

Chapter 3: High CPU Utilization

A CPU-bound system is relatively easy to spot, but not always as easy to diagnose. If you notice that one or more of the CPUs are working at close to maximum capacity, along with a dramatic decrease in server performance, then you've likely got a CPU issue. The CPU is involved in almost all SQL Server activity, from running queries to moving data in and out of memory, and so on, which means that an over-taxed CPU can have dire consequences.

Unfortunately, the source of CPU pressure is not always easy to pinpoint since what seems like a CPU problem may actually have its root cause elsewhere, such as insufficient memory, causing SQL Server to constantly move data in and out of memory, or poorly written queries, inadequate indexing, or even inappropriate configuration option settings. The source of the CPU pressure may also be a non-SQL Server process running on the server.

Regardless of what caused the problem, the goal of the investigation stage of troubleshooting excessive CPU utilization in SQL Server is to isolate the problem to a specific source. Generally, this will require the collection of multiple pieces of information, using tools such as Performance Monitor (PerfMon), SQLTrace and several of the SQL Server Dynamic Management Views.

Once it has been confirmed that the high CPU usage is due to the SQL Server process, and the problem has been isolated to a specific query (or set of queries), we can seek to alleviate the CPU pressure via design changes, such as tuning CPU-intensive queries, adding appropriate indexes, replacing ad hoc SQL with stored procedures to improve plan reuse and so on, or by tweaking SQL Server and Windows configuration settings.

Investigating CPU Pressure

In this section, we'll discuss the three main tools used to measure CPU usage, and diagnose CPU pressure, in SQL Server:

- **Performance Monitor** – a Windows monitoring tool for measuring the CPU usage by SQL Server and other processes running on the server.

- **SQLTrace** – a set of system stored procedures for real-time tracing events that are executing in SQL Server during periods of high CPU usage.

- **Dynamic Management Views** – a collection of system objects that provide both snapshot and aggregate data regarding resource usage in SQL Server.

Performance Monitor

If your SQL Server system is experiencing excessively high CPU activity, the first tool for which you should reach is **Performance Monitor** (PerfMon). This Windows monitoring tool will confirm whether the excessive CPU usage is due to SQL Server activity, or is caused by other processes on the server, or the operating system itself. There is little point in spending valuable time and energy investigating SQL Server for excessive CPU usage, if the root cause is a non-SQL Server process.

The primary PerfMon counters that are of value for monitoring CPU usage are listed below with brief explanations (quoted from MSDN):

> `Processor/ %Privileged Time` – *percentage of time the processor spends on execution of Microsoft Windows kernel commands such as core operating system activity and device drivers.*
>
> `Processor/ %User Time` – *percentage of time the processor spends on executing user processes such as SQL Server. This includes I/O requests from SQL Server.*
>
> `Process (sqlservr.exe)/ %Processor Time` – *the sum of processor time on each processor for all threads of the process.*

Simply open up PerfMon (**Control Panel | System and Security | Administrative Tools**), click the **Add** button (represented by a green cross) and add the counters, as shown in Figure 3.1.

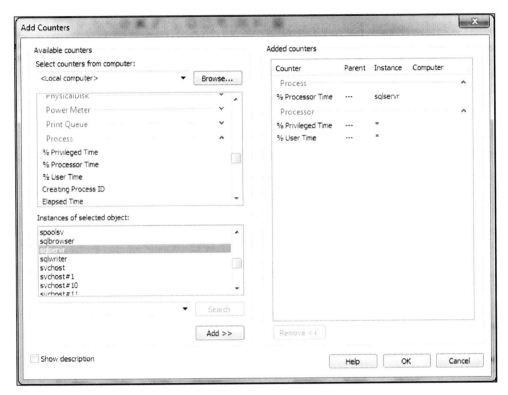

Figure 3.1:   Adding CPU counters in PerfMon.

These three counters are sufficient to monitor the overall CPU usage, as well as the usage by SQL Server. However, there are several SQL Statistics counters (and one Plan Cache counter) that don't directly monitor CPU usage but do monitor events such as compilation and recompilation events, which can eat up a lot of CPU cycles, or are indications of problems that produce high CPU usage. These counters are simply listed here, and discussed in further detail later in the chapter, in direct relation to the issues that they can be used to investigate.

- **SQLServer:SQL Statistics/Auto-Param Attempts/sec**

- **SQLServer:SQL Statistics/Failed Auto-params/sec**

- **SQLServer:SQL Statistics/Batch Requests/sec**

- **SQLServer:SQL Statistics/SQL Compilations/sec**

- **SQLServer:SQL Statistics/SQL Re-Compilations/sec**

- **SQLServer:Plan Cache/Cache hit Ratio**

None of these counters have hard thresholds that indicate "good" or "bad" values; instead they should be evaluated against what is normal for the system in question, and if a certain value falls far outside the normal range, the cause should be investigated further.

Processor usage in virtual machines

With a virtual machine (VM), the `%ProcessorTime` *is the percentage of the resources allocated to the VM that is being used, not the percentage allocated to the actual hardware. Hence, if the VM has been allocated very minimal CPU resources, PerfMon may show very high* `%ProcessorTime` *even though the actual CPUs are barely being used. One of the first steps when investigating high CPU usage in a virtual machine is to check the hardware usage of the virtual machine as a whole and ensure that the resource allocations are reasonable.*

SQL Trace

The Profiler utility included with SQL Server can be used to examine the details of what commands are running against a SQL Server. It is a useful tool for digging into details of specific problems once the general problem has been identified. The Profiler GUI makes use of a set of stored procedures, collectively known as **SQL Trace**. The GUI itself should be used with caution on busier servers, as it can have an adverse effect on the overall performance and stability of the server. Instead, a server-side trace should be run, with output directed to a file on a fast, local drive.

The main usage for SQL Trace is to identify specific queries that are consuming large amounts of CPU. It is less useful for a point-in-time analysis than the Dynamic Management Views are, and is more useful for capturing workloads for analysis. With the Dynamic Management Views (such as `sys.dm_exec_requests`) the rising resource usage can be watched while the query is still running, while with SQL Trace the statement or batch must complete before the event that shows the total resource usage is fired.

To capture a set of queries that are using excessive amounts of CPU, a trace needs to be run during times of high CPU usage. The details on how to set up and run a trace are given in *Chapter 5*, and will not be repeated here. The one additional consideration in running a trace to investigate queries that are consuming large amounts of CPU is that a trace filter should be added on the **CPU** column to avoid capturing large numbers of uninteresting queries.

Dynamic Management Views

Various Dynamic Management Views (DMVs) provide a range of information that can help diagnose CPU-related issues. This information includes aggregated query performance statistics, aggregated wait statistics, details of what is running, what is waiting for processing time, what is waiting for other resources, and other information that is hard or impossible to get in any other way. We can investigate high CPU usage by SQL Server by examining the CPU-related wait statistics, the scheduler details and the aggregated query performance statistics, as follows:

- Verifying the extent of CPU pressure via signal waits, using `sys.dm_os_wait_stats`.

- Diagnosing a CPU-bound system according the types of wait observed, using `sys.dm_os_wait_stats` and `sys.dm_os_schedulers`.

- Identifying high-CPU cached plans, and associated queries, using `sys.dm_exec_query_stats` and `sys.dm_exec_sql_text`.

- Identifying currently waiting tasks, especially ones waiting on CPU-related wait types using `sys.dm_os_waiting_tasks`.

- Observing the resource usage of currently executing queries with `sys.dm_exec_requests`.

Investigating CPU-related wait statistics

Whenever a session has to wait before the requested work can continue, SQL Server records the reason for the wait (the resource that is being waited on) and the length of time waited. The `sys.dm_os_wait_stats` DMV exposes these wait statistics, aggregated across all sessions since the server last restarted or the wait statistics were cleared out with the `DBCC SQLPERF('sys.dm_os_wait_stats', CLEAR);` command. This DMV can be used, among other things, to confirm CPU pressure and establish the most common wait types that are being experienced by a CPU-bound system.

It's worth noting that some third-party monitoring tools rely on the statistics in this DMV not being cleared out between server restarts as, if they are cleared out, it may impact the accuracy of the information shown by these monitoring tools.

Signal wait time

Along with a `wait_type` column, indicating the type of wait, the `sys.dm_os_wait_stats` DMV returns several useful wait times, including:

- **wait_time_ms** – total amount of time that tasks have waited on this given wait type; this value includes the time in the `signal_wait_time_ms` column. The value increments from the moment a task stops execution, to wait for a resource, to the point it resumes execution.

- **`signal_wait_time_ms`** – the total amount of time tasks took to start executing after being signaled (i.e. after the resource it was waiting for became available); this is time spent on the runnable queue, and is pure CPU wait.

If the signal wait time is a significant portion of the total wait time, it means that tasks are waiting a relatively long time to resume execution after the resources that they were waiting for became available. This can indicate either that there are lots of CPU-intensive queries, which may need optimizing, or that the server needs more CPU. The query in Listing 3.1 will provide a measure of how much of the total wait time is signal wait time.

```
SELECT   SUM(signal_wait_time_ms) AS TotalSignalWaitTime ,
         ( SUM(CAST(signal_wait_time_ms AS NUMERIC(20, 2)))
          / SUM(CAST(wait_time_ms AS NUMERIC(20, 2))) * 100 )
                    AS PercentageSignalWaitsOfTotalTime
FROM     sys.dm_os_wait_stats
```

Listing 3.1: Verifying CPU pressure via signal wait time.

Since this DMV shows aggregated wait times and counts since the statistics were cleared or since the server started, a point-in-time view of the wait stats is generally not that useful. What is most useful is to compare the wait stats at a particular time with the stats at an earlier time and see how they changed. The other option is to clear the wait stats DMV, using **`DBCC SQLPERF("sys.dm_os_wait_stats",CLEAR);`**, wait a while, then query and see what's accumulated in that known and set period of time.

Tracking session and statement-level waits

Since the wait times in this DMV are aggregated, it is hard to relate a wait time to a specific query, unless you're on a test system with only one session running. However, in SQL Server 2008, it's possible to do this if you use Extended Events. See my blog post: HTTP://SQLBLOG.COM/BLOGS/JONATHAN_KEHAYIAS/ ARCHIVE/2010/12/30/AN-XEVENT-A-DAY-30-OF-31-TRACKING-SESSION-AND-STATEMENT-LEVEL-WAITS. ASPX.

We can also use the **sys.dm_os_wait_stats** DMV to find out which resource waits are the most common in our CPU-bound system, as shown in Listing 3.2, where we identify the top wait events, ordered according to the total amount of time processes have waited (**wait_time_ms**) on this event. It is important to ignore the benign waits, typically ones caused by system processes that are expected to be waiting most of the time. We're also subtracting out the **signal_wait_time** as that portion of the wait time is not waiting for the particular resource, but waiting for time on the scheduler.

```
SELECT TOP ( 10 )
        wait_type ,
        waiting_tasks_count ,
        ( wait_time_ms - signal_wait_time_ms ) AS resource_wait_time ,
        max_wait_time_ms ,
        CASE waiting_tasks_count
          WHEN 0 THEN 0
          ELSE wait_time_ms / waiting_tasks_count
        END AS avg_wait_time
FROM    sys.dm_os_wait_stats
WHERE   wait_type NOT LIKE '%SLEEP%'       -- remove eg. SLEEP_TASK and
                                           -- LAZYWRITER_SLEEP waits
        AND wait_type NOT LIKE 'XE%'
        AND wait_type NOT IN -- remove system waits
( 'KSOURCE_WAKEUP', 'BROKER_TASK_STOP', 'FT_IFTS_SCHEDULER_IDLE_WAIT',
  'SQLTRACE_BUFFER_FLUSH', 'CLR_AUTO_EVENT', 'BROKER_EVENTHANDLER',
  'BAD_PAGE_PROCESS', 'BROKER_TRANSMITTER', 'CHECKPOINT_QUEUE',
  'DBMIRROR_EVENTS_QUEUE', 'SQLTRACE_BUFFER_FLUSH', 'CLR_MANUAL_EVENT',
  'ONDEMAND_TASK_QUEUE', 'REQUEST_FOR_DEADLOCK_SEARCH', 'LOGMGR_QUEUE',
  'BROKER_RECEIVE_WAITFOR', 'PREEMPTIVE_OS_GETPROCADDRESS',
  'PREEMPTIVE_OS_AUTHENTICATIONOPS', 'BROKER_TO_FLUSH' )
ORDER BY wait_time_ms DESC
-- **** Author: Jonathan Kaheyias ****
```

Listing 3.2:   Finding the top 10 wait events (cumulative).

Three interesting wait types to look out for, in regard to CPU pressure, are SOS_SCHEDULER_YIELD, CXPACKET and CMEMTHREAD.

SOS_SCHEDULER_YIELD waits

The SQL scheduler is a cooperative multi-tasking scheduler. This means that it relies on the executing queries to voluntarily relinquish the CPU after a specific amount of running time. By contrast, the Windows scheduler is a pre-emptive multi-tasking scheduler, which means it removes tasks from the CPU after a specific amount of time.

When a task voluntarily relinquishes the CPU and begins waiting to resume execution, the wait type assigned to the task is SOS_SCHEDULER_YIELD. The relinquishing task goes back onto the runnable queue and another task gets its allocated time on the CPU.

If overall wait times are low, this type of wait is benign, simply indicating that the query spent longer than allowed on the CPU without having to wait for other resources (disk I/O, locks, latches, memory grants and so on).

If queries show high wait times in sys.dm_exec_requests or sys.dm_os_waiting_tasks for the SOS_SCHEDULER_YIELD wait type, it's an indication that the query is extremely CPU-intensive. If there are high wait times for this wait type overall on the server it can indicate either that there are lots of CPU-intensive queries, which may need optimizing, or that the server needs more CPU. Scheduler activity can be investigated further using the sys.dm_os_schedulers DMV (discussed shortly).

CXPACKET waits

CXPACKET waits occur during synchronization of the query processor exchange iterator between workers, for a query running in parallel across multiple processors. If the server hosts a data warehouse or reporting type of database that receives a low volume of queries but processes large amounts of data, parallelism can substantially reduce the time it takes to execute those queries. In contrast, however, if the server hosts an OLTP database that has a lot of small queries and transactions, then parallelism can kill throughput and negatively impact performance. For further discussion of high CXPACKET waits and how to deal with this issue see the section *Inappropriate parallelism*, later.

CMEMTHREAD waits

CMEMTHREAD waits are waits for synchronized memory objects. Some memory objects can be accessed by multiple threads simultaneously, some cannot. When multiple threads are trying to access a memory object, typically a cache, which must be accessed by one thread at a time, the waiting threads get a CMEMTHREAD wait.

In general, CMEMTHREAD waits are not common or long-lasting. However, there is a known memory issue with SQL Server 2005 where, under certain circumstances, a server would show very high CPU usage, very high CMEMTHREAD waits, and very poorly performing queries. The details of this will be discussed later, in the *TokenAndPermUserStore* section.

Investigating scheduler queues

The sys.dm_os_schedulers DMV can identify whether or not a SQL instance is CPU-bound. This DMV returns one row for each of the SQL Server schedulers and it lists the total number of tasks that are assigned to each scheduler, as well as the number that are runnable.

A runnable task is one that is in the runnable queues, waiting for CPU time. Other tasks on the scheduler that are in the current_tasks_count but not the runnable_tasks_count are ones that are either sleeping or waiting for a resource (lock, latch, I/O, memory, and so on).

```sql
SELECT   scheduler_id ,
         current_tasks_count ,
         runnable_tasks_count
FROM     sys.dm_os_schedulers
WHERE    scheduler_id < 255
```

Listing 3.3:   Investigating scheduler queues.

Again, there is no threshold value that represents the boundary between a "good" and "bad" number of runnable tasks, but the lower the better. A high number of runnable tasks, like a high signal wait time, indicates that there is not enough CPU for the current query load.

The filter for schedulers below 255 removes, from the result set, the numerous hidden schedulers in SQL Server, which are used for backups, the Dedicated Administrator Connection (DAC), and so on, and are not of interest when investigating general CPU load.

Identifying CPU-intensive queries

In order to determine the worst-running queries in the plan cache of SQL Server, the DMVs `sys.dm_exec_query_stats` and `sys.dm_exec_sql_text` can be used. The `sys.dm_exec_query_stats` DMV provides aggregated statistics and returns one row for each query statement in the cached plan. Many of the columns are incremented counters, and provide information about how many times a query has been executed and the resources that were used. For example, the `*_worker_time` columns represent the time spent on the CPU, and the `*_elapsed_time` columns show the total execution time.

The query shown in Listing 3.4 returns the top ten most costly queries in cache by total worker time. We join to the `sys.dm_exec_sql_text` and `sys.dm_exec_query_plan` functions to retrieve the text and execution plans for these queries, within the batch.

```
SELECT TOP ( 10 )
        SUBSTRING(ST.text, ( QS.statement_start_offset / 2 ) + 1,
            ( ( CASE statement_end_offset
                WHEN -1 THEN DATALENGTH(st.text)
                ELSE QS.statement_end_offset
              END - QS.statement_start_offset ) / 2 ) + 1)
        AS statement_text ,
```

```
        execution_count ,
        total_worker_time / 1000 AS total_worker_time_ms ,
        ( total_worker_time / 1000 ) / execution_count
               AS avg_worker_time_ms ,
        total_logical_reads ,
        total_logical_reads / execution_count AS avg_logical_reads ,
        total_elapsed_time / 1000 AS total_elapsed_time_ms ,
        ( total_elapsed_time / 1000 ) / execution_count
               AS avg_elapsed_time_ms ,
        qp.query_plan
FROM    sys.dm_exec_query_stats qs
        CROSS APPLY sys.dm_exec_sql_text(qs.sql_handle) st
        CROSS APPLY sys.dm_exec_query_plan(qs.plan_handle) qp
ORDER BY total_worker_time DESC
```

Listing 3.4:   Finding the top ten CPU-consuming queries.

The execution plan can be viewed by clicking the XML link to open the plan in its graphical form. The execution plan returned is for the entire batch, not just the high-CPU statement.

When querying the plan cache in order to investigate sub-optimal plans, note that some queries may not be listed. Execution plans are retained in cache until SQL Server decides that the plan has aged to a point where it should be removed to allow for new execution plans to be cached, or the cache is fully or partially cleared by DBCC commands, database state changes (restoring a database, detaching or taking a database offline, and so on) or certain server-wide configuration changes, or SQL Server is restarted. SQL Server will also remove execution plans from the cache if it finds that extra memory is required elsewhere in the system.

Clearing the plan cache

You can flush all plans from the cache using, DBCC FREEPROCCACHE, *or supply a* plan_handle *or* sql_handle *to remove a plan for a specific batch. Alternatively,* DBCC FREEPROCINDB(db_id) *can be used to remove plans for a specific database.*

It's also important to note that some queries may never appear in the cache at all. Procedures marked `WITH RECOMPILE` and queries with the hint `OPTION (RECOMPILE)` are never cached. Also, the query stats for a query are cleared when the query recompiles for any reason, for example due to changing statistics or schema changes. As a result, queries that are subject to many recompilation events may also show a very low total for elapsed time, because that total is only for the current plan, which may not have been in cache very long.

This problem extends beyond just recompilation; the results you receive from queries such as Listing 3.4 will be skewed towards plans that have been in the cache the longest. An often-used plan that's been in the cache a long time will appear higher in the list than a really bad plan that has only recently been added to the cache.

You can still get a good idea of what queries have run and how they have run, but the only way to ensure a truly level playing field is to flush the cache and then perform the analysis after a set period of time. However, flushing the cache on a production server may not be the best idea, especially if that server is already known to be CPU-bound. That's why, if a comprehensive analysis is needed, I recommend you use server-side tracing to capture all of the executing queries for a period of time.

Common Causes of High CPU Usage

Regardless of the size and expense of the hardware and technology that underpins your SQL Server installations, there is always the risk that one or more poorly tuned T-SQL statements will cause severe overutilization of resources.

For every statement sent to SQL Server for execution, the query optimizer attempts to find the most efficient way to retrieve the data, i.e. the one that is the least expensive in terms of use of CPU, I/O and memory resources. The plan it produces will only be as good as the data access paths that are available to it, and the information it has regarding the data and its distribution. If appropriate indexes are missing, or queries are written in such a way that potentially-useful indexes are ignored, then the optimizer will not be able to come up with a truly optimal plan. Likewise, if the information the optimizer has regarding the data, via index statistics, is inaccurate, then the optimizer may select a sub-optimal plan, since the information that it is using to calculate the cost of plans is inaccurate.

Another possibility is that the optimizer will produce a plan that is optimal for one execution of the query (typically the one that triggered the optimization) and not for others. This is commonly known as "parameter sniffing," though it should more accurately be referred to as "inappropriate parameter sniffing," since parameter sniffing is in general a good thing, as we'll discuss later in the chapter.

Missing indexes

It might surprise some people to learn that missing indexes can cause high CPU usage but, in fact, a lack of appropriate indexing is one of the most common causes of heavy CPU and I/O utilization in SQL Server. When an appropriate index doesn't exist to satisfy a query, the table scans that result can cause significant CPU usage, as SQL has to read and process far, far more rows than is actually necessary to satisfy the query.

Using the execution plans obtained from the plan cache, as shown in Listing 3.4, we can find any operations that can be replaced with more efficient operations, by adding covering indexes, or in some cases changing the indexes that are in place. Let's consider a simple query against the **Adventureworks2008** database, as shown in Listing 3.5.

```
SELECT   per.FirstName ,
         per.LastName ,
         p.Name ,
         p.ProductNumber ,
         OrderDate ,
         LineTotal ,
         soh.TotalDue
FROM     Sales.SalesOrderHeader AS soh
```

```
        INNER JOIN Sales.SalesOrderDetail sod
                   ON soh.SalesOrderID = sod.SalesOrderID
        INNER JOIN Production.Product AS p ON sod.ProductID = p.ProductID
        INNER JOIN Sales.Customer AS c ON soh.CustomerID = c.CustomerID
        INNER JOIN Person.Person AS per
                   ON c.PersonID = per.BusinessEntityID
WHERE   LineTotal > 25000
```

Listing 3.5: A simple query in `AdventureWorks`.

This query causes a table scan on the `SalesOrderDetail` table, as there is no index on the `LineTotal` column. The execution characteristics (with all the necessary pages in the data cache, so no I/O waits) are as follows:

```
SQL Server parse and compile time:
   CPU time = 0 ms, elapsed time = 0 ms.

 SQL Server Execution Times:
   CPU time = 452 ms,  elapsed time = 458 ms.
```

Almost half a second of CPU time to return 24 rows; that's not good. Now let's add a simple index, as shown in Listing 3.6.

```
CREATE NONCLUSTERED INDEX idx_SalesOrderDetail_LineTotal
ON Sales.SalesOrderDetail (LineTotal)
```

Listing 3.6: Adding an index to the `LineTotal` column in `AdventureWorks`.

Now, if we run the same query again, the performance characteristics will be very different:

```
SQL Server parse and compile time:
   CPU time = 0 ms, elapsed time = 0 ms.

 SQL Server Execution Times:
   CPU time = 0 ms,  elapsed time = 8 ms.
```

This was a simplistic example, but it serves to demonstrate the point, and one of the major problems I see when investigating high CPU scenarios is very simply missing indexes.

Please refer to *Chapter 5* for further information on missing indexes.

Outdated statistics

The SQL Server Optimizer uses statistics to calculate the estimated cardinality for various query operators. That cardinality, essentially number of rows, affects the cost of the operators. The cost of the operators, in turn, determines the cost of the plan. If the cardinality estimation is wrong, because of outdated statistics, the cost that the optimizer calculates for the operators will also be wrong, leading the optimizer to select a plan that has a low estimated cost, but a very high actual cost when it is executed.

The most common side effect of incorrect statistics is that the optimizer estimates on the low-side for the number of rows, and so chooses operators that are very good for small numbers of rows, such as nested loop joins and key lookups. When the query is executed and it turns out that a large number of rows need to be processed, the chosen operators scale badly and the plan is highly inefficient.

One way to tell if there is a problem with statistics for a particular query, is to run the query in Management Studio, return the actual execution plan and examine the estimated and actual row counts for any index seek and scan operations within the execution plan. If the two counts are significantly different, bearing in mind that the estimated count is per execution of the operator and the actual count is a total for all executions of the operator, then one possibility is that the statistics are outdated.

Fixing outdated statistics is done via the **UPDATE STATISTICS** statement. This can be run for all the statistics on a table (**UPDATE STATISTICS <Table name>**) or just for one specific statistics set (**UPDATE STATISTICS <Table name> <statistic name>**).

If the problem is due to stale statistics, i.e. an update of the statistics fixes the problem, then you need to prevent a recurrence of the problem, and there are three ways to do it:

1. If the database setting, `Auto_Update_Statistics`, is off, consider turning it on. Alternatively, a database-wide statistics update job can be run on a regular basis.

2. If automatic updates are disabled for a particular index of set of statistics, as a result of rebuilding the index with the `NORECOMPUTE` option, they should be enabled.

3. A job can be created that updates the specific statistics that suffer from insufficient updates, and so result in performance problems. This job can be scheduled as often as necessary. I have heard of cases where such a job is run hourly.

Non-SARGable predicates

SARGable, where SARG stands for Search Argument, is one of those annoying made-up terms that we, as IT people, love to use; it simply means that that a predicate can be used in an index seek operation. The rules for SARGable predicates, in general, are that the column should be directly compared (equality or inequality) to an expression, and that any functions specified on the column will make the predicate non-SARGable. In other words, `WHERE SomeFunction(Column) = @Value` is not SARGable, whereas `WHERE Column = SomeOtherFunction(@Value)` is SARGable. Note that SARGability doesn't rule out the use of operators such as `LIKE` or `BETWEEN` (both inequality comparisons) or `IN` (treated as a set of equality comparisons).

Non-SARGable predicates can result in table or index scans and, similar to the case of missing indexes, this will cause significant CPU usage as SQL has to read and process far more rows than necessary. Listing 3.7 shows an example of a `WHERE` clause predicate that is non-SARGable due to the usage of some date-manipulation functions on the `ModifiedDate` column. This example assumes that an index has been added on `ModifiedDate`, as there is not one in the standard `AdventureWorks` database.

```
SELECT    soh.SalesOrderID ,
          OrderDate ,
          DueDate ,
          ShipDate ,
          Status ,
          SubTotal ,
          TaxAmt ,
          Freight ,
          TotalDue
FROM      Sales.SalesOrderheader AS soh
          INNER JOIN Sales.SalesOrderDetail AS sod
                  ON soh.SalesOrderID = sod.SalesOrderID
WHERE     CONVERT(VARCHAR(10), sod.ModifiedDate, 101) = '01/01/2010'
```

Listing 3.7:   A non-SARGable predicate in the search condition.

From the execution plan, we can see that use of the functions on the `ModifiedDate` column meant that an index seek operation was not possible; the entire index was scanned in order to locate the matching values, as shown in Figure 3.2.

Index Scan (NonClustered)	
Scan a nonclustered index, entirely or only a range.	
Physical Operation	Index Scan
Logical Operation	Index Scan
Actual Number of Rows	0
Estimated I/O Cost	1.69053
Estimated CPU Cost	1.06775
Estimated Number of Executions	1
Number of Executions	1
Estimated Operator Cost	2.75828 (69%)
Estimated Subtree Cost	2.75828
Estimated Number of Rows	2241.42
Estimated Row Size	19 B
Actual Rebinds	0
Actual Rewinds	0
Ordered	False
Node ID	12

Predicate
CONVERT(varchar(10),[Adventureworks].[Sales].
[SalesOrderDetail].[ModifiedDate] as [sod].
[ModifiedDate],101)='2010/01/01'
Object
[Adventureworks].[Sales].[SalesOrderDetail].
[idx_SalesOrderDetail_ModifiedDate] [sod]
Output List
[Adventureworks].[Sales].
[SalesOrderDetail].SalesOrderID

Figure 3.2:   An index scan on the `SalesOrderDetail` index.

This is a fairly common problem in SQL code. Dates can be difficult to work with and often people take the easiest approach, not realizing the impact it will have on performance. The change in this case is easy; modify the predicate to be a range (inequality) search for date and times within the desired day.

```
SELECT     soh.SalesOrderID ,
           OrderDate ,
           DueDate ,
           ShipDate ,
           Status ,
           SubTotal ,
           TaxAmt ,
           Freight ,
           TotalDue
FROM       Sales.SalesOrderheader AS soh
           INNER JOIN Sales.SalesOrderDetail AS sod ON soh.SalesOrderID = sod.
SalesOrderID
WHERE      sod.ModifiedDate >= '2010/01/01'
           AND sod.ModifiedDate < '2010/01/02'
```

Listing 3.8: A SARGable predicate in the search condition.

Figure 3.3 confirms that we now see an index seek operation.

This is a fairly common problem in many databases; I often see functions such as UPPER, LTRIM, ISNULL being used in queries, either in the joins or in the WHERE clause, and in many cases there is simply no need for them. If the columns use a case-insensitive collation, then uppercase and lowercase values are considered equal, and the use of the UPPER or LOWER functions do nothing other than degrade performance. Similarly, with string comparisons SQL ignores trailing spaces, removing the need for the RTRIM function.

Index Seek (NonClustered)

Scan a particular range of rows from a nonclustered index.

Physical Operation	Index Seek
Logical Operation	Index Seek
Actual Number of Rows	0
Estimated I/O Cost	0.003125
Estimated CPU Cost	0.0001581
Estimated Number of Executions	1
Number of Executions	1
Estimated Operator Cost	0.0032831 (50%)
Estimated Subtree Cost	0.0032831
Estimated Number of Rows	1
Estimated Row Size	11 B
Actual Rebinds	0
Actual Rewinds	0
Ordered	True
Node ID	2

Object
[Adventureworks].[Sales].[SalesOrderDetail].[idx_SalesOrderDetail_ModifiedDate] [sod]

Output List
[Adventureworks].[Sales].[SalesOrderDetail].SalesOrderID

Seek Predicates
Seek Keys[1]: Start: [Adventureworks].[Sales].[SalesOrderDetail].ModifiedDate >= Scalar Operator('2010-01-01 00:00:00.000'), End: [Adventureworks].[Sales].[SalesOrderDetail].ModifiedDate < Scalar Operator('2010-01-02 00:00:00.000')

Figure 3.3: An index seek on the `SalesOrderDetail` index.

Dealing with `NULL`s is always a fun one. The `ISNULL` function is often used unnecessarily due to a misunderstanding of how `NULL`s work in predicates. For example, the following two `WHERE` clause predicates are completely equivalent in function.

```
WHERE ISNULL(SomeCol,0) > 0
WHERE SomeCol > 0
```

In the first one, any row with a `NULL` value will be excluded because the `NULL` is converted to zero and the filter is for values greater than zero. In the second one, any row with a `NULL` value will be excluded because `NULL`s do not ever return `true` when compared to any value using the =, <>, <, > or any of the other comparison operators. They can only return `true` for `IS NULL` or `IS NOT NULL` checks. Hence, both predicates achieve the same result, but only the second one allows use of index seeks.

Implicit conversions

An implicit conversion results from a comparison of unequal data types. SQL cannot compare values of differing types and it must convert one of the columns involved to the same data type as the other, in order to do the comparison.

When an implicit conversion occurs on a column that is used in a WHERE or FROM clause, the SQL Server Optimizer dictates a conversion of all the column values before the filter can be applied. This means that, during the query execution, the query processor will convert the lower precedence data type to the higher precedence data type before applying the filter or join condition. This means that, as with the case of functions on the column, the predicate is considered non-SARGable and so index seeks cannot be used, SQL must process more rows than necessary to get the results, and this leads to higher CPU usage.

A common manifestation of this problem is the comparison of NVARCHAR parameters to columns that are of type VARCHAR. There are some data access libraries (JDBC springs immediately to mind) that pass string constants as Unicode (NVARCHAR), by default. The problem is demonstrated in Listing 3.9, where the AccountNumber column is a VARCHAR and the parameter is a Unicode string (NVARCHAR), so designated by the N before the opening quote.

```
SELECT   p.FirstName ,
         p.LastName ,
         c.AccountNumber
FROM     Sales.Customer AS c
         INNER JOIN Person.Person AS p ON c.PersonID = p.BusinessEntityID
WHERE    AccountNumber = N'AW00029594'
```

Listing 3.9: An implicit data type conversion in the search condition.

The relevant section of the execution plan, shown in Figure 3.4, confirms that we get an index scan operation.

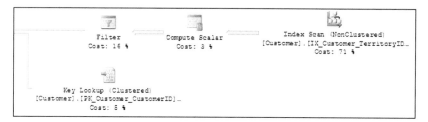

Figure 3.4:   The non-SARGable predicate results in an index scan.

The **Filter** properties window, in Figure 3.5, shows the implicit conversion.

Filter	
Restricting the set of rows based on a predicate.	
Physical Operation	Filter
Logical Operation	Filter
Actual Number of Rows	1
Estimated I/O Cost	0
Estimated CPU Cost	0.0114956
Estimated Number of Executions	1
Number of Executions	1
Estimated Operator Cost	0.0114956 (16%)
Estimated Subtree Cost	0.0637468
Estimated Number of Rows	1
Estimated Row Size	25 B
Actual Rebinds	0
Actual Rewinds	0
Node ID	3
Predicate	
CONVERT_IMPLICIT(nvarchar(10),[Adventureworks]. [Sales].[Customer].[AccountNumber] as [c]. [AccountNumber],0)=N'AW00029594'	
Output List	
[Adventureworks].[Sales].[Customer].CustomerID, [Adventureworks].[Sales].[Customer].AccountNumber	

Figure 3.5:   The filter predicate dictates the need to convert all the rows in
the AccountNumber column to NVARCHAR.

The fix for implicit conversions is to ensure that columns used in joins are always of the same type and that, in the WHERE clause, any variables, parameters or constants are of the same type as the columns to which they are being compared. If they are not, make careful use of conversion functions (CAST, CONVERT) on the variables, parameters or constants so that they match the data type of the column.

If using data access libraries like JDBC, check the properties to ensure that they are not passing all string values as **NVARCHAR** regardless of the underlying column data type.

Parameter sniffing

Parameter sniffing is a process used by SQL Server when creating an execution plan for a stored procedure, function, or parameterized query. The first time the plan is compiled, SQL Server will examine, or "sniff", the input parameter values supplied, and use them, in conjunction with the column statistics, to estimate the number of rows that will be touched by the query. It then uses that estimate in its costing of various possible execution plans. A problem only arises if the values that were passed as input parameters on initial plan creation, result in a row count that is atypical of that which will result from future executions of the procedure. Parameter sniffing only occurs at the time a plan is compiled or recompiled, and all subsequent executions of the stored procedure, function, or parameterized query will use the same plan.

During the initial compile, only the values of the input parameters can be sniffed as any local variables will have no value. If a statement within the batch is recompiled, both parameter and variable values can be sniffed, as the variables will, by that time, have values.

By way of an example, we'll use the **AdventureWorks** database again, and specifically the **ShipDate** in the **Sales.SalesOrderHeader** table. This column has a minimum date of 2011/07/08 and maximum date of 2004/08/07. Listing 3.10 shows a stored procedure to find all sales order numbers (also in this table) that are between two given ship dates.

```
CREATE PROCEDURE user_GetCustomerShipDates
    (
        @ShipDateStart DATETIME ,
        @ShipDateEnd DATETIME
    )
AS
    SELECT  CustomerID ,
```

```
            SalesOrderNumber
    FROM    Sales.SalesOrderHeader
    WHERE   ShipDate BETWEEN @ShipDateStart AND @ShipDateEnd
GO
```

Listing 3.10: The user_GetCustomerShipDates stored procedure.

This would be supported by a non-clustered index on ShipDate, as shown in Listing 3.11.

```
CREATE NONCLUSTERED INDEX IDX_ShipDate_ASC
    ON Sales.SalesOrderHeader (ShipDate)
GO
```

Listing 3.11: A non-clustered index on the ShipDate column.

Now, we'll execute the stored procedure twice, as shown in Listing 3.12, with the first query spanning a date range of several years, and so returning many rows, and the second one only covering a range of ten days. Be sure to retrieve the actual execution plan with the results.

```
DBCC FREEPROCCACHE
EXEC user_GetCustomerShipDates '2001/07/08', '2004/01/01'
EXEC user_GetCustomerShipDates '2001/07/10', '2001/07/20'
```

Listing 3.12: Executing the user_GetCustomerShipDates stored procedure, with the large date range query first.

Note that we ran DBCC FREEPROCCACHE to clear the plan cache and ensure a new plan is created. The plan is identical in each case, as shown in Figure 3.6

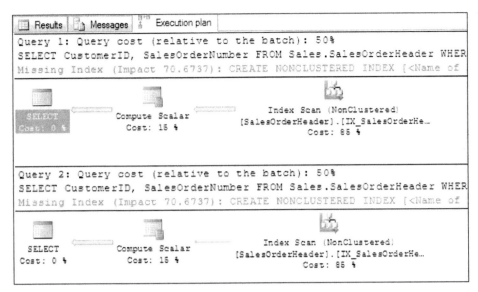

Figure 3.6: Execution plans for the user_GetCustomerShipDates stored procedure.

In the plan we see that optimizer has chosen *not* to use the non-clustered index on the ShipDate column, which we created especially for this procedure. The reason is that it is not a covering index (it doesn't include the SalesOrderNumber column) and the number of rows that the optimizer estimated, based on the parameter values for the initial execution, along with the statistics, was too high to make the combination of index seek/key lookup optimal. Hence the optimizer ignores that index and scans a different one.

Now, run Listing 3.12 again, this time not returning the execution plan, but with STATISTICS IO and STATISTICS TIME enabled. The reason we're doing a separate run is that returning the actual execution has an impact on the query's performance, so executions that return the execution plan should not also be used to check the query's performance statistics. The results are as follows (the separating headers were added manually, for clarity).

```
===FIRST EXECUTION (LARGE DATE RANGE)===

(Table 'SalesOrderHeader'. Scan count 1, logical reads 686, physical reads 0.

 SQL Server Execution Times:
   CPU time = 16 ms,  elapsed time = 197 ms.

 SQL Server Execution Times:
   CPU time = 16 ms,  elapsed time = 197 ms.

===SECOND EXECUTION (SMALL DATE RANGE)===

Table 'SalesOrderHeader'. Scan count 1, logical reads 686, physical reads 0.

 SQL Server Execution Times:
   CPU time = 15 ms,  elapsed time = 5 ms.

 SQL Server Execution Times:
   CPU time = 15 ms,  elapsed time = 5 ms.
```

The logical reads are shown as 686 reads for both, but it's the CPU time that is of far more interest here. It's worth noting that the majority of the elapsed time is actually the transmission and display of the rows, hence this time will be far larger for 17,000 rows (the first set) than for 40 rows (the second).

Now, we'll clear the cache again and flip the order of execution, so the shorter date range query is executed first, as shown in Listing 3.13. This means that, this time, the parameter sniffing process will result in a much lower estimated number of rows.

```
DBCC FREEPROCCACHE
EXEC user_GetCustomerShipDates '2001/07/10', '2001/07/20'
EXEC user_GetCustomerShipDates '2001/07/08', '2004/01/01'
```

Listing 3.13: Executing the user_GetCustomerShipDates stored procedure, with the shorter date range query first.

As expected, the execution plan has changed dramatically, as shown in Figure 3.7. The smaller number of estimated rows leads the optimizer to use an index seek on our IDX_ShipDate_ASC index, followed by a key lookup to retrieve the remaining rows.

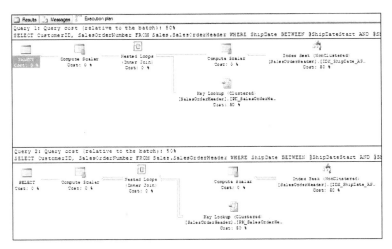

Figure 3.7: New execution plans for the user_GetCustomerShipDates stored procedure.

Run Listing 3.13 again, this time without the execution plan but with the statistics, and you'll see that the plan works just fine for the first execution, but causes problems for the next one.

```
===FIRST EXECUTION (SMALL DATE RANGE)====

Table 'SalesOrderHeader'. Scan count 1, logical reads 127, physical reads 0, read-
ahead reads 0, lob logical reads 0, lob physical reads 0, lob read-ahead reads 0.

 SQL Server Execution Times:
   CPU time = 0 ms,  elapsed time = 0 ms.

===SECOND EXECUTION (LARGE DATE RANGE)====

Table 'SalesOrderHeader'. Scan count 1, logical reads 52429, physical reads 0.

 SQL Server Execution Times:
   CPU time = 47 ms,  elapsed time = 182 ms.
```

Now that's not a huge jump in CPU time, but remember that even the second execution is dealing with 17,000 rows in the result set. At larger row counts, this problem can have a very significant impact.

This is a classic, though small-scale, example of parameter sniffing working against us. The plan with the key lookups is only optimal for small row counts (typically < 1% of the table). Above that, the additional I/O and additional CPU required for the key lookups becomes very significant.

There are several different ways to tackle parameter sniffing problems, depending on the situation and on the version of SQL Server you're using.

Trace Flag 4136

SQL Server 2008 introduced an option to turn parameter sniffing off altogether for a SQL Server instance, by simply enabling Trace Flag 4136. This option was added in SQL Server 2008 SP1 CU7, and SQL Server 2008 R2 CU2, and also back-ported into SQL Server 2005 in SP3 CU9.

When the query optimizer is able to "sniff" the value of a parameter, it uses this value, along with the statistics histogram, to provide an accurate estimate of the number of records that will be returned. As discussed earlier, this is only problematic if the initial parameter value turns out to be completely atypical.

When parameter sniffing is prevented, the optimizer can't find out the parameter value and so can't use the statistics histogram. Instead, it makes what is often a less accurate estimation of the number of rows that will be returned, by assuming a uniform data distribution across all data values. For example, consider a column X, containing 10 rows with values 1, 2, 3, 3, 3, 3, 3, 4, 5, 5. The optimizer would always estimate that a "WHERE X=value" query will return 2 rows (total number of rows divided by number of distinct values), and so the plan would always be optimized for this number of rows.

In short, although this option is available, parameter sniffing is beneficial to most procedures that are written to use typical values. Turning parameter sniffing off may inadvertently affect these plans in a negative way. As such, this Trace Flag should be considered an absolute last resort if nothing else fixes the problem.

Using the OPTIMIZE FOR hint

In SQL Server 2005 and later, we can use the OPTIMIZE FOR hint to specify a parameter value for the optimizer to use when compiling a plan, as shown in Listing 3.14.

```
CREATE PROCEDURE user_GetCustomerShipDates
    (
        @ShipDateStart DATETIME ,
        @ShipDateEnd DATETIME
    )
AS
    SELECT   CustomerID ,
             SalesOrderNumber
    FROM     Sales.SalesOrderHeader
    WHERE    ShipDate BETWEEN @ShipDateStart AND @ShipDateEnd
    OPTION   ( OPTIMIZE FOR ( @ShipDateStart = '2001/07/08',
                              @ShipDateEnd = '2004/01/01' ) )
GO
```

Listing 3.14: Using the OPTIMIZE FOR query hint.

This allows the optimizer to optimize the plan for a parameter value that is known to be more typically used. This will remove the possibility for parameter sniffing, but at the same time may still lead to a plan that is not as efficient, if atypical values are used.

In SQL Server 2008, this was "extended" to provide the OPTIMIZE FOR UNKNOWN hint, which instructs SQL Server to not use parameter sniffing at all. This allows for a query-by-query control of parameter sniffing, whereas the aforementioned Trace Flag controls the setting for the entire instance. In most cases, the hint is a more desirable solution as, in general, parameter sniffing is a good thing.

Recompilation options

We can use the `WITH RECOMPILE` option, when creating a stored procedure, as another possible solution to parameter sniffing issues. This will mean a plan is never cached for the procedures, since it forces a recompile, and generation of a new plan on every execution. This means that row estimations will always be based on the current parameter value, but at the cost of increasing the execution time of the procedure.

```
CREATE PROCEDURE user_GetCustomerShipDates
    (
      @ShipDateStart DATETIME ,
      @ShipDateEnd DATETIME
    )
    WITH RECOMPILE
AS
    SELECT   CustomerID ,
             SalesOrderNumber
    FROM     Sales.SalesOrderHeader
    WHERE    ShipDate BETWEEN @ShipDateStart AND @ShipDateEnd
GO
```

Listing 3.15:   Using the `WITH RECOMPILE` option.

The `OPTION(RECOMPILE)` query hint can be used in much the same way, and may be a better option if there are multiple queries within the procedure and only a portion of them suffer from parameter sniffing problems.

```
CREATE PROCEDURE user_GetCustomerShipDates
    (
      @ShipDateStart DATETIME ,
      @ShipDateEnd DATETIME
    )
AS
    SELECT   CustomerID ,
             SalesOrderNumber
    FROM     Sales.SalesOrderHeader
    WHERE    ShipDate BETWEEN @ShipDateStart AND @ShipDateEnd
    OPTION   ( RECOMPILE )
GO
```

Listing 3.16:   Using the `OPTION(RECOMPILE)` query hint.

These techniques are useful when the overhead of the additional compilations is small in comparison with the performance degradation caused by reuse of inappropriate plans. The OPTION(RECOMPILE) hint should be used where possible, in preference to WITH RECOMPILE for a stored procedure, in order to keep the impact of the repeated compilation process as low as possible.

Ad hoc non-parameterized queries

Ad hoc queries are statements sent to the optimizer that are not predefined by using stored procedures, sp_executesql or other ways to force reuse of execution plans. The SQL Server will always check on the plan cache to see if a suitable plan can be reused for a given query, before going through the full process of generating a new execution plan and storing it in cache.

Ad hoc queries will cause execution plans to be generated for each and every statement. This causes excessive use of resources, especially CPU. Consider the three queries shown in Listing 3.17.

```
SELECT   soh.SalesOrderNumber ,
         sod.ProductID
FROM     Sales.SalesOrderHeader AS soh
         INNER JOIN Sales.SalesOrderDetail AS sod
             ON soh.SalesOrderID = sod.SalesOrderID
WHERE    soh.SalesOrderNumber = 'SO43662'

SELECT   soh.SalesOrderNumber ,
         sod.ProductID
FROM     Sales.SalesOrderHeader AS soh
         INNER JOIN Sales.SalesOrderDetail AS sod
             ON soh.SalesOrderID = sod.SalesOrderID
WHERE    soh.SalesOrderNumber = 'SO58928'

SELECT   soh.SalesOrderNumber ,
         sod.ProductID
FROM     Sales.SalesOrderHeader AS soh
```

```
         INNER JOIN Sales.SalesOrderDetail AS sod
            ON soh.SalesOrderID = sod.SalesOrderID
WHERE    soh.SalesOrderNumber = 'SO70907'
```

Listing 3.17: Three simple but non-parameterized queries.

These three statements should produce the same execution plan, but they don't. The different values hard-coded into value assignment in the WHERE clause mean that they are considered by the optimizer to be three different queries, and hence get separate execution plans.

For very simple queries, SQL Server can use a technique called **simple parameterization** to replace the fixed values with parameters, and so allow for plan reuse. However, even the queries in Listing 3.17 are too complex to qualify for simple parameterization.

The problem with non-parameterized queries is two-fold:

1. **The plan cache fills up with lots of single-use plans from ad hoc queries.** This means that the memory is used less efficiently. It also means that plans that might have been reusable can get discarded from cache due to memory pressure, requiring them to be compiled again when the queries are rerun.

2. **The compilation of these single-use plans wastes CPU.** Compilation is expensive, using relatively large amounts of CPU, and the repeated compilation of plans for ad hoc queries, which are unlikely to be reused, is just a waste of resources.

Cases where a lack of parameterization is causing excessive plan compilation, or where simple (or forced) parameterization is attempted but fails, can be identified using the following counters from the SQL Statistics objects in Performance Monitor:

*   **SQLServer: SQL Statistics: SQL Compilations/Sec**
*   **SQLServer: SQL Statistics: Auto-Param Attempts/Sec**
*   **SQLServer: SQL Statistics: Failed Auto-Param/Sec**

Reference: HTTP://MSDN.MICROSOFT.COM/EN-US/LIBRARY/MS190911(SQL.100).ASPX.

If the non-parameterized ad hoc queries are causing a problem, there are a couple of options for fixing it. The first and best option is to fix the problem at source, in the calling application. If that is not an option, there are settings in SQL Server that can be changed to alleviate the problem.

Fixing the application

If it is possible to change the application that is sending these non-parameterized queries to SQL Server, then that option should be the one chosen. This can involve moving data access from ad hoc queries embedded in the front-end code into stored procedures, or it may just involve changing the ad hoc queries that are embedded in the front-end code to their parameterized versions. Listing 3.18 shows an unparameterized query being sent to SQL Server.

```
cmd.CommandType = CommandType.Text;
cmd.CommandText = @"SELECT soh.SalesOrderNumber,
                           sod.ProductID
                 FROM Sales.SalesOrderHeader AS soh
                       INNER JOIN Sales.SalesOrderDetail AS sod
                             ON soh.SalesOrderID = sod.SalesOrderID
                 WHERE soh.SalesOrderNumber = '" + txtSalesOrderNo.Text + "'";

dtrSalesOrders = cmd.ExecuteReader();
```

Listing 3.18: An unparameterized query being sent to SQL Server.

Listing 3.19 shows the same query, but now in a parameterized form that will allow plan reuse.

```
dtrSalesOrders.Close();
cmd.CommandType = CommandType.Text;
cmd.CommandText = @"SELECT soh.SalesOrderNumber,
                           sod.ProductID
                 FROM Sales.SalesOrderHeader AS soh
                       INNER JOIN Sales.SalesOrderDetail AS sod
```

```
                                    ON soh.SalesOrderID = sod.SalesOrderID
                    WHERE soh.SalesOrderNumber = @SalesOrderNo";

cmd.Parameters.Add("@SalesOrderNo", SqlDbType.NVarChar, 50);
cmd.Parameters["@SalesOrderNo"].Value = txtSalesOrderNo.Text;

dtrSalesOrders = cmd.ExecuteReader();
```

Listing 3.19: A parameterized query being sent to SQL Server.

If changing the application is not possible, as is often the case with vendor applications, or where the source code for the application is unavailable, then there are two options in SQL Server that can help alleviate the problem: **forced parameterization** and **optimize for ad hoc workloads**.

Forced parameterization in SQL Server

SQL Server 2005 and above offers the ability to set the database-level PARAMETERI-ZATION option to FORCED, using the ALTER DATABASE statement, as shown in Listing 3.20. This will force all ad hoc queries against that database to be parameterized before the compile process starts.

```
ALTER DATABASE AdventureWorks SET PARAMETERIZATION FORCED
```

Listing 3.20: Setting the PARAMETERIZATION option to FORCED.

If you run this command and then rerun the three queries from Listing 3.17, the query that the SQL Query Optimizer gets to optimize will be the parameterized version, and you'll find that there's only one plan created in cache, not three.

There are potential downsides to using forced parameterization, in that this setting forces SQL to use one plan for all matching queries, no matter what the literal values, so there is a possibility for the same parameter sniffing problems to which stored procedures are susceptible. If such a problem does occur, it can be investigated and resolved in much the same way as with stored procedures, discussed earlier in this chapter.

Optimize for ad hoc workloads

In SQL Server 2008 and later, we can use `optimize for ad hoc workloads`, which is a server-level setting, i.e. it will affect every single database on the server (as opposed to forced parameterization, which is database-specific).

With this setting enabled, SQL Server does not cache the plan of an ad hoc query the first time it is encountered. Instead, a plan-stub is cached that just indicates that the query has been seen before. Only if the query is seen a second time is the plan cached. This won't reduce the number of compiles for ad hoc queries, but it will make it less likely that the plan cache will grow as much, since the initial stub takes up very little memory. As such, it reduces the chances that other plans which could be reusable will be discarded due to memory pressure.

To enable the `optimize for ad hoc workloads` setting, use `sp_configure`, as shown in Listing 3.21.

```
EXEC sp_configure 'show advanced options',1
RECONFIGURE
EXEC sp_configure 'optimize for ad hoc workloads',1
RECONFIGURE
```

Listing 3.21: Enabling the `optimize for ad hoc workloads` setting.

Inappropriate parallelism

SQL Server is designed to be able to make use of multiple processors when processing user requests. Query parallelism is the mechanism used by the SQL query execution engine to split the work of a query into multiple threads, each of which will execute on a separate scheduler. Queries are parallelized at the operator level; in other words, if the query runs in parallel, some of the query operators may run in their parallel form, while others may not.

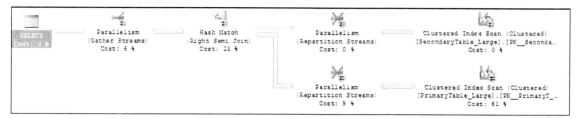

Figure 3.8: Execution plan showing that operators are running in parallel.

When a query is submitted to SQL Server for processing, the query optimizer compiles an execution plan that has been optimized to allow the query to execute in the fastest manner possible. If the estimated cost of executing the plan serially exceeds the 'cost threshold for parallelism' sp_configure option, the number of logical CPUs available to SQL Server is greater than one, and the 'max degree of parallelism' sp_configure option is set to the default of zero or greater than one, the plan produced will include parallelism. The Degree of Parallelism (DOP) is not included as a part of the plan; this is, instead, determined at the time of execution based on the number of logical processors, the 'max degree of parallelism' sp_configure or, if the MAXDOP query hint is being used, the value specified by the hint, and the number of available worker threads.

Parallel query processing can reduce the time required to process a query by horizontally partitioning the input data, distributing the partitions across multiple logical CPUs, and simultaneously executing the same operation across multiple processor cores. This can be very beneficial to data warehouse and reporting operations, which have a few large queries that deal with volumes of data and only a few requests occur concurrently. By splitting the request across multiple OS threads on multiple processor cores, the optimizer increases the utilization of the hardware resources by spreading the load across all of the processors on the server, resulting in a reduction of total execution time.

The specific impact of a parallel workload depends on a number of factors, not the least of which is the ability of the remaining hardware components in the system to cope with the heavy demands for memory allocation and disk I/O that a parallel workload can generate. When parallelism is used appropriately, on high-cost queries, it can have a very beneficial effect on overall server performance. However, it can be very detrimental to OLTP environments where the workload consists of lots of smaller queries executing concurrently, since the parallel operation can utilize up to all of the processor cores on the server, causing other requests to wait to execute. If the primary use of the server is for an OLTP database that has a lot of smaller concurrent requests, parallelism of a single common query can sink throughput.

As noted above, SQL Server has two configuration options that control the parallel execution of queries by the engine. They are the `cost threshold for parallelism` and the `max degree of parallelism` options of sp_configure. The `max degree of parallelism` option exists to prevent a single query from utilizing all of the processor cores on a SQL Server. The `cost threshold for parallelism` option exists to control the threshold for a query that causes the optimizer to use parallelism to execute a query.

Too often, when CPU issues related to "inappropriate parallelism" arise, the suggested solution seems to focus solely on changing the value for `max degree of parallelism`. For example, a quick online search of the problem, especially the `CXPACKET` wait type (a classic indicator of parallelism-related issues, as discussed a little later) will result in numerous posts that recommend reducing the `max degree of parallelism` to one half or one fourth the number of logical processors or processor cores on the server, or even to completely disable parallelism by setting it to 1. While this may solve the problem, it may not be the ideal solution. The best solution is to consider, in tandem, the appropriate value for each of these options.

Cost threshold for parallelism

As discussed, the `cost threshold for parallelism` option determines a threshold "cost" which, when exceeded, will cause a parallel execution plan to be generated, in order to execute the user request. Since parallel execution is only possible on multi-processor systems, the `cost threshold for parallelism` option is only used by the engine when multiple processors exist, the server is not affinitized to a single processor and `max degree of parallelism` is set to a value other than 1.

The "cost" is the estimated amount of time in seconds that it would take to execute the query serially with a given execution plan. The default value is five, meaning that a parallel plan will only be generated and used by queries that are estimated to take longer than five seconds to execute serially on the given system. On larger databases, this threshold may be low enough to cause multiple concurrent executions of common queries, and so to cause contention in the system.

To determine what might be an appropriate setting for the `cost threshold for parallelism` option, it is possible to query the existing plans in the plan cache to determine the costs associated with the plans that have been executing with parallelism, as shown in Listing 3.22.

```
SET TRANSACTION ISOLATION LEVEL READ UNCOMMITTED ;

WITH XMLNAMESPACES
    (DEFAULT 'http://schemas.microsoft.com/sqlserver/2004/07/showplan')
SELECT query_plan AS CompleteQueryPlan ,
        n.value('(@StatementText)[1]', 'VARCHAR(4000)') AS StatementText ,
        n.value('(@StatementOptmLevel)[1]', 'VARCHAR(25)')
                AS StatementOptimizationLevel ,
        n.value('(@StatementSubTreeCost)[1]', 'VARCHAR(128)')
                AS StatementSubTreeCost ,
        n.query('.') AS ParallelSubTreeXML ,
        ecp.usecounts ,
        ecp.size_in_bytes
FROM    sys.dm_exec_cached_plans AS ecp
        CROSS APPLY sys.dm_exec_query_plan(plan_handle) AS eqp
```

```
        CROSS APPLY query_plan.nodes
                ('/ShowPlanXML/BatchSequence/Batch/Statements/StmtSimple')
        AS qn ( n )
WHERE   n.query('.').exist('//RelOp[@PhysicalOp="Parallelism"]') = 1
```

Listing 3.22: Determining the estimated cost of parallel execution plans.

Analysis of the most commonly executed statements that result in parallel queries can guide the appropriate setting of the cost threshold for parallelism option to minimize the impact of multiple concurrently executing parallel requests which drive CPU and I/O contention in the system.

Max degree of parallelism

Whenever the estimated cost of executing a query serially exceeds our carefully-evaluated value for cost threshold for parallelism, the database engine can spread the execution load for that query across multiple available processors, according to the degree of parallelism dictated by the max degree of parallelism option. The number of processors used will be determined by the lowest of the following three values:

- number of available processors

- max degree of parallelism option

- MAXDOP query hint provided for the query being executed (which overrides the value specified by max degree of parallelism).

Generally speaking, as we have discussed, the appropriate value for the max degree of parallelism option depends largely on the type of workload being executed, and the ability of the other hardware subsystems to cope with the additional workload associated with parallel execution in the system. If your system is experiencing parallelism-related issues (see the *Diagnosing inappropriate parallelism* section), then it may be necessary to limit the degree of parallelism, in conjunction with tuning the cost threshold for parallelism to resolve the problem.

One of the more common online recommendations is to disable parallelism entirely by setting the `max degree of parallelism` to 1. There are cases where this configuration might make sense, for example, true OLTP workloads where all of the transactions are small and there are a lot of transactions executing concurrently. These types of database rarely exist today and disabling parallelism entirely is more likely to reduce performance in the long term.

Over the years I've made a number of different recommendations about how to configure `max degree of parallelism`. For example, in a SMP system, setting it to half the number of available physical processor cores, or to the number of physical cores on a single processor die, or even setting it to 1 to disable parallelism entirely. Today, I only make a recommendation based on analysis of the query workload, and a review of the wait types of associated workers and subtasks which are executing using parallelism.

In particular, I'll analyze occurrences of the **CXPACKET** session wait type. In most systems, **CXPACKET** is the symptom and not the problem; there is often a different underlying wait type that can be seen in **sys.dm_os_waiting_tasks** for the session. By focusing on this wait type, a better decision regarding the appropriate `max degree of parallelism` option can be made. For example, if the underlying wait type, is **PAGEIOLATCH_SH** then the parallel operation is waiting on a read from the disk I/O subsystem, and reducing the `max degree of parallelism` won't resolve the root problem; it will just reduce the number of workers being used in the system, and reduce the accumulated wait time for the **CXPACKET** wait type. However, this may reduce the additional load the parallelism operations place on the disk I/O subsystem, and buy you time to scale up the I/O performance of the server.

There are, however, some specific considerations, relating to the memory architecture of the processors. On NUMA-based (Non-Uniform Memory Access) systems, the `max degree of parallelism` option should be set to the minimum number of processors available on a single NUMA node. This is done to prevent cross-node parallel processing of a request from occurring, which incurs significant expense since sharing memory across nodes is an expensive operation.

On Symmetric Multiprocessing (SMP) systems, one of the trade-offs with multiple processor cores on a single die is the usage of shared L2 caches across multiple cores, which can result in cache misses for memory-consuming applications such as SQL Server, and which affects the performance of highly concurrent workloads, under higher levels of parallelism. Here, the appropriate value for this option depends largely on the type of workload being executed and the ability of the other hardware subsystems to cope with the added workload associated with parallel execution in the system.

Finally, note that on SQL Server 2008 and above, the resource governor can be used to enforce a `max degree of parallelism` for groups of queries, based on various connection properties. Hence it would be possible to limit queries from one application, a specific set of logins or specific hostnames, to a certain max degree of parallelism and let other queries be unlimited.

Hyper-threading and parallelism

Hyper-threading is an Intel technology designed to improve parallel execution by presenting to the operating system two logical cores for each physical core. This means that instead of one scheduler per processor core you get two, and so two threads can be executed "simultaneously."

AMD processors and two strong threads

*Modern AMD processor architectures, such as Bulldozer, use a different approach to threading, called **two strong threads**, with a design that offers dedicated hardware to each of two threads. We won't discuss this topic further here, but further information can be found on the AMD website:* HTTP://WWW.ANAND-TECH.COM/SHOW/3863/AMD-DISCLOSES-BOBCAT-BULLDOZER-ARCHITECTURES-AT-HOT-CHIPS-2010.

A question that is commonly asked in the online forums is whether or not hyper-threading should be enabled for SQL Server, and how such decisions are affected by workload type.

As discussed earlier, for an OLAP or DSS workload, query execution performance will benefit from allowing the query optimizer to parallelize individual queries. This is certainly true when there exist a large number of true, physical CPU cores but, on early hyper-threading implementations, it was the experience of most DBAs that the often complex queries that comprised a typical OLP/DSS workload performed poorly when parallelized across multiple hyper-threaded cores. A typical, short OLTP query was less affected by running on a logical core, as opposed to a physical one, so enabling hyper-threading for an OLTP workload could see a benefit from parallelization in the sense that more cores were available to process more queries in a given time.

Nevertheless, several architectural problems with early hyper-threading implementations, which became more and more problematical as the CPU load on a server increased, meant that most DBAs simply disabled hyper-threading in the BIOS, regardless of workload type.

As recently as a few years ago, when SQL Server 2008 RTM first released, advice to disable hyper-threading for SQL Server, especially for DW/OLAP/DSS workloads, was generally correct. The biggest problem with older processors and hyper-threading related to the size of the onboard caches, which are shared when hyper-threading is enabled. The smaller cache size meant that cache misses were common place for memory-dependent applications like SQL Server. Another issue early on was that Windows Server 2000 wasn't hyper-threading aware so, when you had a dual processor server with hyper-threading enabled, Windows thought it had four physical processors, and would schedule concurrent execution on both threads of a processor when under load.

However, recent advances and improvements in hardware and in Windows, as well as in hyper-threading implementation mean that it is simply incorrect to disable hyper-threading as a matter of course. Many of the early problems no longer exist. For example, Windows Server 2003 and later are hyper-threading aware and so will see two physical and two logical processors, and will handle scheduling differently to accommodate the fact that two of the logical processors are from hyper-threading. Also, newer processors have much larger caches (MB instead of KB); they are less prone to the cache-miss issues and are much better suited for using hyper-threading with memory dependent implementations like SQL Server, especially on Windows Server 2008.

In fact, with recent processor architectures, especially Intel Nehalem and later, my advice is to enable hyper-threading unless you find a good reason to turn it off. It's certainly a mistake to disable hyper-threading without first thoroughly testing your application workload with hyper-threading enabled, then disabled, in order to truly know whether or not there is a benefit to having hyper-threading turned on or off.

Of course, as processors with eight or even twelve physical cores emerge onto the market, it becomes easier to achieve high levels of parallelism without the need for hyper-threading. However, the technology remains fundamental to Intel's modern processors (for example, the Xeon E7-4870 processor, for 4-socket servers, boasts ten physical core *plus* hyper-threading), and with most recent processor architectures, there is a good chance that you'll see a performance and/or throughput benefit for both DW/OLAP and OLTP workloads.

Diagnosing inappropriate parallelism

The best way to determine if parallel processing is causing a resource bottleneck in a specific system is to look at the wait statistics and latch statistics for an instance of SQL Server. When a bottleneck exists during the parallel execution of a query, the CXPACKET wait type shows up as one of the top waits for SQL Server. This wait type is set whenever a parallel process has to wait in the exchange iterator for another worker to continue processing. As previously discussed, when this happens, there is generally an underlying, non-CXPACKET wait type, which is associated with the stalled worker. However, since multiple workers are forced to wait when this occurs, the volume of CXPACKET waits will generally exceed the underlying root wait type being exhibited.

Whenever possible, it is best to isolate and troubleshoot the underlying wait type, since this will lead to overall system throughput improvements. The CXPACKET waits are simply a symptom of a problem in most cases, not the actual problem. There are scenarios where it may not be possible to eliminate the underlying wait type; for example, when the disk I/O subsystem can't keep up with the demand required by the parallel execution of a query, the root wait type may be an `IO_COMPLETION`, `ASYNC_IO_COMPLETION`, or `PAGEIOLATCH_*` wait type, and scaling out the I/O subsystem is not possible. When this occurs, reducing the level of parallelism to a degree that still allows parallel processing to occur without bottlenecking in the disk I/O subsystem can improve overall system performance. It is possible that `CXPACKET` waits in conjunction with other wait types, for example `LATCH_*` and `SOS_SCHEDULER_YIELD`, do show that parallelism is the actual problem, and further investigation of the latch stats on the system will validate if this is actually the case. The `sys.dm_os_latch_stats` DMV contains information about the specific latch waits that have occurred in the instance, and if one of the top latch waits is `ACCESS_METHODS_DATASET_PARENT`, in conjunction with `CXPACKET`, `LATCH_*`, and `SOS_SCHEDULER_YIELD` wait types as the top waits, the level of parallelism on the system is the cause of bottlenecking during query execution, and reducing the 'max degree of parallelism' `sp_configure` option may be required to resolve the problems.

Resolving parallelism issues

As discussed earlier, larger, long running queries will generally benefit from parallel execution, since the cost of executing the query serially outweighs the cost associated with initialization, synchronization and termination of the parallel workers, for parallel execution of the query. Inappropriate parallelism most commonly arises in cases where the nature of the workload is "mixed," i.e. we have what is essentially an OLTP workload, characterized by a large number of short transactions, but where some of those transactions are actually complex enough that the `cost threshold for parallelism` is exceeded and SQL Server parallelizes their execution across all available cores, so tying up CPU resources.

When parallelism-related issues are diagnosed, the first possible remedy that should be investigated is optimizing the queries that are parallelizing inappropriately, if they are not already tuned. Inappropriate parallelism can easily be a result of missing/inadequate indexes, outdated statistics or badly written queries. In other words, by tuning these queries, they'll cease to exceed the `cost threshold for parallelism`, and so will naturally execute on a single CPU core.

If the workload is as tuned as it can be, and parallelism issues persist, then the `cost threshold for parallelism` option should be used in conjunction with the `max degree of parallelism` option to manage parallel execution in the system overall.

TokenAndPermUserStore

The `TokenAndPermUserStore` cache was introduced in SQL 2005 as an optimization that would allow caching of the results of permissions checks by users against database objects. This cache, however, could be the cause of performance problems, especially in earlier builds of SQL Server 2005, because the limits on the size of the cache were too high. The performance problems typically manifested as excessively high CPU usage and threads with high **CMEMTHREAD** waits. This section will cover how to identify problems associated with the `TokenAndPermUserStore` cache, short-term work-arounds, hot fixes from Microsoft for the problem, as well as how to solve the problem in the long term.

The problem is discussed in the Knowledge Base article 927396 (HTTP://SUPPORT.MICROSOFT.COM/KB/927396) and tends to materialize under the following circumstances:

- large amounts of non-AWE memory allocated to SQL Server (this means the problem is specific to 64-bit SQL)
- lots of dynamic or ad hoc SQL queries
- many different database users.

To investigate possible problems related to the `TokenAndPermUserStore` cache, track the size of the cache over a period of time, using the query shown in Listing 3.23.

```
SELECT    SUM(single_pages_kb + multi_pages_kb) / 1024.0 AS CacheSizeMB
FROM      sys.dm_os_memory_clerks
WHERE     [name] = 'TokenAndPermUserStore'
```

Listing 3.23: Finding the size of the `TokenAndPermUserStore` cache.

If the cache constantly grows in size, and that growth is accompanied by queries waiting with a **CMEMTHREAD** wait type, then the size of the cache may be the cause of the high CPU usage.

If you're using a SQL Server 2005 and the patch level is below SP2, the first thing to do is apply SP2 at the very least, and preferably SP4, since improvements in the management of this cache were made in SP2.

A best long-term fix, however, is an architectural change to reduce the usage of ad hoc or dynamic SQL, and move as much logic as possible into stored procedures. Depending on the application architecture this may be anything from trivial to impossible, but it should be considered, as doing so almost completely removes the chance of running into this problem.

Short-term fixes in SQL Server 2005

If these measures aren't immediately possible, there are a couple of short-term work-arounds to this problem in SQL Server 2005.

Use the sysadmin server role

By making the application service account a member of the **sysadmin** server role, any permissions checking is bypassed and the problem is resolved. The assumption is that the account can perform any operation inside of SQL Server and therefore does not require additional permissions checks.

This solution is very far from ideal, since it provides elevated permissions to the service account. In a pinch, it will provide short-term relief to the problems associated with high CPU utilization. However, if it works, proving that the `TokenAndPermUserStore` cache is the root cause, then you should immediately determine if another solution can be utilized instead, to solve the problem.

Regularly clear the cache

Using a SQL agent job and the command shown in Listing 3.24, you can regularly free up space in the `TokenAndPermUserStore` cache.

```
DBCC FREESYSTEMCACHE ('TokenAndPermUserStore')
```

Listing 3.24: Freeing space in the `TokenAndPermUserStore` cache.

Again, this should only is done in extreme cases and as a temporary solution. However, it will control the cache size until a long-term resolution can be applied.

Trace Flags

On SQL 2005 SP2 or above, Trace Flag 4618 and/or Trace Flag 4610 can be enabled. Trace Flag 4618 restricts the number of entries that the cache will hold to 1024 and, if both flags are enabled, the number of cache entries is limited to 8192. Restricting the number of entries the cache will hold should be used temporarily, while other fixes are taken into consideration.

One last configuration change option on SQL 2005, if on SP3 or above, is that Trace Flag 4621 can be enabled. This allows a custom quota to be set. For the details of configuring this, see Knowledge Base article 959823 (HTTP://SUPPORT.MICROSOFT.COM/KB/959823).

Configuration options in SQL Server 2008

With SQL Server 2008, the configuration options `access check cache bucket count` and `access check cache quota` were introduced. These options control the number of entries and number of hash buckets used for the `TokenAndPermUserStore` cache. The cache should not cause the same problems on SQL 2008 as it did on SQL 2005, but if the problems do manifest, the quota can be set to a lower number and/or the number of hash buckets can be increased. Changing these settings can reduce the time necessary to locate cache entries. This configuration change is, however, not a recommended change unless directed under the guidance of Microsoft Customer Support, but IT should be noted as an area for your troubleshooting.

Windows Server and BIOS power saving options

As a part of the green computing initiatives, many hardware manufacturers ship new desktops, laptops, and even servers intended for datacenter use, with the advanced power control configuration set such that the operating system, or the hardware itself, can automatically reduce power consumption and cooling requirements of the system by turning off devices that are not being used, and under-clocking the processors installed in the server. Unfortunately, this can have quite a negative impact on your processor performance.

These hardware-based power-saving settings can be configured in the main system BIOS to allow the hardware to control power consumption (**Hardware**), the Windows operating system to control power management (**OS Control**), or to disable power management features completely (**None**). In general, the default option for the BIOS is to allow the operating system to control the power management features of the system, based on its configured options.

Windows Server 2008 and 2008 R2 default the power management configuration setting (the Windows Power Plan feature) to **Balanced**, which allows the system to switch to a low performance state to reduce power consumption. One of the surprises that many people have had, on upgrading their systems on newer server hardware that has Windows Server 2008 or 2008 R2 installed on it, is that overall performance decreases after a period of time and ends up being significantly lower than when the server first started up. This is a direct result of power management features causing under-clocking of the processors on the server.

To identify if this is a problem on your system, a free tool named CPU-Z, available from HTTP://WWW.CPUID.COM/SOFTWARES/CPU-Z/VERSIONS-HISTORY.HTML, can be used to collect information about the current state of the processors installed in a server. We won't discuss this tool in detail here, but the important values to look out for, in regard power management problems, are the **CPU Specification**, which will show the type of processor and its rated clock speed, and the **Core Speed**, which shows the current clock speed of the processors in the system. If the Core Speed is lower that the rated specification, then power management is reducing the performance of the system.

The first thing to do is to check the current Windows power management scheme. If it is set to **Balanced**, change it to **High Performance**, which prevents the system from switching to a low performance state and ensures the performance characteristics of the system are consistent (see HTTP://SUPPORT.MICROSOFT.COM/KB/2207548). If **High Performance** is being used by Windows, the BIOS setting should be checked. If it's set to **Hardware**, change it to **OS Control**.

What is insidious here is the impact that power saving has on the `% Processor Usage` performance counter. The value for this counter is calculated based on the currently used CPU frequency, divided by the available CPU frequency. As such, an under-clocked CPU causes Windows to report higher CPU usage values, leading people to believe that the server is under heavier load than it is in reality.

Summary

Poor management of CPU utilization can and will often have a dramatic impact on SQL Server performance. In general the sustained CPU usage of a SQL Server machine should not exceed 60–70%. Occasional spikes to higher values should not be a problem, but sustained heavier usage is an indication that the server is under severe CPU load.

When CPU issues arise, and having confirmed that the high CPU usage is due to the SQL Server process, the first job is to isolate the source of the problem, using information from tools such as Performance Monitor (PerfMon), SQLTrace and the SQL Server Dynamic Management Views, many of which have been greatly enhanced with the releases of SQL Server 2005 and 2008.

With the problem located, the appropriate measures can be taken to relieve the CPU pressure, ranging from adding useful indexes and tuning CPU-hungry queries, to changing configuration settings. If all of this fails, it may simply be that you need more or faster CPUs along with a better balancing of the load across CPUs, and better scheduling of CPU-intensive queries.

Additional Resources

- Implicit data conversations

  - HTTP://SQLBLOG.COM/BLOGS/JONATHAN_KEHAYIAS/ARCHIVE/2010/01/08/FINDING-IMPLICIT-COLUMN-CONVERSIONS-IN-THE-PLAN-CACHE.ASPX

- Query tuning

  - HTTP://WWW.STRAIGHTPATHSQL.COM/PRESENTATIONS/UCANDOIT/

  - HTTP://WWW.SIMPLE-TALK.COM/SQL/PERFORMANCE/SIMPLE-QUERY-TUNING-WITH-STATISTICS-IO-AND-EXECUTION-PLANS/

- HTTP://WWW.SIMPLE-TALK.COM/SQL/T-SQL-PROGRAMMING/13-THINGS-YOU-SHOULD-KNOW-ABOUT-STATISTICS-AND-THE-QUERY-OPTIMIZER/
  - HTTP://WWW.SIMPLE-TALK.COM/AUTHOR/GAIL-SHAW/
- Estimated vs. actual row counts
  - HTTP://SQLINTHEWILD.CO.ZA/INDEX.PHP/2009/09/22/ESTIMATED-ROWS-ACTUAL-ROWS-AND-EXECUTION-COUNT/
- Cost threshold for parallelism
  - HTTP://SQLBLOG.COM/BLOGS/JONATHAN_KEHAYIAS/ARCHIVE/2010/01/26/21172.ASPX
- Max degree of parallelism
  - HTTP://MSDN.MICROSOFT.COM/EN-US/LIBRARY/MS181007.ASPX
- Query hints
  - HTTP://MSDN.MICROSOFT.COM/EN-US/LIBRARY/MS181714.ASPX
- Guidelines for modifying MAXDOP
  - HTTP://SUPPORT.MICROSOFT.COM/KB/329204
- Limiting MAXDOP with the Resource Governor
  - HTTP://WWW.SQLMAG.COM/BLOG/SQL-SERVER-QUESTIONS-ANSWERED-28/DATABASE-ADMINISTRATION/CONTROLLING-MAXDOP-EXECUTING-QUERIES-140163
- Parallelism/MAXDOP configuration
  - HTTP://MSDN.MICROSOFT.COM/EN-US/LIBRARY/MS178065.ASPX
  - HTTP://MSDN.MICROSOFT.COM/EN-US/LIBRARY/MS188611.ASPX
  - HTTP://BLOGS.MSDN.COM/B/JOESACK/ARCHIVE/2009/03/18/SHOULD-YOU-WORRY-ABOUT-SOS-SCHEDULER-YIELD.ASPX

- SQLOS architecture

  - HTTP://BLOGS.MSDN.COM/B/SQLOSTEAM/ARCHIVE/2010/06/23/SQLOS-RESOURCES.ASPX

  - HTTP://SQLBLOGCASTS.COM/BLOGS/SQLWORKSHOPS/ARCHIVE/2007/11/25/FINDING-OPTIMAL-NUMBER-OF-CPUS-FOR-A-GIVEN-LONG-RUNNING-CPU-INTENSIVE-DSS-OLAP-LIKE-QUERIES-WORKLOAD.ASPX

- System Monitor CPU counters

  - HTTP://MSDN.MICROSOFT.COM/EN-US/LIBRARY/MS178072.ASPX

- DMV usage for CPU usage from ring buffers

  - HTTP://TROUBLESHOOTINGSQL.COM/2009/12/30/HOW-TO-FIND-OUT-THE-CPU-USAGE-INFORMATION-FOR-THE-SQL-SERVER-PROCESS-USING-RING-BUFFERS/

  - HTTP://MSDN.MICROSOFT.COM/EN-US/LIBRARY/MS175048(SQL.90).ASPX

  - HTTP://TECHNET.MICROSOFT.COM/EN-US/LIBRARY/CC966540.ASPX

- Forced parameterization

  - HTTP://TECHNET.MICROSOFT.COM/EN-US/LIBRARY/MS175037(SQL.90).ASPX

- Fixing `TokenAndPermUserStore` problems

  - Identification and overview

    - HTTP://SUPPORT.MICROSOFT.COM/KB/927396

  - Access check result cache

    - HTTP://SUPPORT.MICROSOFT.COM/KB/955644

    - HTTP://MSDN.MICROSOFT.COM/EN-US/LIBRARY/CC645588.ASPX

  - Purging the cache whenever it reaches a certain size

    - HTTP://BLOGS.MSDN.COM/CHRISSK/ARCHIVE/2008/06/19/SCRIPT-TO-PURGE-TOKENANDPERMUSERSTORE.ASPX

- SQL Server 2008 sp_configure options

  - HTTP://SUPPORT.MICROSOFT.COM/KB/955644/EN-US

- Hot-fixes associated with this problem

  - HTTP://SUPPORT.MICROSOFT.COM/KB/959823

Chapter 4: Memory Management

Memory allocation and consumption in SQL Server is a constant source of questions in the online forums. It is very common for SQL Server to use large amounts of memory, and once it allocates that memory, it doesn't release it. This is different behavior from that exhibited by most other applications and it leads some users to believe that SQL Server has a memory leak when this is not the case.

This chapter will take a look at how SQL Server actually allocates memory, how this affects ongoing server operations and, specifically, the differences between memory allocations on 32-bit servers and 64-bit servers.

We'll then move on to discuss how to diagnose memory pressure in SQL Server, where SQL Server is forced to operate with an insufficient amount of memory, using memory-related performance counters and Dynamic Management Views.

Finally, we'll discuss some common problems associated with memory allocations from SQL Server on the various platforms, and how to resolve these problems by, for example, tuning memory-related configuration options in SQL Server. As you progress through the chapters, it is important to pay close attention to the specific cases where changing the memory configuration options is being recommended. Incorrect configuration of the memory options can cause more problems than the default options, depending on the change being made.

Memory allocation and usage in SQL Server is a complex topic, and we're only going to go deep enough to allow a basic understanding of the SQL Server memory issues that can arise. If you're hungry for more after reading this chapter, I recommend the work of Mark Russinovich (for example, HTTP://BLOGS.TECHNET.COM/B/MARKRUSSINOVICH/ARCHIVE/2008/07/21/3092070.ASPX) and Christian Bolton, especially his presentation, A Walk Down Memory Lane, from SQLBits III (HTTP://SQLBITS.COM/SESSIONS/EVENT3/A_WALK_DOWN_MEMORY_LANE).

The Self-Tuning Database Engine

For a long time, Microsoft has been committed to the vision of a self-tuning SQL Server database engine, as a way to reduce the total cost of ownership of the product. Starting with SQL Server 2005, SQL Server manages memory usage dynamically, and can change its memory usage without requiring a restart of the database engine. SQL Server simply does not offer the configuration options for fine-tuning the memory allocations that are prevalent in other RDBMS platforms. Instead, the amount of memory allocated to individual components, for example the plan cache, is controlled automatically and entirely by the database engine, depending on the current SQL Server workload and on other activities on the server. Memory cannot be allocated manually.

While SQL Server lacks the knobs to control specific memory allocations, there are still a few configuration options that affect how the database engine utilizes memory. Whether or not these configuration options require changes from the default values specified during the installation of the system, depends on a number of factors including the versions and editions of Windows Operating System and SQL Server being used, the amount of physical memory installed in the server, and the processor architecture (x86, x64, IA64).

How SQL Server Allocates Memory

The first time someone glances at the **Processes** tab in Windows Task Manager on a typical SQL Server machine, as shown in Figure 4.1, he or she is generally shocked by the amount of memory that is being used on the server; generally by the `sqlservr.exe` process. The first instinct of someone who doesn't understand how SQL Server works, is that SQL Server has a memory leak, which is not the case.

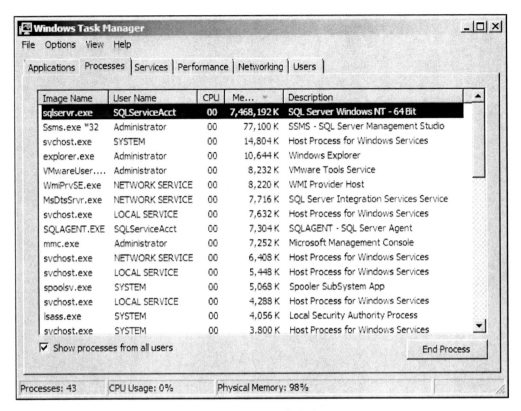

Figure 4.1: SQL Server Process memory usage (default settings).

There is a big difference between high memory usage and a memory leak, and SQL Server is designed to use memory in large quantities, in order to cache information, such as recently used data pages. This improves performance by reducing the need to consistently read data from disk; a much slower and more expensive operation than accessing it from memory.

As a general rule, SQL Server will use as much memory as you can give it, and it will not release the memory that it has allocated under normal operations, unless the operating system has set the **memory low** resource notification flag, which triggers SQL Server to reduce its memory allocations. One of the self-tuning features added to the SQLOS in SQL Server 2005 was a dedicated thread that monitors memory notifications issued by the Windows operating system, to inform other applications of the status of memory usage in the operating system. Two such memory notifications are set by the Windows OS:

- **memory high** lets SQL Server know that it can grow its working set and use additional memory

- **memory low** lets SQL Server know that the operating system is under memory pressure and that SQL should try to reduce its working set to return memory to the operating system.

If neither flag is set by Windows, then memory usage is stable and SQL Server will continue to operate inside of its existing process space. This functionality did not exist prior to Windows Server 2003 and SQL Server 2005. Slava Oks, a developer on the SQLOS team for SQL Server 2005, has a blog post on memory pressure (HTTP://BLOGS.MSDN.COM/B/SLAVAO/ARCHIVE/2005/02/01/364523.ASPX), which explains the basic types of memory pressure and possible consequences (see Figure 4.2). The "memory low" notification, for example, is a result of what Slava terms **external** (OS) dynamic memory pressure. The post also discusses the need to receive notifications of such pressure, and how SQL Server was designed to dynamically manage its memory usage based on the Windows memory notifications.

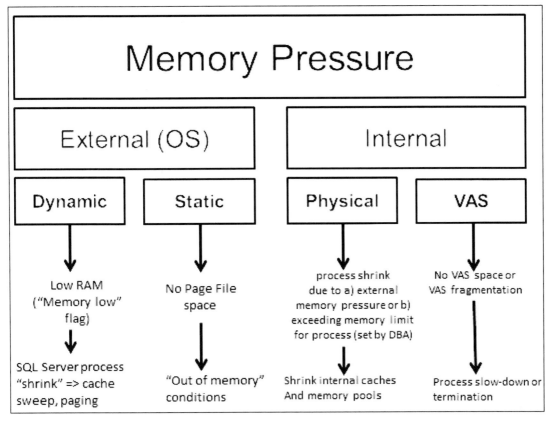

Figure 4.2: Summary of basic types of SQL Server memory pressure.

The amount of memory that SQL Server can use depends on several factors:

- amount of physical memory installed in the server

- memory limits of the installed Windows operating system (see HTTP://MSDN. MICROSOFT.COM/EN-US/LIBRARY/AA366778.ASPX)

- SQL Server architecture (32-bit versus 64-bit)

- SQL Server configuration options that control memory usage

- SQL Server version and edition.

These have been listed in the order of limitation; for example, if the server only has 4 GB of physical memory (RAM) installed, that's going to be the upper limit for SQL Server.

If a server has 64 GB of RAM, and the Windows operating system is Windows Server 2008 64-bit Standard Edition, then the OS limit is 32 GB and that is the most that could be used by SQL Server.

If a 32-bit edition of SQL Server is installed on a Windows Server 2008 x64 Enterprise Edition system with 128 GB RAM, the maximum amount of memory that SQL Server could address, under the default settings for WOW64, would be 4 GB, since a 32-bit pointer can only ever "see" a maximum of 4 GB (232/10243). However, by setting the appropriate SQL Server configuration options (namely, by enabling AWE (Address Windowing Extensions), as discussed later), SQL Server can access additional memory via Physical Address Extensions (PAE). This changes the pointer to 36-bit and, with the use of AWE to allocate the memory, raises the maximum amount of memory to 64 GB (236/10243).

The SQL Server version and edition will occasionally have an impact on the memory limit for SQL Server. For example, in SQL Server 2000 the ability to enable AWE memory usage was an Enterprise Edition-only feature, so if you were using Standard Edition, SQL Server would not have access to this additional memory. In SQL Server 2005, use of AWE became a Standard Edition feature, and so this edition limitation was removed. Another example is that, in SQL Server 2005 and 2008, 64-bit editions running Enterprise Edition can make use of Large Pages (discussed later in this chapter).

32-bit Virtual Address Space limitations

The Windows OS runs every process, including the SQL Server process, in its own dedicated area of virtual memory, known as the Virtual Address Space (VAS). One of the biggest challenges with memory management for 32-bit SQL Server is the limited amount of VAS to which a 32-bit process has access. A 32-bit process can only ever address a maximum of 4 GB of memory and so a 32-bit SQL Server process only has access to 4 GB of VAS. The VAS is divided into two regions; **kernel mode** (or system) space and **user mode** (or application) space.

The kernel mode VAS is used by the OS, for mapping various system data structures such as the file cache, Paged and Non-Page pools (discussed briefly later). The user mode VAS is used to map memory for the currently-executing application process (in our case, SQL Server).

By default, Windows divides the VAS evenly into 2 GB kernel mode VAS and 2 GB user mode VAS. In other words, the total VAS is 4 GB but a single 32-bit SQL Server process can only address 2 GB in the user mode VAS for its working set. Using the default config-uration, SQL Server allocates memory in this 2 GB of user mode VAS for the buffer pool (data and plan cache), with a smaller amount of memory required for non-buffer pool (multi-page) allocations.

Over the coming sections, we'll discuss the following topics:

- How SQL Server allocates memory in the user mode VAS.

- Memory reservation for non-buffer pool allocations.

- How to extend user mode VAS to a maximum of 3 GB, using VAS tuning.

- How to make available to the SQL Server process a separate, larger (>4 GB) area of memory, called AWE memory, for data cache allocations.

Please note that many of the concepts and limitations discussed in this section apply **only** to 32-bit installations of SQL Server. Please refer to the *Using 64-bit SQL Server* section for details of 64-bit installations.

User mode VAS allocation and VirtualAlloc

SQL Server reserves 2 GB of user mode VAS but doesn't commit that memory until a physical memory allocation occurs. SQL Server allocates memory in the user mode VAS by making calls to the `VirtualAlloc` function in the Windows API. If you're running a 32-bit version of either Windows OS or SQL Server, then a call to `VirtualAlloc` returns a 32-bit pointer and so, as discussed, this limits the amount of user mode VAS that SQL Server can use to 2 GB.

Memory allocated by `VirtualAlloc` doesn't have to be physically present, so 2 GB of user mode VAS would still be reserved by Windows for SQL Server use, regardless of how much physical memory (RAM) was installed. However, when that memory is committed (used), it needs to be backed by RAM (or the page file) and Windows ensures that the amount of memory committed by SQL Server and any other processes will be less than, or equal to, the installed physical memory, plus page file capacity.

However, if you happen to have less than 2 GB of RAM installed (rare, these days) then the RAM limit becomes the hard upper limit of memory that SQL Server will commit. During initial memory ramp up, SQL Server will ensure that the buffer cache is smaller than the physical RAM available; SQL Server isn't going to commit memory that is guaranteed to be paged out for the buffer cache, since the whole point of having the buffer cache in memory is to reduce the physical disk activity. In fact, your buffer pool will be somewhat smaller than the installed RAM, due to additional memory requirements of SQL Server which are discussed in more detail in the next section, *Non-buffer pool allocations (MemToLeave)*.

Finally, note that any memory allocated by `VirtualAlloc` is pageable; this means that the Windows OS can force this memory to be paged to disk, in response to memory pressure.

Non-buffer pool allocations (MemToLeave)

As discussed, the largest memory allocations made by SQL Server are generally to the buffer pool, for data pages and execution plan caching. However, any user mode VAS memory allocation that required more than 8 KB of contiguous memory would be a non-buffer pool allocation, made by the multi-page allocator. Examples of such multi-page allocations include thread stack allocations, heap allocations, extended stored procedures, SQLCLR, linked servers, and backup buffers. Of these, the backup buffers, i.e. the series of buffers allocated at the start of a database backup, are one of the most common consumers of non-buffer pool memory, with the total space required by the backup buffers being the number of buffers times the maximum data transfer size (`MaxTransferSize*BackupBufferCount`). It is not uncommon for a backup operation to reserve 16 backup buffers; with each backup buffer being 4 MB in size, this on its own will eat up 64 MB of non-buffer pool memory.

To ensure that sufficient VAS is available for non-buffer pool allocation requirements, 32-bit editions of SQL Server, upon startup, reserve a contiguous portion of the VAS that is commonly referred to as the `MemToLeave`.

MemToLeave (*or VAS Reservation*) *calculation*

This only applies to 32-bit instances of SQL Server and is not performed on 64-bit instances of SQL Server.

Once this reservation is taken, the size of the buffer pool is determined based on the amount of physical memory that is installed in the server and the remaining VAS.

For SQL Server 2005 and 2008, the calculation for the `MemToLeave` is calculated from the required thread stack size in MB, which is:
`MaxWorkerThreads` * 0.5 MB + default reservation size (256 MB).
where `MaxWorkerThreads` = (`ProcessorCount`-4)+256).

For SQL Server 2000, the calculation is `MaxWorkerThreads`=256.

In general, for 32-bit SQL Server installations using the default configuration options for Windows and SQL Server, the amount of the `MemToLeave` reservation is at least 384 MB ((256*0.5) + 256), and generally less than 432 MB, depending on the number of processors installed in the server. The −g startup parameter for the SQL Server service, covered shortly, can be used to increase the amount of VAS that is reserved by the `MemToLeave` calculation.

When this is subtracted from the 2 GB of user mode VAS, the remaining portion is available to the buffer pool, up to the available physical memory installed in the server. So, for servers with 2 GB of RAM, or more, this means that about 1.6 GB of RAM will be available to the buffer pool.

To allow 32-bit SQL Server to utilize any additional memory for buffer pool allocations, two options exist, and the appropriate option depends on the amount of memory that is installed on the server.

For servers with 4 GB of RAM, we can apply the concept known as **4 Gigabyte Tuning (4GT)** or, more generally, as **VAS tuning** in order to gain extra user mode VAS (at the expense of kernel mode VAS). For servers with more than 4 GB of RAM, we can make available a separate area of memory that can be used exclusively for allocations to the data cache portion of the buffer pool, by enabling AWE.

VAS tuning

For servers with 4 GB of memory, it's possible to change the way VAS is allocated between user mode and kernel mode processes. Instead of a 50:50 split, up to 1 GB of additional space can be allocated to user mode VAS for the buffer pool. In Windows Server 2008 this process is generally referred to as VAS tuning, though in earlier Windows version it was called 4 Gigabyte Tuning (4GT).

Of course, the trade-off with VAS tuning is that you end up with up to 1 GB less space for kernel mode VAS, and this can have significant consequences. When the kernel mode VAS is reduced, the number of system **Page Table Entries** (PTEs) is reduced, and this in turn reduces the total amount of memory that SQL Server can address.

Critical concepts: Page Table Entries

PTEs allow the mapping of virtual memory addresses to physical memory addresses. If there are an insufficient number of PTEs within the Windows kernel address space, the amount of physical memory that can be stably addressed by the system is limited. The PTEs used to map AWE memory, for example, must remain memory resident to provide system stability.

In short, if insufficient address space is allocated to kernel mode VAS, it can lead to system instability, so care must be taken when using VAS tuning.

In Windows Server 2008, VAS tuning for 32-bit servers is accomplished through the use of `BCDEdit /set` from the command prompt to set the value for the `increaseuserva` option to between 2048 and 3072 MB.

In Windows Server 2000 and beyond, two switches can be added to the `boot.ini` file to control how the VAS is split. The `/3GB` switch in the `boot.ini` changes the allocation so that 3 GB is allocated to the user mode VAS and 1 GB is allocated to kernel mode. In cases where the 3 GB:1 GB split proves problematic, the `/USERVA` switch can be used in conjunction with the `/3GB` switch in order to tune the split, and allocate additional VAS to the kernel mode address space, increasing slightly the number of PTEs and the size of the Non-Paged Pool.

For more on 4GT tuning...

...see the Books Online, "Topic: 4 Gigabyte Tuning" (HTTP://MSDN.MICROSOFT.COM/EN-US/LIBRARY/ BB613473(V=VS.85).ASPX).

The case for AWE

On 32-bit servers on which more than 4 GB of RAM is installed, SQL Server can utilize the memory over 4 GB through the use of Address Windowing Extensions (AWE), assuming the Windows operating system supports it. AWE is significantly more flexible, and allows for more memory to be made available than is the case with 4GT. However, AWE requires additional configuration of the OS to use Physical Address Extensions (PAE) to work.

PAE is enabled on Windows Server 2008 through the use of **BDCEdit /set** from the command prompt, to set the **PAE** option to **ForceEnable.** On Windows Server 2000 and 2003, PAE is enabled through the use of the **/PAE boot.ini** switch. When PAE is used by the OS, the 32-bit pointer used for memory management is expanded by 4 bits, to 36 bits, allowing the OS to address up to 64 GB of RAM. However, for applications to make use of this additional memory, they must use AWE.

While VAS tuning is concerned with reallocation of VAS, memory allocated using AWE is entirely separate. When allocating memory above the 4 GB limit using AWE, SQL Server does not use calls to **VirtualAlloc**, but instead calls the **AllocateUserPhysical-Pages** function in Windows. Unlike memory allocated using **VirtualAlloc**, memory allocated using **AllocateUserPhysicalPages** is mapped using PTEs and has to be physically available on the server to be allocated. Also, once the allocation is made, the memory is locked and non-pageable by Windows.

Memory allocated by SQL Server using AWE can be used *only* for the data cache portion of the buffer pool. So, when using AWE, all data cache is allocated in AWE memory (and is non-pageable), and the rest of the buffer pool (mainly the plan cache), and any non-buffer pool allocations that require user mode Virtual Address Space, will continue to be mapped within the 2 GB of user mode VAS.

In order for SQL Server to be able to use AWE to allocate memory, PAE must first be enabled, as described earlier. Next, the **'awe enabled' sp_configure** option must be set inside of SQL Server, and the SQL Server service account must have the **Lock Pages** in `Memory` user right, found in the User Rights Assignment of the Local Security Policy assigned to it in Windows (using the Windows Group Policy tool, `gpedit.msc`). If you enable either of these options, or to enable both of them at the same time, you must then restart the database engine in order for the change(s) to take effect.

As previously hinted, one of the side effects of granting the `Lock Pages in Memory` user rights to the SQL Server service account, is that the memory allocated to the buffer pool using AWE is locked and cannot be paged out if the Windows operating system gets into memory pressure. For this reason, whenever AWE is being used, it is recommended that the 'max server memory' `sp_configure` option be set in order to set a firm upper limit for memory that can be allocated to the buffer pool and so ensure that sufficient memory is available to the operating system after the SQL Server memory ramp up completes. If the Windows OS experiences memory pressure, it will set the **memory low** notification flag. SQL Server will always respond to this by performing a cache sweep and trying to free up memory (down to the value specified by the `min server memory` setting). In the meantime, however, the OS is unable to page out the AWE memory, as it is locked. If SQL Server is unable to free up enough memory quickly enough, the OS can reach an unstable state where it can't page, and can't allocate more memory.

For systems with less than 16 GB of RAM, it's possible to use the 4GT methods discussed in the previous section, in conjunction with AWE, but it is not generally recommended. One of the side effects of including the `/3GB` switch in the boot file, for 4GT tuning, is that the total amount of memory that can be managed by Windows is reduced from 64 GB to 16 GB due to the reduction in the number of PTEs caused by the lower kernel mode address space. On systems with more than 16 GB of RAM, the use of 4GT tuning in conjunction with AWE is unsupported by Microsoft (see HTTP://SUPPORT.MICROSOFT. COM/KB/274750).

The –g startup parameter

Earlier in this chapter, it was noted that during startup of 32-bit SQL Servers, a portion of the user mode VAS is reserved (a process called **VAS Reservation**) for non-buffer pool memory allocations. The size of this `MemToLeave` reservation is generally very small compared to the amount of memory that a SQL Server may have installed, and compared to the size of the buffer pool.

For most systems, this is not a problem, since the majority of memory consumed by SQL Server is not from this region of reserved address space, but from the buffer pool. However, as applications have increased in complexity, so have the databases that support them, and it is possible that the default VAS Reservation for a SQL Server instance is not large enough to support the requirements for non-buffer pool memory allocations.

Compounding the problem of inadequate size of the non-buffer pool VAS, is fragmentation of the VAS Reservation that does exist. Memory allocations from VAS must be contiguously allocated, and it is possible that sufficient VAS is available, but it has become fragmented and the appropriate contiguous size required for a memory allocation is not available.

Determining which of these two problems exists can be accomplished by querying the `sys.dm_os_virtual_address_dump` DMV to find the size of the available VAS on the system, and the size of the largest contiguously available space.

Determining available VAS

*SQL Server MVP, Christian Bolton, provides a script to determine the amount of available VAS to SQL Server, and the size of the largest contiguous block of VAS on his blog post: "SQL Server memtoleave, VAS and 64-bit" (*HTTP://SQLBLOGCASTS.COM/BLOGS/CHRISTIAN/ARCHIVE/2008/01/07/SQL-SERVER-MEMTOLEAVE-VAS-AND-64-BIT.ASPX*).*

The —g startup parameter for the SQL Server service can be used to increase the amount of VAS reserved by the `MemToLeave` startup VAS Reservation. This parameter can be used with an integer value greater than 256, to specify the size in megabytes to be used for the base reservation variable of the `MemToLeave` sizing calculation. By default, the base reservation is 256 MB in size, to which the calculated thread stack size (as shown earlier) for the instance is added to get the total size of the `MemToLeave` VAS Reservation. When this option is used, it reduces the user mode VAS available to the buffer pool, and therefore reduces the maximum size of the buffer pool for the SQL instance.

`MemToLeave` fragmentation is a more difficult problem to handle; if you call Microsoft support with this issue, you'll probably be told that the only answer is to upgrade to 64-bit SQL Server. The reason that this recommendation is made is that the size of the VAS on a 64-bit server is 8 TB, which exceeds the amount of physical RAM currently possible in a server, meaning that there will always be available VAS for non-buffer pool allocations by SQL Server. If you can't immediately upgrade to 64-bit SQL Server, your only options, currently, are to schedule frequent instance restarts or use the —g startup parameter to assign more memory to `MemToLeave` with the idea that the fragmentation will have less of an effect.

Using 64-bit SQL Server

The first 64-bit version of SQL Server 2000 was released in 2003 and it changed memory management for SQL Server significantly. Over the coming sections, we'll discuss some of the most significant changes, a few of which have caught some DBAs off-guard.

Higher VAS memory limits

One of the benefits of 64-bit systems is that the VAS limits are substantially higher. Where 32-bit systems only have 4 GB of Virtual Address Space, 64-bit systems have 16 exabytes (2^{64}) of VAS making it virtually unlimited in comparison to the amounts of physical RAM that can currently be installed in a server. In reality, managing this much VAS poses significant challenges, and the sizes of the kernel mode and user mode address spaces are currently limited to 8 TB each on x64 systems, and 7 TB each on IA64 (Itanium) systems.

This vastly higher VAS means that 64-bit SQL Server instances do not require any additional configuration in order to allocate memory over 4 GB; the `AWE enabled` option has no application for these instances. The `Lock Pages in Memory` option may, however, still be relevant (discussed shortly).

High amounts of pageable memory under default configuration

As with 32-bit SQL Server, the default behavior for 64-bit SQL Server is to allocate VAS memory using the `VirtualAlloc` Windows function. This means that all of this memory is not locked and is pageable. This caught many administrators off-guard; on 32-bit SQL Server they had up to 2 GB of user mode VAS-allocated memory, and then an additional, larger amount that was enabled using AWE and so was locked. Now, on 64-bit SQL Server, all memory can be committed using VAS only, making it all pageable, which can create significant problems for SQL Server if the OS is under memory pressure and decides to hard page out the SQL Server working set.

This was one of the problems that became apparent early on with 64-bit SQL Servers that were installed using the default configuration and left to run. We'll discuss this issue in more depth shortly, in the *Lock pages in memory* section.

No MemToLeave calculation for non-buffer pool allocations

The size of the Virtual Address Space on a 64-bit server guarantees that even after the buffer pool memory has been allocated by SQL Server, there will still be sufficient user mode VAS available to handle non-buffer pool memory requests. This means that the concept of a VAS Reservation (`MemToLeave`) for non-buffer pool allocations does not apply to 64-bit SQL Servers (and so the —g startup parameter has no significance, either). This issue is discussed in more detail shortly, with regard to setting `max server memory` in 64-bit SQL Server, but basically the lack of VAS Reservation means that it's important to account for non-buffer pool and non-SQL memory allocations by monitoring the `Memory/Available Mbytes` counter to ensure it remains above 150–300 MB as you gradually increase the value of `max server memory`.

Significantly larger procedure cache

Since the user mode VAS is significantly larger, the procedure cache in SQL Server, where execution plans are stored, can allocate significantly more memory on 64-bit systems, which was a surprise to many DBAs who upgraded their hardware while using SQL Server 2005 RTM or Service Pack 1. If their database had an ad hoc workload that generated a large number of single use plans, they found that these plans began consuming as much as half the memory available on their server.

Understanding changes to procedure cache sizing in SQL Server

*The SQL Server Programmability Team blogged about the challenges associated with the sizing of the procedure cache on 64-bit SQL Servers due to the size of the user mode VAS and how the cache sizing algorithms were changed in SQL Server 2005 Service Pack 2 to reduce the problems associated with cache bloat for ad hoc workloads on their blog post: "Changes in Caching Behavior between SQL Server 2000, SQL Server 2005 RTM and SQL Server 2005 SP2" (*HTTP://BLOGS.MSDN.COM/B/SQLPROGRAMMABILITY/ ARCHIVE/2007/01/22/3-0-CHANGES-IN-CACHING-BEHAVIOR-BETWEEN-SQL-SERVER-2000-SQL-SERVER-2005-RTM-AND-SQL-SERVER-2005-SP2.ASPX*).

Memory configuration options with 64-bit SQL Server

The following sections cover special considerations for setting important memory config-uration options when using 64-bit SQL Server, namely `max` (and `min`) `server memory` and `Lock Pages in Memory`. It also briefly discusses a special Trace Flag (834) that, when enabled on 64-bit servers, causes SQL Server to use Windows Large Page Allocations for buffer pool allocations.

Min and max server memory

SQL Server offers two instance-level settings that can be used to control how memory is allocated to, and removed from, the buffer pool: the `min server memory` and `max server memory sp_configure` options. Note that in SQL Server 2000, 2005, 2008 and 2008 R2, these settings apply *only* to the buffer pool size and do not include the memory that may be allocated by SQL Server outside of the buffer pool.

The `min server memory` option specifies the minimum size to which SQL Server can shrink the buffer pool when under memory pressure; it does not specify the minimum amount of memory that SQL Server will initially allocate. During memory ramp up, the memory usage of an instance slowly increases and the buffer pool is grown to meet the needs of the requests being executed. The `max server memory` option specifies the maximum amount of memory that SQL Server can use for the buffer pool, which is primarily used for caching data pages in memory.

The appropriate setting for each of these configuration options depends on the SQL Server implementation. It is common to find recommendations online that state something along the lines of:

> *"If a SQL Server is dedicated to running only the SQL Server database engine then, generally, each of these options can be configured to have the same value, so that the SQL Server allocates memory for the buffer pool and then does not shrink its memory usage once that level has been met."*

While this information is technically correct, it is not the recommended configuration that I would make for a dedicated SQL Server. The problem I have with this configuration is that, when `Lock Pages in Memory` is being used, this configuration limits how far SQL Server can respond to OS low memory notifications by sweeping its caches and reducing its memory usage to free memory back to the OS for use. This can result in system instability issues and, for this reason, I would recommend that the `min server memory` configuration be set lower than the `max server memory` configuration by a couple of gigabytes of memory, to allow SQL Server to resize the buffer pool as needed to respond to OS low memory notifications.

If the SQL Server also runs Reporting Services, Integration Services, or other applications that require memory from Windows, these options should be configured with a range so that the `min server memory` is configured at an acceptable lower limit for memory allocated to the buffer pool and the `max server memory` is set a higher limit, allowing the SQL Server to grow or shrink the memory usage within the established range as needed while other processes are running.

One of the popular questions on online SQL Server forums is: *"What is the proper max server memory setting for a SQL Server with N gigabytes of installed RAM?"* Unfortunately there is no single setting that applies to every environment for this option; different servers have different processes running and what is best for one server will not be the same for a different server. The best answer is to set the initial value low enough to ensure that the operating system doesn't have memory pressure issues and then monitor the `Memory\Available Mbytes` performance counter on the server (along, possibly, with counters like `Total Server Memory` and `Target Server Memory`, covered later) to determine the value for `max server memory` that leaves at least 150–300 MB of memory available at all times for the memory requirements of non-buffer pool and non-SQL memory allocations, for Windows and other applications.

As a general base configuration, for a dedicated SQL Server machine, reserve 1 GB of RAM for the OS, 1 GB for each 4 GB of RAM installed from 4–16 GB, and then 1 GB for every 8 GB RAM installed above 16 GB RAM. This means that, for a server with 64 GB RAM, the starting point for `max server memory` should be in the 54 GB range, and then tuned higher based on monitoring the `Memory\Available Mbytes` performance counter.

Lock pages in memory

While the SQL Server process is designed to be self-tuning with regard to its own memory allocation needs, it can't account for memory demands made by other processes running on the server, or by operations such as file copies. Its self-tuning nature means that it will respond to memory pressure, as and when signaled by the operating system.

This means that, ultimately, the operating system is in control of the response to memory pressure, and one of the ways that the OS responds is by trimming, and possibly paging out, the working set of processes that are consuming memory, including, of course, the SQL Server process. When this occurs, memory allocations that are backed by physical memory are written to virtual memory in the system page file on disk. If the process's working set is relatively small, this is not generally a big problem, but on 64-bit SQL Servers with large amounts of RAM installed, where all memory is committed using VAS only and so is pageable, this can significantly impact performance.

If SQL Server experiences a working set trim, or memory gets paged out, SQL will write a message in the error log as follows:

A significant part of sql server process memory has been paged out. This may result in a performance degradation. Duration: 0 seconds. Working set (KB): 16484, committed (KB): 6239692, memory utilization: 0%.

If this message is frequently seen, it indicates there is a problem with SQL getting paged out.

On 32-bit SQL Servers this wasn't generally a big issue since the pageable memory that could be allocated by SQL Server was limited to 2 GB of user mode VAS. However, on 64-bit systems, the SQLOS can, by default, allocate all of the memory on the server using calls to `VirtualAlloc`, which are non-locked and pageable. On a server with 16 GB of RAM, this can result in a significantly sized, pageable working set for the SQL Server process. This was especially problematic on Windows Server 2003 where the operating system responded aggressively to memory pressure by trimming working sets. First, Windows would ask SQL Server to trim its working set, which would prompt de-allocation of memory down to the `min server memory` setting. If SQL Server didn't trim enough memory, or didn't trim fast enough, the OS could force part of SQL Server's memory allocation out of physical memory and into the paging file. At this point, the buffer cache is still allocated, but it is not backed by physical memory, it is backed by page file on disk which is very slow and causes the performance issues.

To prevent this from happening on 64-bit SQL Servers, the `Lock Pages in Memory` privilege can be assigned to the SQL Server service account, in which case memory is allocated to the buffer pool using the Win32 function `AllocateUserPhysicalPages`, which is provided by the AWE API. This is the same function that is used in 32-bit SQL Servers that have AWE enabled in order to allocate memory above 4 GB. Even though the same function is used to perform the memory allocations, it is important to note that AWE is not being used by the 64-bit SQL Server and the `'awe enabled'` `sp_configure` option does not have to be set. The function is being used simply so that the allocated pages are locked and cannot be paged to disk.

Do NOT enable AWE on 64-bit SQL Server

The ability to lock pages in 64-bit SQL Server requires only the `Lock Pages in Memory` *privilege for the service account; it does not require setting the* `'awe enabled'` `sp_configure` *option, which is a no-op in the SQL Server code for 64-bit systems.*

One of the problems that people often run into when running SQL Server using Lock Pages in Memory is that the information returned by Task Manager no longer reflects the total memory use by the sqlservr.exe process. The information shown in Task Manager is only for the non-buffer pool memory usage by the sqlservr.exe process and does not include the memory allocated to the buffer pool using locked pages, as shown in Figure 4.3.

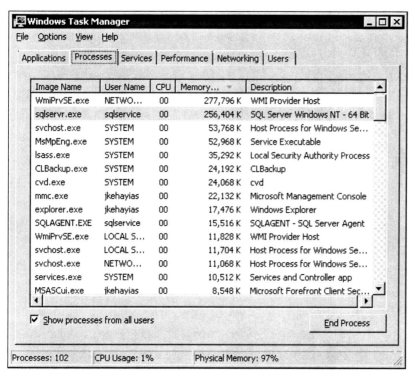

Figure 4.3: SQL Server Process memory usage (locked pages).

The server shown in Figure 4.3 has 64 GB of RAM installed in it, of which 97% is currently allocated, primarily by SQL Server. To determine the total amount of memory that is being used by SQL Server, the SQL Server:Memory Manager\Total Server Memory performance counter should be used.

Initially, in SQL Server 2005 and 2008, `Lock Pages in Memory` was an Enterprise-only feature. However, it was added to SQL Server Standard Edition in SQL Server 2008 R2, and can be used in SQL Server 2008 SP1 with Cumulative Update 2 or later, and in SQL Server 2005 SP3 with Cumulative Update 4 or later. Having applied the appropriate update to the server, the startup Trace Flag –T845 must be added to the SQL Server service startup parameters for the instance, in order to begin using the feature. Since the memory allocated using `Lock Pages in Memory` is locked and cannot be paged, it is recommended that the `max server memory sp_configure` option be set to limit the amount of memory that SQL Server can use, and so prevent starving the OS of memory.

Additional references for `Lock Pages in Memory` *and how to reduce paging*

How to reduce paging of buffer pool memory in the 64-bit version of SQL Server: HTTP://SUPPORT. MICROSOFT.COM/KB/918483.

Support for locked pages on SQL Server 2005 Standard Edition 64-bit systems and on SQL Server 2008 Standard Edition 64-bit systems: HTTP://SUPPORT.MICROSOFT.COM/KB/970070.

Using Large Pages (-T834 startup parameter)

If this specific topic had not been addressed in a published Microsoft Knowledge Base article (HTTP://SUPPORT.MICROSOFT.COM/KB/920093), and subsequently referenced by VMware as a best practice for virtualized SQL Servers (HTTP://WWW.VMWARE.COM/FILES/ PDF/SQL_SERVER_VIRT_BP.PDF), it would probably never have made it into this book, and I'm not going to discuss this complex issue in a lot of detail.

There is much debate regarding whether or not the use of Large Page Allocations (LPA) with SQL Server is beneficial to a given workload, but I'll defer to Bob Ward, a Senior Customer Support Services Engineer at Microsoft, who provides further information about this feature on his blog (HTTP://BLOGS.MSDN.COM/B/PSSSQL/ARCHIVE/2009/06/05/ SQL-SERVER-AND-LARGE-PAGES-EXPLAINED.ASPX), and concludes that you should "use with caution."

Even though the LPA option is used during TPC-related benchmarks by Microsoft, the real truth is that any configuration option utilized during one of these benchmarks has to be documented by the software manufacturer and, had this not been used to attain the published results of the benchmark, it would probably never have been documented.

The problem with this is that the documentation breeds confusion about whether or not this configuration option is truly beneficial to SQL Server or not. One of the constraints associated with using Large Pages with SQL Server is that the buffer pool cannot be dynamically sized when Large Pages are in use, and if a sufficient contiguous allocation of physical memory does not exist to back the configuration of the `'max server memory'` `sp_configure` option, the amount of memory allocated to the buffer pool can be significantly lower than expected. The use of this feature of SQL Server should be thoroughly evaluated to ensure that an actual benefit is realized for your specific workload prior to this option being enabled on a production SQL Server, even when running under VMware virtualization.

Diagnosing Memory Pressure

If SQL Server is forced to operate with an insufficient amount of memory, it will be able to store fewer data pages in the buffer pool. As a result, higher physical I/O is needed to bring data pages from disk into the buffer pool as they are requested, and performance will degrade. These data pages may soon be subsequently flushed from the buffer pool, to make room for other pages, only to be then read back into the buffer pool, in a repetitive cycle known as **buffer pool churn**. The heightened disk I/O observed during buffer pool churn often means that it's easily mistaken for a disk I/O subsystem problem, rather than a memory pressure problem.

If a system consistently performs read operations that require more memory than is available to SQL Server, each read of the data will result in flushing the buffer cache, and cause physical I/O against the disk subsystem. In addition, if the workload requires significant amounts of data in sort or aggregate operations during query processing, the data can spill over to `tempdb` work tables due to a lack of available memory to accommodate that processing, again further increasing the I/O demand on the system.

The best way to tell if SQL Server is under memory pressure and needs more memory is to review a number of critical performance counters related to the health of the SQL Server instance's buffer pool.

Memory-related counters

In this section, we'll review some of the critical performance counters related to memory usage. It's important to realize that there is no single performance counter that can be used in isolation to determine if SQL Server is under memory pressure, and there is no single point-in-time snapshot of the counters that will allow you to diagnose the "health" of the server in regard to memory use. Diagnosing memory pressure requires tracking several counter values across a period of time (a day, week, or even a month) that represents the normal operations of the database.

SQL Server:Buffer Manager

There are a number of useful counters belonging to the `SQL Server:Buffer Manager` object that, when monitored collectively, can help uncover problems relating to buffer pool churn.

Buffer Cache Hit Ratio

The `SQL Server:Buffer Manager\Buffer Cache Hit Ratio` counter provides a database-wide measure of how often SQL Server gets data from memory (buffer cache) as opposed to disk. There are a ton of references on the Internet suggesting that this counter should be greater than 95% for OLTP systems and greater than 90% for OLAP systems.

Unfortunately, none of those references explain the meaning of this counter and how its value is affected by read ahead pre-fetch operations performed by the database engine to read pages into the buffer pool before they are actually used by an executing statement. The fact that this counter shows a 95% hit rate for the buffer cache indicates nothing more than the fact that SQL Server is working as designed to read pages into memory before they are needed. To see a significant drop in the value of this counter, you'd have to have some serious memory problems with SQL Server, and you'll spot this problem much more easily and quickly using counters other than this one.

On its own, this performance counter doesn't tell you anything about the health of your SQL Server, or whether or not it is under memory pressure.

Page Life Expectancy

The `Page Life Expectancy` counter provides the time in seconds that a page exists in cache before being aged out to allow reuse of the cache space. Again, there are numerous references out there on the Internet, suggesting that the value for this counter should generally be greater than 300 (i.e. five minutes).

However, most of those references are based on a recommendation made by Microsoft over a decade ago, for SQL Server 2000, in a time when 4 GB of RAM was considered to be a lot of memory, and SQL Server was only allocating 1.6 GB of memory to the buffer pool. If SQL Server has to read 1.6 GB of data from disk every five minutes, the impact is minimal.

However, fast-forward ten years, and servers today commonly have 64 GB of RAM, or more, and SQL Server is commonly configured to use a majority of this memory for the buffer pool. If SQL Server has to read 50 GB or more of data from disk every five minutes, then the impact to the I/O subsystem is going to be substantially greater than it would have been when Microsoft made the original recommendation.

The value of this counter reflects the Page Life Expectancy (PLE) at that exact point in time, and it is not uncommon to see periodic drops in the value returned by this performance counter, especially when a large query is executing a table scan, reading new pages into the buffer pool from disk. This counter must be monitored over long periods of time in order to properly identify normal trends.

Free Pages

The **Free Pages** counter reflects the total number of free pages that exist for the SQL Server buffer pool, allowing for immediate allocations by an executing request without having to release additional pages from cache to satisfy the request. The number of free pages in the system should never reach zero. This counter should be monitored in conjunction with the **Page Life Expectancy** counter and the **Free List Stalls** counter, to gauge whether the system is actually under memory pressure. If the PLE experiences drops in value that correlate to low or zero values for **Free Pages**, and the system is also experiencing **Free List Stalls** at the same time, then these are a sure sign that the instance is experiencing memory pressure and could benefit from having addition memory allocated to the buffer pool.

Free List Stalls/sec

Free List Stalls occur whenever a request has to wait for a free page in the buffer pool. If the number of stalls exceeds zero frequently or consistently over a period of time, this is a sign of memory pressure.

Lazy Writes/sec

The **Lazy Writes/sec** counter reflects the number of buffer pages that have been flushed by the Lazy Writer process, outside of a normal checkpoint operation, allowing the buffer to be reused for other pages. If you observe Lazy Writes occurring in conjunction with a low PLE, a low number of free pages, and the occurrence of Free List Stalls, this is a sign that the workload is exceeding the amount of memory that is available to the buffer pool, and additional memory needs to be added to the server.

SQL Server:Memory Manager

The counters relating to the `SQL Server:Memory Manager` object provide useful insight into overall memory consumption and memory management issues on the server.

Total Server Memory (KB) and Target Server Memory (KB)

Respectively, these counters represent the total amount of memory that has been allocated by SQL Server and the amount of memory that SQL Server wants to commit. When the `Target Server Memory (KB)` counter exceeds the `Total Server Memory (KB)` counter, the SQL Server process wants to commit more memory than is available on the server, which can be a sign of memory pressure.

Generally, SQL Server will reduce its memory demands to match the available memory on the server, or what is specified by the 'max server memory' option of sp_configure, so these two counters are not the first places to start, when looking to confirm a memory pressure issue on SQL Server.

Memory Grants Outstanding

This counter measures the total number of processes that have successfully acquired a workspace memory grant. Low values for this counter, under periods of high user activity or heavy workload, may be a sign of memory pressure, especially if there are a high number of memory grants pending.

Memory Grants Pending

This counter measures the total number of processes that are waiting for a workspace memory grant. If this value is non-zero, it is a sign that tuning or optimization of the workload should be performed if possible, or that additional memory needs to be added to the server.

Memory-related DMVs

There is also some information regarding memory-related waits and non-buffer pool memory allocations and so on, that can be extracted from the DMVs, such as the **sys. dm_os_memory_*** objects in the Operating System-related DMVs, or the **sys.dm_ exec_query_memory_grants** DMV. For example:

- **sys.dm_exec_query_memory_grants** can be used to find queries that are waiting (or have recently had to wait) for a memory grant, especially those requesting relatively large memory grants.

- **sys.dm_os_memory_cache_counters** provides a snapshot of current usage of the memory cache. Includes the `multi_pages_kb` column showing the amount of memory allocated by the multiple-page allocator.

- **sys.dm_os_sys_memory** summarizes the overall memory condition of the system, including current levels of memory in the system, the cache, and so on.

- **sys.dm_os_memory_clerks** provides information related to memory clerk processes that manage SQL Server memory. For example, significant memory allocation in the buffer pool associated with the MEMORYCLERK_ SQLQERESERVATIONS may indicate insufficient memory in the buffer pool for certain queries to execute.

We'll not discuss these objects any further here, since I've generally found the information in these objects to be harder to analyze and interpret than that which is easily available from the memory counters. As a result, I always use the PerfMon memory counters, in preference to these DMVs, in order to determine whether or not a SQL Server instance has memory issues.

Common Memory-Related Problems

One of the hardest challenges in selecting a list of common problems was categorizing the list of common problems as misconceptions, misconfigurations, or true problems in SQL Server. In the end, only a few problems stood out in the myriad list of problems that people report related to memory management and SQL Server.

The SQL Server memory leak myth

While this topic has already been addressed in this chapter, the prevalence of the notion that SQL Server has a memory leak based on its memory consumption on a server made it one of the top picks for common problems for memory management with SQL Server. To oversimplify this subject, SQL Server does not have a memory leak. However, it is possible for an extended stored procedure or in-process linked server driver to have a memory leak that usually leads to system instability and service crashes. It is not uncommon or abnormal for SQL Server to allocate as much memory as it possibly can, up to and including the physical memory limit installed in the server on which SQL Server is running. Further details about this were given earlier in this chapter.

Paging problems

Starting with SQL Server 2005 Service Pack 2, if a working set trim occurs SQL Server will, as discussed earlier, write a message to the error log to the effect that "a significant part of SQL Server process memory has been paged out."

Whenever these messages appear in the error log, performance degradation has occurred as a result of the working set for SQL being paged out to disk. There are a number of causes of working set trims of the SQL Server process, but the most common ones are:

- incorrect settings for the `max server memory sp_configure` option, when `Lock Pages in Memory` is not being used
- a large system cache in Windows caused by caching of non-buffered I/O operations such as file copy operations
- hardware driver issues that result in memory leaks or excessive memory allocations by the driver.

The fastest way to resolve problems related to the OS trimming the working set of the SQL Server process is to use brute force, and enable `Lock Pages in Memory` for the SQL Server service.

However, as recommended in the previous preference paper on reducing paging of buffer pool memory in the 64-bit version of SQL Server (HTTP://SUPPORT.MICROSOFT.COM/KB/918483), it is better to identify the actual root cause of the working set trim issues, and resolve those problems, rather than falling back on `Lock Pages in Memory`. Nevertheless, practical experience from the field has shown that enabling `Lock Pages in Memory` may be the only way to resolve working set trim issues for the SQL Server process.

OS instability due to Lock Pages in Memory plus unlimited max server memory

When `Lock Pages in Memory` is being used for a SQL Server instance, the default configuration for the `max server memory sp_configure` option must be changed to limit the amount of memory that the SQL Server instance can allocate for the buffer pool. If the `max server memory` configuration option is not set for the instance, under the default configuration the instance will allocate all of the memory available on the server for use by the SQL Server buffer pool. The problem with this scenario is that when the Windows OS gets into memory pressure (and it certainly will, as SQL Server commits all of the memory available on the server), it can't page out or trim the SQL Server working set in response to the memory pressure. This leaves the OS at the mercy of SQL Server to respond to the memory pressure fast enough to prevent the Windows OS from crashing. The same scenario can occur if an inappropriately high value has been set for `max server memory` for the instance. For this reason, it is critical that when `Lock Pages in Memory` is set for a SQL Server instance, the `max server memory` configuration option should be set low enough to ensure that the Windows OS never gets into memory pressure.

App Domain is marked for unload due to memory pressure

This error is related to SQLCLR and can be triggered by a number of factors. It is generally seen on 32-bit installations of SQL Server, though it may occur on 64-bit installations where the `max server memory` configuration of SQL Server limits the amount of physical memory that can be allocated by SQLCLR. A majority of the times that this error shows up the problem can be tracked to one of two problems: inefficient memory utilization by the SQLCLR assembly or limitations of the VAS that is available for allocation by the SQLCLR assembly.

When this error is encountered on 32-bit installations of SQL Server, the prevailing recommendation is to upgrade the server to a 64-bit installation to realize the benefits of the increased size of the user mode VAS provided by the 64-bit installation. However, if the SQLCLR code excessively utilizes memory by using objects like a `DataSet`, which uses excessive amounts of memory in the CLR stack to store all of the results from a query's execution, over a `SqlDataReader`, even an upgrade from 32-bit to 64-bit is unlikely to resolve the problem. One way to identify if this is the problem is to utilize the code of the SQLCLR assembly outside of the SQL Server process, in a Console or WinForms application, and profile its memory usage.

Depending on the purpose of the SQLCLR assembly being affected, this error message in the error log may be benign in nature, or could be significantly problematic. For example, if a SQLCLR stores state across executions and its Code Access Security (CAS) declaration is UNSAFE, then having it unload would lose the state information and cause significant problems.

In either case, repeated App Domain unloads and reloads do impact performance and they should be eliminated if possible. If a migration from a 32-bit installation to a 64-bit installation is not immediately possible, one potential remediation is to use the –g startup parameter, discussed earlier in this chapter to increase the size of the MemToLeave VAS Reservation, providing additional Virtual Address Space to SQLCLR for memory allocations.

Error 701 and FAILED_VIRTUAL_RESERVE

When SQL Server fails to allocate a contiguous region of VAS for an operation, it raises a 701 error and outputs the information about the size of the allocation request into the SQL Server error log. This problem generally only occurs on 32-bit SQL Servers, where the VAS is limited, and can be associated with a number of different factors, including backups that are using larger-than-default configuration values for maxtransfersize and buffer count, as well as SQLCLR, XML, spatial data types, linked servers, or large query plans being generated by the system. This error is not related to the buffer pool in SQL Server, it is specific to allocation requests outside of the buffer pool that are generally larger than 8 KB in size.

If a migration from a 32-bit installation to a 64-bit installation is not immediately possible, one remediation is to use the –g startup parameter, discussed earlier, to increase the size of the `MemToLeave` VAS Reservation, providing additional VAS to the multi-page allocator for memory allocations.

Over-provisioned virtual machines

In late 2008, Microsoft added virtualization support (Hyper-V) to SQL Server 2005 and 2008, then expanded its support to cover validated configurations using other virtualization technologies, via its Server Virtualization Validation Program (SVVP). After that, it was only a matter of time before virtualized SQL Server implementations became common in business datacenters.

Depending on the hypervisor being used, advanced features like "memory overcommit" can lead to problems for SQL Server, when the amount of memory allocated to the virtual machines running on the hypervisor exceeds the actual physical memory installed in the host server.

Hypervisors that support options such as "memory overcommit" implement additional functionalities that allow the host server to respond to physical memory pressure, and so stabilize the system. In general, there are two ways the hypervisors cope with physical memory pressure on the host server: **memory ballooning** and **memory paging**.

Memory ballooning of the guest virtual machines is a process where a specialized "balloon driver," installed as a part of the VM tools in each guest, begins acquiring memory from the VM. This leads to memory pressure inside the VM, which causes "low memory" resource notifications to be set by the Windows OS which, in turn, forces processes running under the guest OS to release memory, which can then be returned to the host server.

Memory ballooning is the preferred option, but when ballooning of the guest VMs can't release memory fast enough to cope with the host-level memory pressure, the alternative method used by hypervisors is to actively page the guest memory allocations out to disk, which results in severe degradation of performance of the paged-out guests on the system.

SQL Servers that are running as VMs require special considerations with regard to their memory configurations in the hypervisor, in order to minimize problems associated with ballooning and paging when the host hypervisor comes under memory pressure.

When a SQL Server VM voluntarily reduces its memory usage as a result of ballooning, this can, in extreme cases, result in SQL Server reducing its buffer pool allocations to the point that little to no memory is being used by SQL Server for caching data. This, in turn, will result in excessive physical disk I/O operations by the instance.

All of the hypervisors currently supported by Microsoft provide mechanisms for reserving a minimum amount of memory for the VM that is hosting SQL Server, which prevents the hypervisor from ballooning or paging the VM in the event that the host experiences memory pressure. Setting the appropriate reservation for SQL Server is a recommended best practice by the hypervisor vendors. In addition, setting the correct `min server memory` configuration inside of SQL Server can allow for partial ballooning to occur, while ensuring that SQL Server continues to allocate the buffer pool memory needed to meet the environmental SLAs.

Memory settings for multiple instances

One of the selling points that Microsoft marketing uses for SQL Server is the ability to install multiple named instances of SQL Server on a single, large server. Consolidating multiple SQL Server instances onto a single server or a failover cluster can lead to a substantial reduction in SQL Server licensing costs.

However, when multiple instances are being run on the same physical server, it is very important that the `min server memory` and `max server memory sp_configure` options are set appropriately for each instance, based on workload, in order to avoid competition for memory resources, and one instance starving others of memory. Each of the instances should be monitored using the performance counters discussed in the *Diagnosing Memory Pressure* section, to determine where the `max server memory` value should be set. The aggregate total of the `max server memory sp_configure` options for all of the instances on the server should be low enough to ensure that the Windows OS still has sufficient available memory, as tracked by the `Memory\Available Mbytes` counter, to prevent the OS low memory notifications.

It is also recommended that `min server memory` be configured for each instance, to guarantee a minimum amount of memory to the buffer pool if the Windows OS sets the low memory notification, and the SQL Server instances reduce their memory allocations in response. If the `min server memory` configuration option is not set, a single instance of SQL Server may voluntarily reduce its memory usage to the point that it experiences performance degradation. Setting `min server memory` for all of the instances will prevent this from occurring, and instead cause the other instances to reduce memory usage appropriately, in response to the OS low memory notification.

Summary

Without a doubt, some of the most important configuration options for SQL Server relate to memory management, and the advent of 64-bit SQL Server changed memory management for SQL Server significantly.

When SQL Server is a 32-bit process, its memory usage for the buffer pool is limited to 2 GB, the size of the Virtual Address Space (VAS), minus the size of the Virtual Address Space Reservation (also known as the `MemToLeave`) for non-buffer pool memory allocations for the SQL Server process. If the installed RAM is lower than 2 GB then memory usage is limited to RAM minus the `MemToLeave`. This chapter discussed the two options that will allow 32-bit SQL Server to utilize additional memory for buffer pool allocations, either by decreasing the kernel mode VAS (VAS tuning), or by making available a separate, larger area of PAE memory, using Address Windowing Extensions (AWE).

When SQL Server is a 64-bit process, VAS is essentially unlimited but the physical memory limitation still applies to the environment. We covered some of the significant memory management changes, and their specific implications for configuration settings and options such as `max server memory`, `min server memory` and `Lock Pages in Memory`.

Memory management of SQL Server continues to be a confusing topic for most people, but the guidelines suggested by this chapter should, in most cases, provide the best practice configuration of SQL Server.

Nevertheless, memory-related problems still can (and probably will) arise, and this chapter covered the most useful PerfMon counters to investigate some issues, as well as some of the most commonly reported problems, and how to fix them.

Chapter 5: Missing Indexes

Indexes in SQL Server provide optimized access to data inside of a database, and one of the common causes of performance problems with a SQL Server database is missing or incorrect indexes on tables within the database.

Great strides have been made in SQL Server 2005 and 2008 to assist in identifying missing indexes, via the use of:

- **the Database Engine Tuning Advisor** – analyses the execution plans generated for a supplied workload, along with the physical characteristics of the database, and recommends a set of indexes
- **the Missing Index feature** – provides information regarding potentially useful indexes, stored in Dynamic Management Views and in XML Showplans.

However, the information provided by these tools, in particular the latter, can cause problems when used incorrectly. We'll cover two of the most critical factors regarding the appropriate structure of the indexes to be created, namely the index key column order and the appropriate use of **included** columns. This will help you to evaluate and verify the index recommendations made by these tools, in light of your knowledge of the data and workload for the given database.

Finally, since indexes come with a maintenance cost, we'll discuss how to identify any unnecessary indexes in your database, either duplicate indexes or those that are being maintained but never used by any queries.

Note that this chapter focuses exclusively on identifying an appropriate set of indexes for a given database; related index issues that could also affect query performance, such as index fragmentation, are not covered.

Index Selection and Design

Selecting the appropriate set of indexes for a database requires an understanding of how the database is used, and the data it contains. An indexing strategy that may be applied to a data warehouse or decision support system will be very different from the strategy that would be appropriate for an online transaction processing (OLTP) system. However, in any type of database, the general indexing strategy should be to establish indexes that are not necessarily query specific, but instead provide the best performance for the overall workload against the database.

In defining an appropriate set of indexes, you will ensure that the most significant queries in your workload are able to read *only* the minimum required amount of data, and in a logical, ordered fashion, enabling them to return that data quickly and efficiently, with minimal read I/O.

Conversely, if a database lacks an appropriate set of indexes for the required workload, then any searches against non-indexed columns will be resolved by performing Clustered Index Scans or Table Scans, reading far more data than is necessary to return the required result set, and leading to high associated read I/O costs.

To understand the overall workload, you have to first know the specific queries that will be executed against the database, and then how frequently each of them will be executed. An index that improves the performance of a single query that is executed once or twice a day may not be worth creating if the query, when it runs, is not impacting the overall performance of the server. If the same query ran a few thousand times an hour, however, the impact of the index would likely be significant enough that creating it would be beneficial.

Remember that, while indexes can improve the performance of specific queries in SQL Server, they are not free. There is a cost associated with maintaining the records contained in each index, and this cost must be balanced against the performance benefits that each individual index provides. A database that has too many indexes will have a large write I/O cost associated with maintaining the indexes, for every `INSERT` and `DELETE` operation, as well as any `UPDATE` operations that affect an indexed column. Furthermore, as your indexes grow larger and more numerous, so the cost of performing routine maintenance work, such as backups, index reorganization and rebuild, and `DBCC CHECKDB` operations, will rise accordingly.

Index key column order

It is fairly common to find recommendations online that state the index key columns should be ordered based on their cardinality (or selectivity), the idea being to reduce the number of pages that have to be read to match a set of filtering or grouping columns.

However, selecting the appropriate key column order is never as straightforward as most online content makes it seem, and you won't generally find a lot of guidance about when and why you might choose to create an index that has the columns in an order that is different from the cardinality order. For example, is it better to create multiple indexes, where each individual index has the optimal key column order, based on column selectivity, or to create a single index that covers multiple queries, but has a less selective column order?

Ultimately, your decision should be based on the type of database for which the index is being implemented. For a data warehouse, where there are significantly more read operations than write operations, the multiple indexes option may be appropriate. For an OLTP system, where there are more writes than reads, a less selective index that covers multiple queries using a less than optimal column order may be most appropriate.

The most important point to understand though, regarding index key column order, is that a query cannot seek on an index unless the query filters on a left-based subset of the index key. To demonstrate this point, let's say we have the index and queries shown in Listing 5.1.

```
CREATE INDEX idx_Test ON TestTable (Col2, Col1, Col3)

SELECT  1
FROM    TestTable
WHERE   Col1 = @Var1
        AND Col2 = @Var2
        AND Col3 = @Var3

SELECT  1
FROM    TestTable
WHERE   Col1 = @Var1
        AND Col3 = @Var3

SELECT  1
FROM    TestTable
WHERE   Col2 = @Var2
        AND Col3 = @Var3
```

Listing 5.1: Various queries against a simple three-column index.

The first query can seek effectively on the index because it filters on all three columns of the index (the order of clauses in the WHERE clause is irrelevant).

The second query cannot seek on that index; the leading column of the index is Col2 and that query does not filter on Col2. The query can use that index, but only via a scan.

The third query can seek on the index, but the seek is not as efficient as it could be, as SQL can only seek for Col2; it would have to do a secondary filter for Col3, since Col3 is not the second column in the index.

If I wanted to create the minimum number of indexes that could allow SQL Server to resolve all three queries as efficiently as possible, i.e. with index seeks, then I could create an index for each query, or I could try several combinations of two indexes, with differing index key ordering. The selectivity of the various columns would help choose which pair were the most appropriate. Some of the options are shown in Listing 5.2.

```
--3 possible pairs of indexes

CREATE INDEX idx_Test1
ON TestTable (Col1, Col3, Col2)
CREATE INDEX idx_Test1
ON TestTable (Col2, Col3)

--OR--

CREATE INDEX idx_Test
ON TestTable (Col2, Col3, Col1)
CREATE INDEX idx_Test1
ON TestTable (Col1, Col3)

--OR--

CREATE INDEX idx_Test
ON TestTable (Col3, Col1, Col2)
CREATE INDEX idx_Test1
ON TestTable (Col2, Col3)
```

Listing 5.2:   Three possible pairs of indexes.

Let's look at a quick **AdventureWorks** example. Listing 5.3 shows three queries, each with a different predicate in the **WHERE** clause.

```
SELECT   BusinessEntityID ,
         PersonType ,
         FirstName ,
         MiddleName ,
         LastName ,
         EmailPromotion
FROM     Person.Person AS p
WHERE    FirstName = 'Carol'
         AND PersonType = 'SC'

SELECT   BusinessEntityID ,
         FirstName ,
         LastName
FROM     Person.Person AS p
WHERE    PersonType = 'GC'
```

169

```
        AND Title = 'Ms.'

SELECT  BusinessEntityID ,
        PersonType ,
        EmailPromotion
FROM    Person.Person AS p
WHERE   Title = 'Mr.'
        AND FirstName = 'Paul'
        AND LastName = 'Shakespear'
```

Listing 5.3: Three queries against `AdventureWorks`.

We could create three indexes, each one perfectly suited to a single query, and in a data warehouse environment that may indeed be the best option. In an OLTP environment where the number of indexes should be kept low, in order to maintain good `INSERT` performance, it may not be such a good idea.

In terms of selectivity, the `LastName` column is the most selective, followed closely by `FirstName`. The `Title` and `PersonType` columns have a much lower selectivity, each having only six distinct values in the table. In this case, we could create just the two indexes shown in Listing 5.4, and have all the queries in Listing 5.3 perform very well.

```
CREATE INDEX idx_Person_FirstNameLastNameTitleType
ON Person.Person (FirstName, LastName, Title, PersonType)

CREATE INDEX idx_Person_TypeTitle
ON Person.Person (PersonType, Title)
```

Listing 5.4: Two indexes, designed based on column selectivity.

The first index satisfies the first and third queries. It's not perfect for the first one, but given how selective the `FirstName` column is, it's likely to be good enough. I've chosen to have `FirstName` as the leading column despite having slightly worse selectivity than `LastName`, because if I put `LastName` as the leading column then the first query would be unable to seek on it and I would need a third index to completely satisfy all queries.

With the second index, the order of columns is arbitrary. Neither the queries nor the selectivity shows a preferred order, so either way works. In a real environment, the order would probably be decided by other indexes or queries.

It should be clear even from this relatively simple example that determining the optimal order of columns for an index can be a complex process and is not something that should be decided on without sufficient analysis and investigation.

More on index selectivity

SQL Server MVP, and Technical Reviewer for this book, Gail Shaw, discusses this topic in further detail on her two blog posts: "Index columns, selectivity and equality predicates" (HTTP://SQLINTHEWILD. CO.ZA/INDEX.PHP/2009/01/19/INDEX-COLUMNS-SELECTIVITY-AND-EQUALITY-PREDICATES/) *and "Index columns, selectivity and inequality predicates"* (HTTP://SQLINTHEWILD.CO.ZA/INDEX.PHP/2009/02/06/ INDEX-COLUMNS-SELECTIVITY-AND-INEQUALITY-PREDICATES/).

Use of included columns

Many of the features described in the remainder of this chapter, for identifying missing indexes in the databases of a SQL Server instance, will make recommendations regarding the use of `include` columns, so a brief discussion of the benefits and impact of included columns is necessary.

Included columns, a new feature in SQL Server 2005, allow creation of non-clustered indexes that contain non-key columns as a part of the index definition, so that a single index can cover more queries. The key columns of an index are stored at all levels of the index, but the included columns are only stored at the leaf level of the index. The typical usage for included columns is in creating indexes that cover queries. A **covering index** is one that contains all of the columns needed by a query, as either key or non-key columns, preventing the need to access the table or clustered index using lookup operations, and so decreasing the number of I/O operations required to return the data.

Included columns can only be created on non-clustered indexes, and the non-key columns do not count towards the limitation of 900 byte key size or 16-columns that exists in SQL Server. The non-key columns can use data types not allowed by index key columns; all data types except the legacy `text`, `ntext`, and `image` are supported. Additionally, in SQL Server 2008, `varbinary (max)` columns that have the `FILESTREAM` attribute cannot be included in an index. While the new large object (LOB) data types are supported as non-key columns, there are performance implications with maintaining the included columns, since the column values are copied into the leaf level of the non-clustered index that contains them. This will result in high disk space requirements to store the index, and also an increase in I/O demands and lower buffer cache efficiency.

Once again, the degree to which you use included columns in your indexing strategy for a database depends on the usage characteristics of that database. The gains in query performance that included columns can provide must be balanced against the cost of higher disk space requirements, lower cache efficiency, and reduced performance of data modification operations. In data warehouse environments, it may be acceptable to have non-clustered indexes with long included column lists to cover the queries that may be executed, if during the extract-transform-load process (ETL) the indexes may be disabled or dropped to eliminate the impact of index maintenance during the data loading. In contrast, transactional databases would generally use fewer included columns due to the impact on the performance of data manipulation operations.

Creating a covering index for a query can be one of the best ways to get a query to perform well, however not all queries can be covered, and not all queries should be covered. In an OLTP environment, this is something that should be considered only for critical queries, i.e. queries that execute often and must run as fast as possible. Trying to cover all queries that run in an environment is almost certain to bloat the database size significantly and have detrimental effects on data modification performance.

So, given that, let's take one of the earlier examples from `AdventureWorks` and see how we can use included columns to make the query in Listing 5.5 even more efficient.

```
SELECT   BusinessEntityID ,
         FirstName ,
         LastName
FROM     Person.Person AS p
WHERE    PersonType = 'GC'
         AND Title = 'Ms.'
```

Listing 5.5: An AdventureWorks query.

The index that we decided on for this query is shown in Listing 5.6.

```
CREATE INDEX idx_Person_TypeTitle
ON Person.Person (Title, PersonType)
```

Listing 5.6: A non-covering index.

That index does not cover the query. While it has all the columns needed for the WHERE clause, it does not have as part of the index the three columns in the SELECT. SQL Server will have to do a lookup to the clustered index to fetch those columns.

Now, if we were to add those three columns to this index it would make the index covering for this query. We don't want them as key columns; doing so would make the key unnecessarily wide. Since those columns are not being filtered or joined on, there is no need to have them as key columns, so we can make them included columns instead, as shown in Listing 5.7.

```
CREATE INDEX idx_Person_TypeTitle
ON Person.Person (Title, PersonType)
INCLUDE (BusinessEntityID, FirstName, LastName)
```

Listing 5.7: Adding included columns to cover a query.

Now the index contains all the columns needed for the query, and the query is as efficient as possible since it no longer needs to do lookups. The trade-off is that the index is slightly larger and that data modifications that affect any of the three include columns have more work to do.

Index width

There is no strict rule governing the width of an index, and we won't discuss the topic in detail here. However, in general, you want the index to be as narrow as possible while still achieving accurate search results. This means that indexes will ideally comprise as few columns as is practical, consisting of smaller rather than larger data types. Of course, the latter is rather dependent on how intelligently the underlying tables have been designed.

While you certainly don't want any columns to be part of the key that don't need to be there, neither is it at all wise to opt for a large number of single-column indexes. Gail Shaw discusses the topic of a single multi-column index versus multiple single-column indexes in further detail on her blog post, *One wide index or multiple narrow indexes?* (HTTP://SQLINTHEWILD.CO.ZA/INDEX.PHP/2010/09/14/ONE-WIDE-INDEX-OR-MULTIPLE-NARROW-INDEXES/), proving in her example that the single, multi-column index is the best approach.

Identifying Missing Indexes

SQL Server 2005 and later offers a number of features that can help identify indexes that may be beneficial to the performance of a specific workload or query.

- **Database Engine Tuning Advisor** – a vastly-improved and expanded version of the old Index Tuning Wizard, the DTA analyses the execution plans generated for a supplied workload, along with the physical characteristics of the database, and recommends a set of indexes.

- **Missing Index feature** – during query optimization, the Query Optimizer identifies indexes that it thinks would have been beneficial to the performance of the specific query being optimized. This information is stored in two places:

  - **the Missing Index Dynamic Management Views** – a group of four DMVs, identified by `sys.dm_db_missing_index_*`, where* is `details`, `columns`, `group_stats` or `groups`

  - **XML showplans** – missing index information can also be extracted from the **MissingIndexGroup** element of these showplans.

It is important to keep in mind that, while these features can be very useful in determining the indexes that may be beneficial to your databases, they can also be a double-edged sword and do more harm than good when used incorrectly. Blindly implementing the recommendations of any of these features will almost always result in duplicate or overlapping indexes in the database, as well as too many, rather than too few, indexes.

Workload analysis with the Database Engine Tuning Advisor

One of the easiest ways to identify the missing indexes for a SQL database, if you don't understand the concepts behind index selection well enough to create indexes manually, is to make use of the Database Engine Tuning Advisor (DTA).

The DTA can be used to analyze a single query or an entire database workload, in the form of a trace file generated by SQL Server Profiler. Of course, this means that the quality of the DTA's index analysis will only be as high as the quality of the workload that is provided to the tool for analysis. If the workload is non-representative of the typical workload for that database, and is missing significant queries, then the index suggestions will likewise be incomplete, inaccurate, or just plain wrong.

Collecting a workload trace

To get the best results and recommendations from the DTA, the workload trace must contain a significant portion of the standard workload for the database being analyzed. As part of its analysis, the DTA estimates the impact of any suggested index changes on the performance of the workload as a whole. This helps it avoid recommending an index that boosts performance for a certain individual query but has an overall negative impact on the workload. As such, if you provide a single query to the DTA for analysis, the recommendations provided by the DTA can be very different from what would be recommended if the same query was analyzed as a part of a complete workload for the database.

SQL Server Profiler supplies a built-in SQL Trace template, the Tuning template, which is designed to capture the necessary events for a workload for analysis by the DTA. To use this template, open SQL Server Profiler and connect to the SQL Server instance. In the **Trace Properties** window (Figure 5.1) select the **Tuning** template in the **Use the template** dropdown.

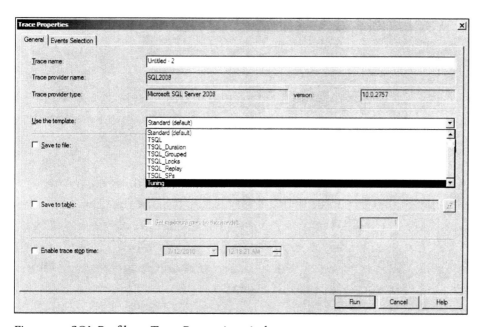

Figure 5.1: SQL Profiler – Trace Properties window.

It is possible to run the tuning trace directly from SQL Profiler and have it save the captured events to a file, or trace table, However, collecting client-side Profiler traces can cause performance deterioration of the server under analysis, due to the additional cost of buffering the events to memory and the network traffic required to send the events to SQL Server Profiler using the rowset provider.

Impact of the rowset provider on Profiler performance

*For further information and analysis of this topic, see SQL Server MVP Grant Fritchey's blog post, "Profiler Research" at (*HTTP://WWW.SCARYDBA.COM/2008/12/18/PROFILER-RESEARCH/*).*

A much better way to capture a workload trace file for analysis by the Database Tuning Advisor is to script the trace definition on the client machine, using Profiler, but then run the trace server-side. To script the trace definition, manually start the tuning trace within Profiler, but then immediately stop it. Next, from the **Export** option in the **File** Menu, select **Script Trace Definition | For SQL Server 2005 – 2008** (Figure 5.2).

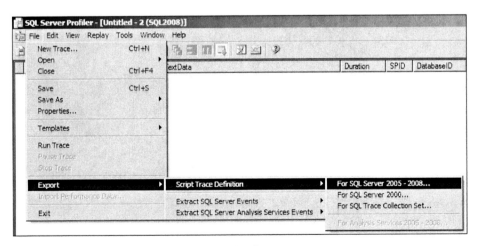

Figure 5.2: SQL Profiler – Script Trace Definition.

This saves a trace definition (`.sql`) file containing all the code necessary to create and start a server-side trace. This generated trace file can be edited as necessary, then run manually, or scheduled as needed. Open the file in SSMS to edit it. Firstly, replace the `@FileName` variable with the path and file name to be created on the server, and then execute the script to start the trace (in Listing 5.8, add the path and file name where the script says `'InsertFileNameHere'`). Only the file name is necessary, as the `.trc` extension will be added automatically.

Once the file has been saved, open the file in SQL Server Management Studio and edit it. Next, change the `@maxfilesize` variable to a size that makes sense, based on the level of activity of the database being traced. Additional options exist for the trace definition, which are not included as a part of the scripted definition provided by SQL Profiler. The `@stoptime` parameter of `sp_trace_create` can be used to specify an automatic stop time for the trace collection. The `@filecount` parameter can be used to specify the number of rollover files to maintain for the trace if the `@options` parameter has been configured to allow rollover to occur.

When these additional options are specified, they must be specified in the exact order that is listed in the Books Online topic for `sp_trace_create` (HTTP://MSDN.MICROSOFT.COM/EN-US/LIBRARY/MS190362.ASPX).

The finished script, shown in Listing 5.8, will output the `traceid` of the trace being created, allowing it to be stopped and deleted using `sp_trace_setstatus` once the collection period has completed.

```
DECLARE @rc INT
DECLARE @TraceID INT
DECLARE @maxfilesize BIGINT
SET @maxfilesize = 50
EXEC @rc = sp_trace_create @TraceID OUTPUT, 0, N'InsertFileNameHere',
    @maxfilesize, NULL
IF ( @rc != 0 )
    GOTO error
-- Client side File and Table cannot be scripted
-- Set the events
```

```
DECLARE @on BIT
SET @on = 1
EXEC sp_trace_setevent @TraceID, 137, 15, @on
EXEC sp_trace_setevent @TraceID, 137, 1, @on
EXEC sp_trace_setevent @TraceID, 137, 13, @on

-- Set the Filters
DECLARE @intfilter INT
DECLARE @bigintfilter BIGINT
-- Set the trace status to start
EXEC sp_trace_setstatus @TraceID, 1
-- display trace id for future references
SELECT  TraceID = @TraceID
GOTO finish
error:
SELECT  ErrorCode = @rc
finish:
go
```

Listing 5.8:   The complete, edited server-side tuning trace.

Analyzing a trace workload

The DTA can be opened from the **Tools** menu in SQL Server Management Studio; a new tuning session is started automatically and the captured workload file can be uploaded. The tuning session configuration screen has two tabs: **General** and **Tuning Options**. The **General** tab (Figure 5.3) contains the name of the session that is running the DTA, the type of workload to be consumed, the source location for the workload, a dropdown for selecting the database to be analyzed, and a grid view to allow the selection of specific databases and tables to tune based on the workload.

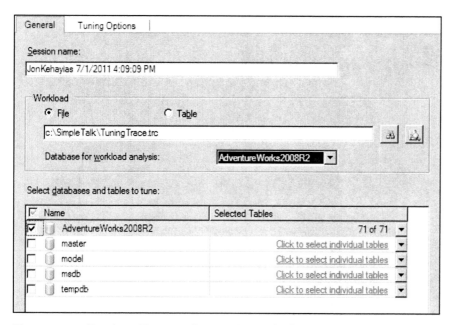

Figure 5.3:   Database Tuning Advisor – General tab.

The **Tuning Options** tab (Figure 5.4) contains the options that will be used during the tuning analysis of the workload. Depending on the size of the workload trace file, the tuning analysis may run for a long time. The **Limit tuning time** check box allows specification of a stop time for the analysis.

In the following sections, you can specify the Physical Design Structures to be used by the DTA when making recommendations (in this case indexes), whether or not partitioning should be used, and which existing Physical Design Structures to keep in the database.

The **Advanced Options** button allows you to define the maximum disk space, in megabytes, that can be used to store the various recommendations, as well as whether or not the indexing recommendations are made for online or offline operations.

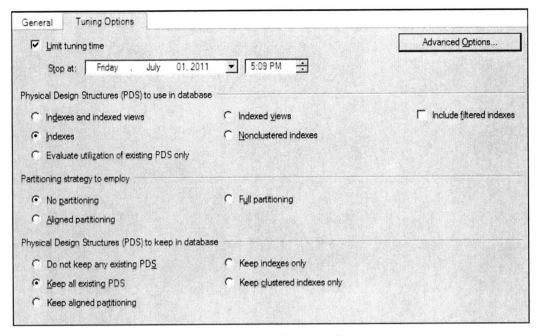

Figure 5.4: Database Tuning Advisor – Tuning Options tab.

Once the appropriate options have been set, you can start the index analysis by clicking **Start Analysis** in the DTA menu bar, and the DTA will begin analyzing the workload. During this analysis, it will create and drop hypothetical indexes and statistics and perform what-if analysis of the impact of each. The DTA tuning log will track the progress of the tuning session, if the option was left checked on the **General** tab of the DTA, and will output messages as the session progresses.

Reviewing index recommendations

When the tuning session completes, the DTA's recommendations regarding indexes and associated statistics will populate the **Recommendations** tab (Figure 5.5). These recommendations can be saved to a file for manual application at a later point in time or applied immediately to the database by selecting the appropriate option in the **Actions** menu. Additionally, the DTA provides the ability to perform another what-if analysis of a subset of the recommendations, allowing you to determine the impact to the estimated improvement caused by removing (unchecking) some of the recommendations from the analysis set. It is strongly recommended that any index recommendations made by the DTA be tested in an isolated test environment before implementing them in production. You can do this either manually, or by using the **Actions | Evaluate Recommendations** option of the DTA to apply the changes, and then evaluating their true impact by rerunning the tuning analysis of the workload.

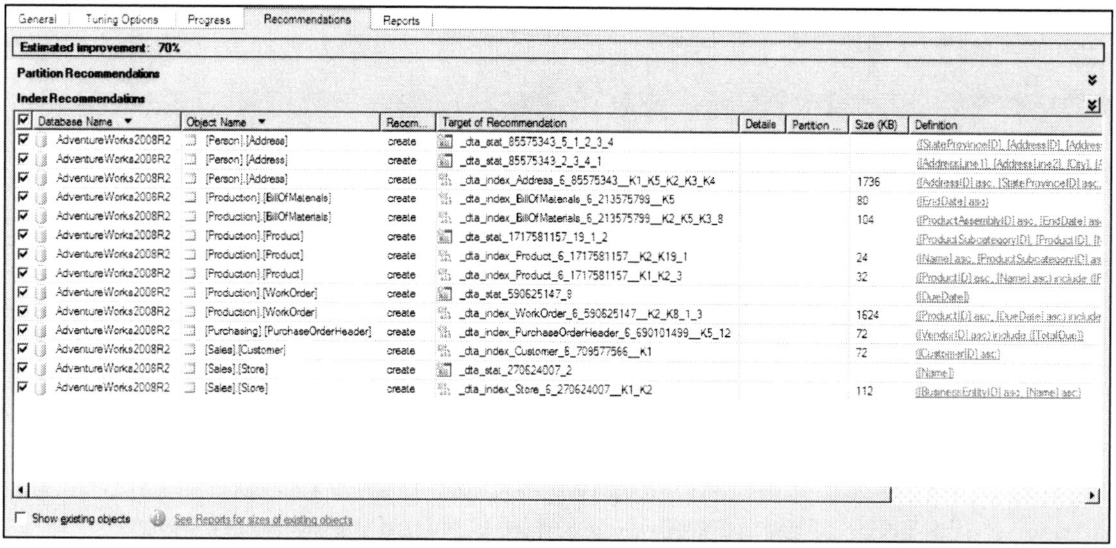

Figure 5.5:   Database Tuning Advisor – Recommendations tab.

Missing index feature

In SQL Server 2005 and later, the database engine tracks information about indexes that do not exist but that the optimizer could have used during query plan optimization to improve the performance of a particular SQL statement.

This information is stored in the missing index DMVs, and in the `MissingIndexGroup` element of the XML showplan for a query, and can, in theory, be used to identify and create beneficial indexes.

It is undoubtedly a useful feature, but I will state up front that if you blindly create all the indexes recommended by this missing index feature, you will likely do more harm than good to your database performance. The biggest problem is that, unlike those arising from the DTA, these missing index recommendations are not workload based; they are derived from the execution of individual queries and take no account of other index recommendations arising from the execution of other queries. As such, it is very common for the missing index feature to recommend overlapping and even duplicate indexes.

However, when used with due care, the missing index feature *can* help you to discover the few indexes that really could make a big difference to the overall performance of your workload, or those indexes that, with a small tweak to their definition, would cover many more queries.

Missing index DMVs

The fastest way to retrieve the information related to missing indexes, as identified by the query optimizer, is to query the missing index DMVs. There are four DMVs associated with the missing index feature in SQL Server:

- **`sys.dm_db_missing_index_details`** – stores detailed information regarding indexes the optimizer would have used had they been available, such as columns that could have been used to resolve equality or inequality predicates, and suggested `INCLUDE` columns for covering a query.

- **`sys.dm_db_missing_index_columns`** – accepts an `index_handle` and returns a list of columns that would comprise the suggested index.

- **`sys.dm_db_missing_index_group_stats`** – returns summary information regarding the potential benefit of a "missing" index, based, for example, on the number of seeks and scans that would have benefited.

- **`sys.dm_db_missing_index_groups`** – a join view between `_group_stats` and `_index_details`.

These views, when joined together, can identify missing indexes and provide the cost reduction, estimated by the optimizer, if the index was created. The `sys.dm_db_missing_index_group_stats` and `sys.dm_db_missing_index_groups` views, despite their names, do not actually contain groups of indexes; the groups (as of SQL Server 2008 R2) relate to only one missing index tracked in the system.

The information stored in these DMVs is certainly useful, but there are a number of limitations that you need to consider when basing your index choices on this data, including the following:

- the information contained in these DMVs is in volatile storage; meaning that it only exists in memory and doesn't exist beyond SQL service restarts, or changes to a database state like restoring the database, detaching the database, taking the database offline, or the database being closed by the `AutoClose` option

- statistics are only stored for a maximum of 500 missing index groups

- index key columns, specified by the equality and inequality column outputs of the `sys.dm_db_missing_index_details` and `sys.dm_db_missing_index_columns` DMVs, are not ordered according to cardinality.

As previously discussed in this chapter, it is often (though not always) best to order the index key columns such that the most selective column is the first column in the index. This reduces the number of database pages that must be read by the database engine while traversing the index, in order to satisfy the query.

However, unlike the DTA recommendations, the missing index recommendations stored in the DMVs do not consider key column cardinality; in other words, they are not based on the data contained in the key columns that it is recommending be created. As such, it is necessary to perform additional manual analysis of the key column cardinality in order to arrive at the optimal index structure.

These limitations mean that this tool is best used to identify gaping holes in an indexing strategy, rather than as a fine-tuning tool. The recommended approach is to identify potentially useful indexes, listing first those that offer the biggest potential performance benefit according to the metrics stored in the `sys.dm_missing_index_group_stats` DMV.

For example, in the `sys.dm_missing_index_group_stats` DMV, the `user_seeks` and `user_scans` columns provide the number of seek and scan operations that would have benefited from a particular index recommendation. The `avg_total_user_cost` column provides the average reduction in query cost as a result of creating the index, and the `avg_user_impact column` provides the percent reduction in query cost, had the index existed.

Together, these columns can be used to generate an overall estimated performance improvement associated with a specific missing index in the database. There are several ways to calculate this estimated performance improvement, but the generally accepted formula, shown in Listing 5.9, was provided by kind permission of Bart Duncan, one of the members of the SQL Server product team at Microsoft, from his MSDN blog post, *Are you using SQL's Missing Index DMVs?* (HTTP://BLOGS.MSDN.COM/B/BARTD/ ARCHIVE/2007/07/19/ARE-YOU-USING-SQL-S-MISSING-INDEX-DMVS.ASPX).

```
SELECT   migs.avg_total_user_cost * ( migs.avg_user_impact / 100.0 )
       * ( migs.user_seeks + migs.user_scans ) AS improvement_measure ,
       'CREATE INDEX [missing_index_'
       + CONVERT (VARCHAR, mig.index_group_handle) + '_'
       + CONVERT (VARCHAR, mid.index_handle) + '_'
       + LEFT(PARSENAME(mid.statement, 1), 32) + ']' + ' ON '
                                            + mid.statement
```

```
              + ' (' + ISNULL(mid.equality_columns, '')
              + CASE WHEN mid.equality_columns IS NOT NULL
                       AND mid.inequality_columns IS NOT NULL THEN ','
                     ELSE ''
                END + ISNULL(mid.inequality_columns, '') + ')'
                                           + ISNULL(' INCLUDE ('
                                              + mid.included_columns
                                              + ')', '')
                                          AS create_index_statement ,
              migs.* ,
              mid.database_id ,
              mid.[object_id]
FROM          sys.dm_db_missing_index_groups mig
              INNER JOIN sys.dm_db_missing_index_group_stats migs
                    ON migs.group_handle = mig.index_group_handle
              INNER JOIN sys.dm_db_missing_index_details mid
                    ON mig.index_handle = mid.index_handle
WHERE         migs.avg_total_user_cost * ( migs.avg_user_impact / 100.0 )
              * ( migs.user_seeks + migs.user_scans ) > 10
ORDER BY      migs.avg_total_user_cost * migs.avg_user_impact
                * ( migs.user_seeks + migs.user_scans ) DESC
```

Listing 5.9: Identifying missing indexes based on query cost benefit.

The calculated `improvement_measure` column provides the estimated improvement value of each index recommendation, based on the average total reduction in query cost that would result, the number of seek and scan operations that could be satisfied by the index, and the percentage benefit the index would provide to the queries being executed. This column makes it easier to focus on those indexers that offer the biggest cost benefit.

When analyzing the output of this query, I focus on the indexes with an impact value higher than 50,000. I then analyze the recommendations carefully, since it's likely that there will be a degree of overlap among the recommended indexes, with several indexes differing only subtly in terms of their index key column definitions and column orders, or included column definitions and orders. It's also likely that I can derive similar performance benefit by modifying an existing index rather than creating a new one. As discussed previously in the *Index Selection and Design* section, every index should be tested, to ensure that it really is useful, before deploying it to production. The goal is to create as few indexes as possible that will satisfy as many as possible of the most significant queries that comprise the SQL Server workload.

Missing index information in XML showplans

When the query optimizer identifies a missing index during query plan generation, it also stores this information within the ShowPlan XML data. This means that we can retrieve this information for any execution plan in the plan cache, with the added bonus that we can tie individual missing index recommendations directly to the statements and execution plans that generated them. If the query that instigated the index recommendation is one that occurs frequently in our normal workload, then it is much more likely to offer a real performance benefit than a recommendation arising from a "one-off" query.

The only downside is that there is often a substantial CPU cost associated with queries that search the plan cache for the entries that contain missing index information, and then shred the ShowPlan XML data to retrieve the actual missing index information.

The ShowPlan XML in SQL Server is a schema-bound XML document, based on Microsoft's published schema (HTTP://SCHEMAS.MICROSOFT.COM/SQLSERVER/2004/07/ SHOWPLAN). A review of the ShowPlan XML schema reveals that the missing index information is captured in the XML document as a complex type, under the `<MissingIndexGroup/>` element. A deeper analysis shows that this complex type can only occur under the `<QueryPlan/>` element with a distinct and predictable relative path. Using this predictable relative path, the individual missing index recommendations can be parsed out of the plan cache and then sub-parsed using XQuery inside of SQL Server, as demonstrated in Listing 5.10.

```
;
WITH XMLNAMESPACES
    (DEFAULT 'http://schemas.microsoft.com/sqlserver/2004/07/showplan')
SELECT MissingIndexNode.value('(MissingIndexGroup/@Impact)[1]', 'float')
                                                    AS impact ,
        OBJECT_NAME(sub.objectid, sub.dbid) AS calling_object_name ,
```

```
        MissingIndexNode.value
            ('(MissingIndexGroup/MissingIndex/@Database)[1]',
             'VARCHAR(128)') + '.'
    + MissingIndexNode.value
            ('(MissingIndexGroup/MissingIndex/@Schema)[1]',
             'VARCHAR(128)') + '.'
    + MissingIndexNode.value
            ('(MissingIndexGroup/MissingIndex/@Table)[1]',
             'VARCHAR(128)') AS table_name ,
    STUFF(( SELECT   ',' + c.value('(@Name)[1]', 'VARCHAR(128)')
            FROM     MissingIndexNode.nodes
                        ('MissingIndexGroup/MissingIndex/
                          ColumnGroup[@Usage="EQUALITY"]/Column')
                     AS t ( c )
            FOR
              XML PATH('')
            ), 1, 1, '') AS equality_columns ,
    STUFF(( SELECT   ',' + c.value('(@Name)[1]', 'VARCHAR(128)')
            FROM     MissingIndexNode.nodes
                        ('MissingIndexGroup/MissingIndex/
                          ColumnGroup[@Usage="INEQUALITY"]/Column')
                     AS t ( c )
            FOR
              XML PATH('')
            ), 1, 1, '') AS inequality_columns ,
    STUFF(( SELECT   ',' + c.value('(@Name)[1]', 'VARCHAR(128)')
            FROM     MissingIndexNode.nodes
                        ('MissingIndexGroup/MissingIndex/
                          ColumnGroup[@Usage="INCLUDE"]/Column')
                     AS t ( c )
            FOR
              XML PATH('')
            ), 1, 1, '') AS include_columns ,
    sub.usecounts AS qp_usecounts ,
    sub.refcounts AS qp_refcounts ,
    qs.execution_count AS qs_execution_count ,
    qs.last_execution_time AS qs_last_exec_time ,
    qs.total_logical_reads AS qs_total_logical_reads ,
    qs.total_elapsed_time AS qs_total_elapsed_time ,
    qs.total_physical_reads AS qs_total_physical_reads ,
    qs.total_worker_time AS qs_total_worker_time ,
    StmtPlanStub.value('(StmtSimple/@StatementText)[1]', 'varchar(8000)') AS
statement_text
  FROM    ( SELECT    ROW_NUMBER() OVER
```

```
                              ( PARTITION BY qs.plan_handle
                                ORDER BY qs.statement_start_offset )
                                AS StatementID ,
                 qs.*
      FROM        sys.dm_exec_query_stats qs
    ) AS qs
    JOIN ( SELECT     x.query('../../..') AS StmtPlanStub ,
                      x.query('.') AS MissingIndexNode ,
                      x.value('(../../../@StatementId)[1]', 'int')
                                                 AS StatementID ,
                 cp.* ,
                 qp.*
         FROM        sys.dm_exec_cached_plans AS cp
                     CROSS APPLY sys.dm_exec_query_plan
                                          (cp.plan_handle) qp
                     CROSS APPLY qp.query_plan.nodes
                            ('/ShowPlanXML/BatchSequence/
                               Batch/Statements/StmtSimple/
                               QueryPlan/MissingIndexes/
                               MissingIndexGroup') mi ( x )
       ) AS sub ON qs.plan_handle = sub.plan_handle
                 AND qs.StatementID = sub.StatementID
```

Listing 5.10: Parsing missing index information out of XML showplans.

This code example will return a similar output to the raw information provided by the missing index DMVs, with the exception that this output will also include the statement text from the plan cache and the associated execution statistics, which are tracked by the `sys.dm_exec_query_stats` DMV.

This level of detail allows for a more focused implementation of the missing index details than is easily available through the missing index DMVs, based on knowledge of the actual SQL statement that was executed in order to generate the index recommendation, as well as information about the query execution stats and impact on the system.

As discussed earlier, this analysis is not free; shredding the XML from the plan cache can be an expensive operation, especially on servers with large amounts of memory installed, and can significantly increase CPU usage.

To minimize the impact on a production server, the execution plans containing the missing index XML nodes can be written to a table, which can then be transferred to a development or test server to perform the XML shredding operation.

Missing indexes on foreign keys

A very common source of performance issues in a SQL Server database is a lack of indexes on FOREIGN KEY columns, which are commonly used to join two tables together. Generally speaking, FOREIGN KEY columns represent parent/child relationships between two tables as one-to-many relationships.

A good rule of thumb is for any FOREIGN KEY columns that are commonly used in JOIN operations to have an associated index, either with the FOREIGN KEY column as the leading column in the index, or as a column further down the index key, depending on the queries.

The code in Listing 5.11 can be used to identify non-indexed FOREIGN KEY columns in a database. The query will match the FOREIGN KEY column to any index with the same column on the same table and returns columns with no matches at all. For a database that is using single-column PRIMARY KEYs, this code can be very effective at identifying any FOREIGN KEY that is potentially problematic for performance, due to the lack of a supporting index on the JOIN. However, for a database with any composite multi-column PRIMARY KEYs, the script will be only partially helpful since it doesn't check the existence of all of the columns within the same index. For more complex key sets, this code can be modified to return information about all of the FOREIGN KEY columns in the database to allow manual validation of the indexing of these keys.

```
SELECT    fk.name AS CONSTRAINT_NAME ,
          s.name AS SCHEMA_NAME ,
          o.name AS TABLE_NAME ,
          fkc_c.name AS CONSTRAINT_COLUMN_NAME
FROM      sys.foreign_keys AS fk
```

```
        JOIN sys.foreign_key_columns AS fkc
            ON fk.object_id = fkc.constraint_object_id
        JOIN sys.columns AS fkc_c
            ON fkc.parent_object_id = fkc_c.object_id
                        AND fkc.parent_column_id = fkc_c.column_id
        LEFT JOIN sys.index_columns ic
        JOIN sys.columns AS c ON ic.object_id = c.object_id
                        AND ic.column_id = c.column_id
                        ON fkc.parent_object_id = ic.object_id
                        AND fkc.parent_column_id = ic.column_id
        JOIN sys.objects AS o ON o.object_id = fk.parent_object_id
        JOIN sys.schemas AS s ON o.schema_id = s.schema_id
WHERE    c.name IS NULL
```

Listing 5.11:   Identifying single-column, non-indexed FOREIGN KEYs.

Identifying Unused Indexes

One of the side effects of adding and modifying indexes in a user database is the possibility that existing indexes stop being used by SQL Server. These unneeded database artifacts offer no benefit in terms of query performance but continue to consume additional I/O operations during data manipulation operations, since any change to the underlying data must also be made to the corresponding data stored in the index. The `sys.dm_db_index_usage_stats` DMV in SQL Server 2005 and 2008 provides a mechanism to determine *how* individual indexes in a specific database have been used.

This DMV provides information about the number of `user_seeks`, `user_scans`, `user_lookups`, and `user_updates` that have been performed against each of the indexes inside a specific database. However, the information contained in the DMV is not persisted and the DMV data is lost whenever the instance is restarted, or the database state changes, for example, being taken offline, restored, detached, or closed. For this reason, the index usage statistics should only be evaluated when the database has been online and under a standard workload that would make use of the indexes that are being evaluated.

What we are looking for, with the query shown in Listing 5.12, is any non-clustered index that has never been used for a seek, scan, or lookup operation by SQL Server, but is associated with a significant number of update operations. These indexes can be considered to be unused and should be dropped from the database.

```sql
SELECT   OBJECT_SCHEMA_NAME(i.object_id) AS SchemaName ,
         OBJECT_NAME(i.object_id) AS TableName ,
         i.name ,
         ius.user_seeks ,
         ius.user_scans ,
         ius.user_lookups ,
         ius.user_updates
FROM     sys.dm_db_index_usage_stats AS ius
         JOIN sys.indexes AS i ON i.index_id = ius.index_id
                             AND i.object_id = ius.object_id
WHERE    ius.database_id = DB_ID()
         AND i.is_unique_constraint = 0 -- no unique indexes
         AND i.is_primary_key = 0
         AND i.is_disabled = 0
         AND i.type > 1 -- don't consider heaps/clustered index
         AND ( ( ius.user_seeks + ius.user_scans +
                   ius.user_lookups ) < ius.user_updates
              OR ( ius.user_seeks = 0
                   AND ius.user_scans = 0
                 )
             )
```

Listing 5.12: Finding unused non-clustered indexes.

Note again that this code should only be used when the database has been online for a significant period of time, in order to ensure that the appropriate workload has been executed. Certain indexes may be used infrequently but when they are required, such as when the weekly, monthly, or even quarterly reporting operations are run, they are vital!

Identifying Duplicate Indexes

Duplicate indexes in a database incur maintenance costs that waste valuable resources on a server. The process of identifying true duplicate indexes in SQL Server is nontrivial at best and incredibly complex when you begin to account for various cases where seemingly duplicate indexes actually aren't duplicate, due to the width and selectivity of the indexes.

Duplicate indexes are primarily a concern for OLTP systems where the performance of INSERT operations is paramount, whereas for data warehouse systems the performance of SELECT operations is critical, data loading occurs less frequently, and so one can have a higher level of tolerance to duplicate indexes.

Many online articles state, incorrectly, that the key columns are the primary point of analysis when identifying duplicate indexes in a database. The truth is that two indexes can have similar key columns, but different width, selectivity, and purpose in a database, and so not be duplicate indexes. To fully identify an index as a duplicate, the leaf level of the index must be investigated to identify which columns are maintained at the leaf level, which also maintains the included columns in the index. Key column order at the leaf level matters, but included column order for the index does not.

Complications of identifying duplicate indexes in SQL Server

In her following two blog posts, Kimberly Tripp offers further insight into the complications of identifying duplicate indexes, and provides a stored procedure for identifying and removing them: "How can you tell if an index is REALLY a duplicate?" (HTTP://SQLSKILLS.COM/BLOGS/KIMBERLY/POST/UNDERSTANDINGDUPLICATEINDEXES.ASPX) *and "Removing duplicate indexes"* (HTTP://SQLSKILLS.COM/BLOGS/KIMBERLY/POST/REMOVINGDUPLICATEINDEXES.ASPX).

Summary

Missing indexes in a SQL Server database can lead to many performance-related problems, including higher than necessary disk I/O operations, excessive CPU usage, caused by unnecessary sort operations, and reduced performance.

Periodic analysis of missing index information, using the available features in SQL Server, will help ensure that the current indexing strategy meets the requirements of the database and the workload being executed. However, due care must be taken when implementing the indexing recommendations made by these features, to ensure that the number of overlapping and duplicated indexes are minimized and that each index created really will have a positive performance benefit. In this way, we can maximize query performance while minimizing the performance impact on data modifications that can arise from over-indexing the tables in a user database.

Chapter 6: Blocking

In a typical, busy database, many user transactions will be competing for simultaneous access to various shared database resources (tables, indexes, and so on). By default, SQL Server mediates access to these resources using various types of locks. These locks prevent competing transactions from "destructively interfering" with each other, and so ensure that each transaction can read and modify data in a consistent fashion.

This locking and blocking activity is a normal part the everyday operation of a database. However, in conditions of highly concurrent user access, the number of locks being taken will increase, and so will the potential for blocking. As the length of time for which processes are blocked increases, so the overall performance of the database declines, and users start to complain.

In systems with many concurrent transactions, some degree of blocking is probably unavoidable, but the situation can be greatly exacerbated by queries that are longer or more complex than they need to be, or read more data than they need to; or by poorly designed databases that lack proper keys and indexing, or by transactions that need to use more restrictive transaction isolation levels (such as `REPEATABLE READ` or `SERIALIZABLE`). All of these factors can increase the number and durations of locks being held, and so will increase the incidence of blocking.

This chapter will describe how to look into SQL Server to verify if a problem is due to blocking, what process is being blocked, and what process is doing the blocking, and then how to resolve some common causes of blocking.

Locks and Concurrency (a Brief Review)

By default, SQL Server uses pessimistic locking to enforce transactional concurrency, whereby all operations in the database acquire locks. For example, when an operation reads data, SQL Server acquires **shared** locks (S) on the rows or pages being accessed by the `SELECT` statement. When an operation changes data, i.e. an `INSERT`, `UPDATE`, or `DELETE`, then an **exclusive** (X) lock is acquired on the row or page in the clustered index or table. An S lock will **block** another transaction from modifying the data while the `SELECT` is running, but does not prevent other transactions reading the data. If a transaction holds an X lock on a resource, any other transaction that wishes to read or write the same data will be **blocked**, until the X lock is released. This ensures that a transaction doesn't read data that is in flux (i.e. "dirty reads" are prevented), and that two transactions can't change the same row of data, or attempt to insert two rows of data into the same location on a page.

A number of factors affect the type and mode of lock used by SQL Server during conditions of competing access for a given resource, and exactly when these locks are taken and released. In this section, we'll just briefly review some of the core concepts behind SQL Server locking and concurrency.

Lock modes

SQL Server employs a number of different **lock modes**, in order to control how concurrent transactions can access a shared resource. Some of the more commonly seen locks are **shared**, **update**, **exclusive** and the associated **intent** locks.

Note that several other modes exist, a full discussion of which is out of scope for this chapter. A complete list and descriptions can be found on MSDN (HTTP://MSDN. MICROSOFT.COM/EN-US/LIBRARY/MS175519.ASPX and HTTP://MSDN.MICROSOFT.COM/EN-US/LIBRARY/MS186396.ASPX).

Shared

A shared lock (shown as S) is a lock that is taken, by default, by queries that are reading from a table or index. Shared locks are compatible with other shared locks and update locks, but not with exclusive locks.

Update

An update lock (shown as U) is taken as part of an update operation. It is compatible with shared locks but not with other update locks or exclusive locks.

Exclusive

An exclusive lock (shown as X) is taken for any data modification (insert, update, delete). It is not compatible with any other lock.

For an update, SQL first takes an update lock and then converts it to an exclusive lock to perform the actual update (the reasons for this are explained in Books Online, HTTP://MSDN.MICROSOFT.COM/EN-US/LIBRARY/MS175519.ASPX, and won't be discussed further here).

Intent locks

Each lock mode has its associated Intent lock (shown as I). Hence you will see IS (Intent Shared) locks, IU (Intent Update) locks and IX (Intent Exclusive) locks.

An intent lock is used to reduce the work SQL must do to tell if a lock can be granted. If a row lock is needed by a query, SQL first takes the appropriate intent lock at the table level, then an appropriate intent lock at the page level and then it will take the necessary row lock.

IS locks are compatible with shared and update locks and all other intent locks. IU locks are compatible with shared locks and other intent locks. IX locks are only compatible with other intent locks.

Lock types

SQL Server can lock a number of different types of resource, the most obvious being **tables** (OBJECT **locks**), **pages** (PAGE **locks**), and **rows** (RID or KEY locks), in order of increasing granularity. Locks are granted and released on these objects as needed, in order to satisfy the requirements of the isolation levels in use by the various sessions. In the locking hierarchy, row and key locks are the lowest level, most granular, forms of lock. The more granular the lock, the higher the degree of concurrent access which can be supported. With that, however, comes a higher memory overhead, from having to manage a large number of individual locks.

SQL Server automatically chooses locks of the **highest possible granularity**, suitable for the given workload. However, if too many individual locks are being held on an index or heap, or if forced to do so due to memory pressure, SQL Server may use lock escalation to reduce the total number of locks being held. For example, a large number of individual row locks may be escalated to a single table lock, or a number of page locks may be escalated to a table lock (escalation is always to a table lock). While this will result in lower overhead on SQL Server, the cost will be lower concurrency. Later in the chapter, we'll show how to investigate lock escalation, and its impact on concurrency.

One other lock type that needs discussion here is the **database-level** lock. People are often concerned when they see a large number of database-level locks listed in the results returned by querying the lock-related DMVs (Dynamic Management Views). These will be described later, in the *Monitoring Blocking* section. In reality this is of no concern at all. Every session takes a shared database lock on the database to which it is connected. This is to ensure that the database cannot be restored, dropped, closed, or detached while there are still sessions using it. These will not cause blocking, except in the case of restoring, dropping, altering, detaching or closing an in-use database.

Lock escalation

Lock escalation is the process in which SQL Server escalates a low-level, granular lock to a higher-level lock. The locks can start as either row or page locks; it makes no difference to the process of lock escalation. If SQL decides to escalate the locks it will in all cases escalate straight to table locks (except when this behavior is explicitly altered using the LOCK_ESCALATION option, discussed shortly). Locks do not, under any circumstances, escalate from row to page and then to table.

In SQL Server, lock escalation is completely dynamic. The thresholds that SQL uses for lock escalation are detailed in Books Online (HTTP://MSDN.MICROSOFT.COM/EN-US/LIBRARY/MS184286.ASPX). For the purposes of this chapter it is enough to say that SQL will attempt to escalate locks when a certain number of locks have been obtained on the table/index, or when the total number of locks, or the amount of lock memory, exceeds configured limits.

In some cases, lock escalation can cause blocking because SQL has escalated locks, and so locked the entire table, with the result that concurrent access to that table is restricted. To identify lock escalations, SQL Trace or Profiler can be used with the Lock:Escalation event, in conjunction with the SP:Started or T-SQL:StmtStarted and SP:Completed or T-SQL:StmtCompleted events, to try to correlate the lock escalation with currently executing statements and procedures.

If this event is logged and there is measurable blocking around the time of the event being logged, then lock escalation may be causing problems, and the procedures that were running at the time of the event being logged may need to be optimized to reduce the amount or duration of the locking.

SQL Server 2008 introduced a new option for altering the way lock escalation occurs in SQL Server. The **ALTER TABLE** statement now has the **LOCK_ESCALATION** option. The options for this setting are **AUTO**, **TABLE** (default) and **DISABLE**. Prior to SQL 2008, lock escalation was only to the table level.

The **TABLE** setting is the default behavior; locks are escalated only to table level. The **DISABLE** setting completely disables lock escalation on this table. This can be useful in some circumstances but must be used with care. Altering lock escalation is discussed later, in the section entitled *Hints, Trace Flags and Other Last Resorts*.

The **AUTO** setting is the one of interest. If a table is partitioned, the **LOCK_ESCALATION** option is set to **AUTO**, and if SQL decides to escalate locks, any locks that are held on the table will escalate to the partition level, not the table level. This can be useful when dealing with a partitioned table where data modifications are confined to one partition but reads are done across many partitions. If the modifications caused an escalation to table level, the reads would be blocked, but if the modifications just escalate to partition level then the reads may not be affected at all. Some caution does need to be employed when considering this setting, as it can, in some cases, result in deadlocks. For an example of such a deadlock see HTTP://WWW.SQLSKILLS.COM/BLOGS/PAUL/POST/SQL-SERVER-2008-PARTITION-LEVEL-LOCK-ESCALATION-DETAILS-AND-EXAMPLES.ASPX.

Concurrency and the transaction isolation levels

The degree to which concurrent sessions can access the same resource simultaneously is dictated by the **transaction isolation levels** in force for the database sessions that are accessing the database.

In the ANSI standards, the isolation levels are defined by what data anomalies they allow, not the manner they are enforced. Each isolation level (from the least restrictive to the most restrictive) allows fewer data anomalies. **SERIALIZABLE** must allow no data anomalies; **REPEATABLE READ** is defined as an isolation level that only allows phantom rows; READ COMMITTED is identified as an isolation level that allows phantom rows and non-repeatable reads; READ UNCOMMITTED is identified as an isolation level that allows phantom rows, non-repeatable reads and dirty reads.

As the isolation level becomes more restrictive, so SQL Server will acquire different modes of lock and hold them for longer periods, in order to ensure the required level is enforced. We'll briefly cover the isolation levels here, and Craig Freedman's blog (HTTP:// BLOGS.MSDN.COM/B/CRAIGFR/ARCHIVE/TAGS/ISOLATION+LEVELS/) is a good source of further reading on this topic.

READ UNCOMMITTED

In this isolation level SQL Server takes no shared locks at all. Since it takes no locks, a session will not get blocked by exclusive locks. Update and exclusive locks are still taken when modifying data. Because no shared locks are taken, this isolation level allows dirty reads (reads of uncommitted data) as well as all of the data anomalies of the higher isolation levels.

READ COMMITED

This is the default mode of operation. SQL Server will prevent "dirty reads" (i.e. it will ensure that transactions can only return committed data). To do this, SQL Server will acquire short-lived S locks on each row that is read, releasing the lock as processing of the statement moves on to the next row, although it may hold these locks till the whole statement has finished processing, should that be necessary in order to guarantee consistent results. The shared locks are retained for, at most, the duration of the executing statement, even if the transaction of which the statement is a part is still active. So if the same statement is run again, as part of the same transaction, it could return different results. This is the data anomaly known as a "non-repeatable read."

REPEATABLE READ

Shared locks are held for longer; for the duration of whole transaction. So, if a statement runs again within the same transaction, you'll get the same result. Hence this isolation level no longer allows non-repeatable reads. It still allows for new rows to have been inserted in the meantime that match the query criteria. These new rows that appear within a result set are known as phantom rows.

SERIALIZABLE

Transaction A will never see any of the effects of Transaction B for the entire duration of Transaction A. In order to enforce this level, Transaction A will cause SQL Server to acquire **key-range locks** on rows that have been read, which prevents any other transaction from modifying them, or inserting new rows, until Transaction A completes. The SERIALIZABLE isolation level allows for no data anomalies at all, at the cost of severely restricting the degree to which the database can support concurrent access.

Optimistic concurrency using row versioning

In addition to the traditional isolation levels discussed in the previous section, SQL Server 2005 introduced two additional isolation levels that use optimistic rather than pessimistic concurrency. Both of these use row versioning rather than locks for concurrency enforcement.

There's far more to row versioning than can be covered here, so this is just a brief summary. For full details on how optimistic concurrency works see the article *SQL Server 2005 Row Versioning-Based Transaction Isolation* at HTTP://MSDN.MICROSOFT.COM/EN-US/ LIBRARY/MS345124(V=SQL.90).ASPX. Despite being written for SQL 2005, it is still valid for SQL 2008.

There are two optimistic concurrency isolation levels: READ_COMMITTED_SNAPSHOT and SNAPSHOT. They are often confused with each other, so I will try to touch on the significant differences here. Both of these isolation levels use row versions for read consistency, not locks. So read queries take no locks. Therefore, instead of blocking when they encounter a row that is subject to an exclusive lock, they will simply "read around" the lock, retrieving from the version store (in TempDB) the version of the row consistent with a certain point in time, either the time the statement started, or the time at which the parent transaction started.

READ_COMMITTED_SNAPSHOT is an optimistic concurrency version of the READ COMMITTED isolation level, so it allows the same data anomalies. However, as discussed earlier, if a statement running under the traditional READ COMMITTED isolation level encounters data that is being modified by another transaction, it must wait until those changes are either committed or rolled back before it can acquire a shared lock and proceed. In the READ_COMMITTED_SNAPSHOT isolation level, when a locked row is encountered, SQL Server fetches the version of the row from the version store, as it existed when the statement began. In other words, data returned will reflect only what was committed at the time the current *statement* began. This means that consistency is guaranteed within the statement, not within the transaction as a whole.

SNAPSHOT isolation is an optimistic concurrency version of the SERIALIZABLE isolation level. As such, it allows no data anomalies at all. In this isolation level, when a locked row is encountered, SQL fetches the latest row version as it existed when the transaction began. In other words, data returned will reflect only what was committed at the time the current *transaction* began.

The other difference between the two levels is in how they are enabled. If the database option READ_COMMITTED_SNAPSHOT is enabled, then the database's default isolation level becomes READ_COMMITTED_SNAPSHOT, and hints or explicit SET TRANSACTION ISOLATION LEVEL statements will be needed to get the READ COMMITTED isolation level (which will use locks). If the database option ALLOW_SNAPSHOT_ISOLATION is enabled, then all that happens is that sessions may request the SNAPSHOT isolation using a SET TRANSACTION ISOLATION LEVEL statement.

Maximizing concurrency

In a busy database, SQL Server must maintain a large number of different types of lock, in order to mediate access to shared resources and ensure consistent results, with minimal blocking. However, even a relatively small number of concurrent sessions can result in the acquisition of a surprisingly high number of locks, however fleetingly held. This is especially true when you consider that it's rarely as simple for SQL Server as acquiring "a single lock on a single target row of data." Consider, for example, that if a modification affects a column that is a part of a non-clustered index, either as a key column or an included column, then the non-clustered index must also be changed to reflect the data change, and this requires an additional exclusive lock on the rows or pages affected by the change.

In general, however, SQL Server will manage all of this seamlessly and will *automatically* choose the modes and types of locks appropriate for the isolation level in use, the type and number of operations being performed, and so on.

We can help it out by, for example, writing fast, efficient SQL, providing useful indexes, and using the least restrictive isolation level compatible with business requirements. This will allow SQL Server to acquire the minimum necessary number of locks, for the shortest duration, and so minimize blocking and maximize concurrent access. However, beyond this, it is only rarely advisable to directly influence the sort of locks that SQL Server acquires. On those rare occasions, SQL Server does provide a number of lock hints that can be used to dictate which locks SQL Server acquires for certain operations and even, for example, to "disallow" page and row locks on a given index. These options will be discussed later in the chapter, in the *Resolving Blocking* section.

Latches and latch contention

Latches can be thought of as light-weight, short-lived locks. Where locks are used to protect the logical and transactional consistency of rows, latches are typically used to protect the physical consistency of pages or memory structures. There are three types of latches that can be encountered in the SQL engine.

For further details see HTTP://BLOGS.MSDN.COM/B/PSSSQL/ARCHIVE/2009/07/08/Q-A-ON-LATCHES-IN-THE-SQL-SERVER-ENGINE.ASPX):

- **Latch** – used to protect various memory structures within SQL Server.
- **Page Latch** – used when SQL is modifying the structure of the page. So, when the page header gets modified, or a row is added to a page, SQL would take a Page Latch before starting and release it once complete.
- **Page I/O Latch** – used when pages are moving between disk and memory. So a Page I/O Latch would be taken before a page is fetched from disk, and released once the page is in the cache.

Latches (usually Page Latch or Page I/O Latch) can cause blocking in much the same way as locks. However, since latches are usually short-lived it is much rarer to encounter blocking due to latches than to locks.

The details around causes and resolutions to latch contention are outside the scope of this chapter, and some specific cases are mentioned elsewhere in the book. For further information, see HTTP://SQLCAT.COM/SQLCAT/B/WHITEPAPERS/ARCHIVE/2011/07/05/DIAGNOSING-AND-RESOLVING-LATCH-CONTENTION-ON-SQL-SERVER.ASPX.

Monitoring Blocking

In this section, we'll cover some of the important tools and techniques that can be used to diagnose, troubleshoot, and resolve blocking issues in a SQL Server database. We'll cover techniques that can be employed to resolve "live" instances of blocking, where important business processes are blocked from proceeding, normal business function is impeded, and end-users (and managers) are complaining. Usually, in such cases, the problem manifests itself as poor performance or timeouts inside the application.

When blocking is actively occurring at the time you are notified, there are several DMVs (or system views, back on SQL 2000) and system stored procedures that can be used to troubleshoot the problem. We'll also look at ways of getting cumulative or aggregated locking, and log wait statistics, to get an overall view of the severity of blocking within the instance.

Of course, our ultimate goal is to monitor possible blocking issues on an ongoing basis, and deal with them before they affect end-users. To that end, we'll move on to discuss ongoing monitoring, using DMVs as well as event notifications, and the `blocked_process_report` and `lock_escalation` events, to get automatic notification when a blocking event occurs.

Before we begin, it's worth briefly noting the way in which the various locks show up in the system views and DMVs, when they appear as wait types. The wait type for locks has the form `LCK_M_<lock type>`. So, a wait to acquire a shared lock appears as `LCK_M_S` (note there's no indication of the lock granularity, only the type requested), a wait for an exclusive lock will appear as `LCK_M_X`, and a wait for an intent shared lock will appear as `LCK_M_IS`. This format can be extrapolated to the other lock types.

```
EXEC sp_lock 52
```

Results | Messages

	spid	dbid	ObjId	IndId	Type	Resource	Mode	Status
25	52	5	318624178	6	KEY	(8a001cb8b537)	X	GRANT
26	52	5	318624178	3	KEY	(e1003ac0408a)	X	GRANT
27	52	5	1918629878	1	PAG	1:26261	IX	GRANT
28	52	5	1509580416	1	PAG	1:10054	IX	GRANT
29	52	5	318624178	6	KEY	(88009770bc9d)	X	GRANT
30	52	5	898102240	0	TAB		IX	GRANT
31	52	5	318624178	6	KEY	(890079df098f)	X	GRANT
32	52	5	1918629878	2	PAG	1:26505	IX	GRANT
33	52	5	1010102639	1	PAG	1:1961	IX	GRANT
34	52	5	318624178	2	PAG	1:35298	IX	GRANT
35	52	5	1918629878	2	PAG	1:26679	IX	GRANT
36	52	5	1918629878	2	KEY	(3802a93d5f0d)	X	GRANT
37	52	5	318624178	1	KEY	(350071742087)	X	GRANT
38	52	5	318624178	1	KEY	(3700fabc292d)	X	GRANT
39	52	5	1010102639	0	TAB		IX	GRANT
40	52	5	1010102639	2	KEY	(37022c28328f)	X	GRANT
41	52	5	1918629878	3	PAG	1:28102	IX	GRANT
42	52	5	898102240	1	KEY	(ac0028fc88c8)	X	GRANT
43	52	5	898102240	5	PAG	1:69558	IX	GRANT

Figure 6.3: Using the `sp_lock` stored procedure.

Prior to SQL Server 2000 SP4, a SPID would only be displayed in the **`blocked`** column in the **`sysprocesses`** view if that session was causing **lock** waits. Post-SP4, the SPID is shown for sessions causing both lock and **latch** waits; in other words, if SPID 53 were waiting to acquire a latch rather than a lock, it would not appear in the **`blocked`** column pre-SP4, but would appear post-SP4.

In most cases, this appears much the same way as with blocking, except that the **`waittype`** column shows a Latch, Page Latch or Page I/O Latch wait rather than a **`LCK`** wait. In some cases, specifically certain I/O-related latches, the value in the **`blocked`** column is the value for the blocked session's SPID instead of the blocking SPID, so it appears to be self-blocking.

For more resources on the changes to SQL Server 2000 blocking and the **sysprocesses** system view, refer to: *The blocked column in the sysprocesses table is populated for latch waits after you install SQL Server 2000 SP4* at HTTP://SUPPORT.MICROSOFT.COM/KB/906344.

Cumulative wait statistics with DBCC SQLPERF (waitstats)

In SQL Server 2000, the cumulative wait statistic information for the instance was only available through the `DBCC SQLPERF(waitstats)` command. It provides the total waiting tasks and total wait time since the instance was started or since the wait stats were cleared using the `DBCC SQLPERF(waitstats, clear)` command.

While this command cannot help diagnose individual blocking problems, it can be used to get an overall picture of the most common waits in the system. This can help in ensuring that it is the actual problem that gets investigated, rather than something that has been incorrectly assumed to be the problem. When blocking is prevalent in one of the databases running in an instance, one of the top wait types for the instance will be a `LCK_*` wait type, which is a wait while attempting to acquire a specific type of lock.

Dynamic Management Views

Although the **sysprocesses** system view, and the `DBCC SQLPERF(waitstats)` command, can still be used to find active blocking in SQL Server 2005 and 2008, Dynamic Management Views (DMVs) offer more in-depth information for troubleshooting the blocking problem.

In order to see this in action, we'll need to create a blocking event in the database. For the purposes of this demo, I'm using the **AdventureWorks** 2008 database (downloadable from HTTP://SQLSERVERSAMPLES.CODEPLEX.COM/).

```
DECLARE @SalesOrderHeaderID INT

BEGIN TRANSACTION

INSERT INTO Sales.SalesOrderHeader
    (RevisionNumber, OrderDate, DueDate, ShipDate, Status,
     OnlineOrderFlag, PurchaseOrderNumber, AccountNumber, CustomerID,
     SalesPersonID, TerritoryID, BillToAddressID, ShipToAddressID,
     ShipMethodID, CreditCardID, CreditCardApprovalCode,
     CurrencyRateID, Comment, rowguid, ModifiedDate)
VALUES
    (5, '2011/06/20', '2011/06/25', '2011/06/30', 5, 0, NULL,
     '10-4030-018749', 18749, NULL, 6, 28374, 28374, 1, 8925,
     '929849Vi46003', NULL, NULL, NEWID(), GETDATE()
    )

SET @SalesOrderHeaderID = @@IDENTITY

INSERT   INTO Sales.SalesOrderDetail
        ( SalesOrderID, CarrierTrackingNumber, OrderQty, ProductID,
          SpecialOfferID, UnitPrice, UnitPriceDiscount, rowguid,
          ModifiedDate )
VALUES  ( @SalesOrderHeaderID, '4911-403C-98', 15, 722, 1, 2039.994, 0,
          NEWID(), GETDATE() ),
        ( @SalesOrderHeaderID, '4911-403C-98', 4, 709, 1, 5.70, 0,
          NEWID(), GETDATE() ),
        ( @SalesOrderHeaderID, '4911-403C-98', 24, 716, 1, 28.8404, 0,
          NEWID(), GETDATE() )
```

Listing 6.2: An uncommitted INSERT transaction in AdventureWorks 2008.

Note that I've left the transaction uncommitted. Hence, the exclusive locks taken on the two tables are still being held. For the sake of a realistic example, we can say that either there's a long-running SELECT after that, or something else that will run for a while, or maybe an error caused the batch to abort leaving the transaction open.

Now, open a new SSMS window and connect to the AdventureWorks 2008 database and run a simple report against one of those tables that was involved in the INSERT transaction.

```
SELECT   FirstName ,
         LastName ,
         SUM(soh.TotalDue) AS TotalDue ,
         MAX(OrderDate) AS LastOrder
FROM     Sales.SalesOrderHeader AS soh
         INNER JOIN Sales.Customer AS c ON soh.CustomerID = c.CustomerID
         INNER JOIN Person.Person AS p ON c.PersonID = p.BusinessEntityID
WHERE    soh.OrderDate >= '2011/01/01'
GROUP BY c.CustomerID ,
         FirstName ,
         LastName
```

Listing 6.3: A query against the `SalesOrderHeader` table.

Right away, we will see that the **SELECT** statement will "hang" whereas, in the absence of blocking, it would complete in milliseconds. Now let's look at the DMVs to see how we would detect that if it were a real system with a real blocking problem.

Using the sys.dm_exec_requests and sys.dm_exec_ sessions DMVs

One of the first places to look is the DMV that shows currently executing tasks. This is the replacement for **sysprocesses** in SQL Server 2005 and above, and shows much the same information that **sysprocesses** did (and a fair bit more).

The script in Listing 6.4 will show a list of all blocked sessions as well as the sessions that are blocking them. This can be very useful when there is a long blocking chain.

```
SELECT   er.session_id ,
         host_name , program_name , original_login_name , er.reads ,
         er.writes ,er.cpu_time , wait_type , wait_time , wait_resource ,
         blocking_session_id , st.text
FROM     sys.dm_exec_sessions es
         LEFT JOIN sys.dm_exec_requests er
                   ON er.session_id = es.session_id
         OUTER APPLY sys.dm_exec_sql_text(er.sql_handle) st
WHERE    blocking_session_id > 0
```

```
UNION
SELECT    es.session_id , host_name , program_name , original_login_name ,
          es.reads , es.writes , es.cpu_time , wait_type , wait_time ,
          wait_resource , blocking_session_id , st.text
FROM      sys.dm_exec_sessions es
          LEFT JOIN sys.dm_exec_requests er
                      ON er.session_id = es.session_id
          OUTER APPLY sys.dm_exec_sql_text(er.sql_handle) st
WHERE     es.session_id IN ( SELECT    blocking_session_id
                             FROM      sys.dm_exec_requests
                             WHERE     blocking_session_id > 0 )
```

Listing 6.4:   Find blocking with **sys.dm_exec_requests** and **sys.dm_exec_sessions**.

The output of this query, for the simulated blocking that we set up earlier, is shown in Figure 6.4.

session_id	host_name	program_name	original_login_name	reads	writes	cpu_time	wait_type	wait_time	wait_resource	blocking_session_id	text
52	MYRLIN	Microsoft SQL Server Manag...	AVALON\Gail	266	131	1500	NULL	NULL	NULL	NULL	NULL
53	MYRLIN	Microsoft SQL Server Manag...	AVALON\Gail	0	0	0	LCK_M_S	2170906	PAGE: 5:1:1961	52	SELECT FirstName, LastName, SUM(soh.TotalDue) AS ...

Figure 6.4:   Details of the blocked and blocking sessions.

This shows the blocked and blocking session. The NULLs visible in the blocking session (52) indicate that it is not currently running any queries and hence has no entry in **sys.dm_exec_requests**. We can get the last command that it ran by querying **sys.dm_exec_connections** and using the **most_recent_sql_handle** column as a parameter to **sys.dm_exec_sql_text**, as shown in Listing 6.5.

```
SELECT    ec.session_id ,
          ec.connect_time ,
          st.dbid AS DatabaseID ,
          st.objectid ,
          st.text
FROM      sys.dm_exec_connections ec
          CROSS APPLY sys.dm_exec_sql_text(ec.most_recent_sql_handle) st
WHERE     session_id = 52
```

Listing 6.5:   Finding the command that caused blocking via **sys.dm_exec_connections**.

This is enough to identify the source of the blocking query, the machine, the login name, and the application name. If this was an ad hoc query run by someone who simply doesn't know better, then the resolution could be as simple as asking that person to stop running the query and to teach them, so that the problem won't reoccur.

If the query is coming from an application, then between the application name and the query text it should be possible to identify the source of the problematic code with a view to fixing it (some options for fixing are given later in the chapter).

Using the sys.dm_os_waiting_tasks DMV

The sys.dm_os_waiting_tasks DMV is primarily used to show all waiting tasks *currently* active or blocked. In order to take full advantage of this DMV, JOIN on the sys. dm_exec_requests DMV and CROSS APPLY to sys.dm_exec_sql_text.

```
SELECT  blocking.session_id AS blocking_session_id ,
        blocked.session_id AS blocked_session_id ,
        waitstats.wait_type AS blocking_resource ,
        waitstats.wait_duration_ms ,
        waitstats.resource_description ,
        blocked_cache.text AS blocked_text ,
        blocking_cache.text AS blocking_text
FROM    sys.dm_exec_connections AS blocking
        INNER JOIN sys.dm_exec_requests blocked
                ON blocking.session_id = blocked.blocking_session_id
        CROSS APPLY sys.dm_exec_sql_text(blocked.sql_handle)
                                            blocked_cache
        CROSS APPLY sys.dm_exec_sql_text(blocking.most_recent_sql_handle)
                                            blocking_cache
        INNER JOIN sys.dm_os_waiting_tasks waitstats
                ON waitstats.session_id = blocked.session_id
```

Listing 6.6: Investigating blocking using the sys.dm_os_waiting_tasks DMV.

The results for our simulated blocking case are shown in Figure 6.5.

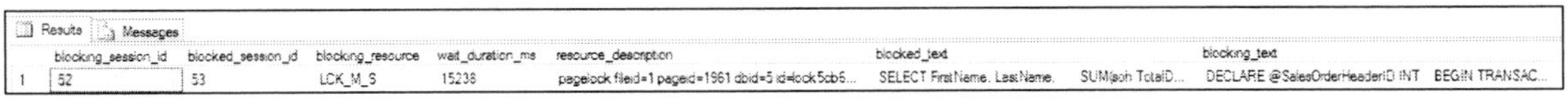
Results Messages

	blocking_session_id	blocked_session_id	blocking_resource	wait_duration_ms	resource_description	blocked_text	blocking_text
1	52	53	LCK_M_S	15238	pagelock fileid=1 pageid=1961 dbid=5 id=lock5cb6...	SELECT FirstName, LastName, SUM(soh.TotalD...	DECLARE @SalesOrderHeaderID INT BEGIN TRANSAC...

Figure 6.5: Results of the `sys.dm_os_waiting_tasks` query.

In the results from the query that takes any match by having a valid blocked `SPID` entry for a `SPID` and matching entry in `sys.dm_os_waiting_tasks`, we can see session 53 is being blocked by session 52. This doesn't give us much more information than the previous query (the additional columns returned in the previous section can be added here too, and were omitted solely for clarity), though it provides more detail on the resource on which blocking is occurring.

We could then use that information to help resolve the problem and stop it from reoccurring. For more on `sys.dm_os_waiting_tasks` refer to Books Online (HTTP://MSDN.MICROSOFT.COM/EN-US/LIBRARY/MS188743.ASPX).

Using the sys.dm_tran_locks DMV

This is not necessarily the first DMV that someone would look at when diagnosing blocking, as it's certainly not as easy to use as the DMVs discussed previously. This is the replacement for the `syslockinfo` system table. It provides a snapshot of the state of locking in a SQL Server instance, across all databases. It returns a row for every *currently active request to the lock manager for a lock that has been granted or is waiting to be granted.* The columns provided offer information regarding both the resource on which the lock is being held (or has been requested), and the owner of the request.

The main use of this DMV is to get further information on the locks held by processes that are known to be blocking each other. Using Listing 6.7, we can take a look at the locks held and requested by the two processes that we already know are blocking.

```
SELECT    request_session_id ,
          resource_type ,
          DB_NAME(resource_database_id) AS DatabaseName ,
          resource_associated_entity_id ,
          resource_description ,
          request_mode ,
          request_status
FROM      sys.dm_tran_locks AS dtl
WHERE     request_session_id IN ( 52, 53 )
          AND resource_type NOT IN ( 'DATABASE', 'METADATA' )
```

Listing 6.7:   Querying the sys.dm_tran_locks DMV.

This reveals details of all the locks held and requested by those two sessions, as shown in Figure 6.6.

	request_session_id	resource_type	DatabaseName	resource_associated_entity_id	resource_description	request_mode	request_status
66	52	KEY	Adventureworks	72057594052345856	(b3009a1c4f3c)	X	GRANT
67	52	PAGE	Adventureworks	72057594052280320	1:5785	IX	GRANT
68	52	PAGE	Adventureworks	72057594053918720	1:47027	IX	GRANT
69	52	PAGE	Adventureworks	72057594045333504	1:10054	IX	GRANT
70	52	PAGE	Adventureworks	72057594052345856	1:5892	IX	GRANT
71	52	KEY	Adventureworks	72057594059358208	(8300a58062aa)	X	GRANT
72	52	OBJECT	Adventureworks	898102240		IX	GRANT
73	52	PAGE	Adventureworks	72057594054574080	1:26505	IX	GRANT
74	52	KEY	Adventureworks	72057594058309632	(03011b83839f)	X	GRANT
75	53	PAGE	Adventureworks	72057594046775296	1:1960	S	GRANT
76	52	PAGE	Adventureworks	72057594046775296	1:1961	IX	GRANT
77	53	PAGE	Adventureworks	72057594046775296	1:1961	S	WAIT
78	52	KEY	Adventureworks	72057594046709760	(a2006a91af48)	X	GRANT
79	52	KEY	Adventureworks	72057594052083712	(d702e0989d06)	X	GRANT
80	52	OBJECT	Adventureworks	1918629878		IX	GRANT
81	52	KEY	Adventureworks	72057594053918720	(d300e16f2b2f)	X	GRANT
82	52	PAGE	Adventureworks	72057594054705152	1:28461	IX	GRANT
83	52	PAGE	Adventureworks	72057594054705152	1:28460	IX	GRANT
84	52	KEY	Adventureworks	72057594059948032	(7001b76c93f1)	X	GRANT

Figure 6.6:   Detailed locking information from the sys.dm_tran_locks DMV.

Just for those two simple queries there are 84 locks at the object, page, or key level. This is why I say this is probably not the first place to look, but a place to look for further information once a problem is identified.

The highlighted line (the sole lock with a wait status) and the row above show the problem in the simulated example. Session 53 wants a shared lock on page 1:1961, but session 52 already has an IX lock on that page and, as mentioned earlier, IX locks are only compatible with other intent locks, not with a shared lock. Hence session 53 will have to wait until session 52 releases that IX lock.

Cumulative wait statistics using sys.dm_os_wait_stats

Any time an executing task is forced to wait for a resource in the engine, the time spent waiting is tracked, accumulatively, by SQL Server 2005 (and later), in the sys.dm_os_wait_stats DMV. The values provided in this DMV are running totals, accumulated across all sessions since the server was last restarted or the statistics were manually reset using the DBCC SQLPERF command, as shown in Listing 6.8.

```
DBCC SQLPERF("sys.dm_os_wait_stats",CLEAR);
```

Listing 6.8:   Clearing existing wait statistics using DBCC SQLPERF.

While the information in this DMV cannot be used on its own to diagnose individual blocking problems, it can be used to find out whether locking waits are one of the most common waits in the system. Simply run the query in *Listing 3.2 (Chapter 3)* and look for high incidences of the LCK_* wait types, which are a sign that a task had to wait for locks held by another task to be released, before continuing to execute. For example, having cleared the existing wait statistics, we can re-create our previous blocking simulation (listings 6.2 and 6.3). As we repeatedly simulate this blocking, we should see rising counts for the LCK_M_IX wait event, as shown in Figure 6.7.

2	LCK_M_IX	1	422513	422513	0
3	MISCELLANEOUS	83	24788	358	0
4	WRITELOG	70	577	202	0

Figure 6.7:   Investigating the `LCK_M_IX` wait event.

In general, high wait time could originate from a single instance of a high wait, from very many processes with very low individual waits, or from a few processes with moderate waits. The `sys.dm_os_wait_stats` DMV can provide a picture of overall, instance-wide behavior.

Performance Monitor

I'm not going to go into much detail here but it is just worth noting that Performance Monitor (PerfMon) has a number of counters that can be used to monitor locking and blocking within a SQL instance. As with the aggregated wait statistics, PerfMon data can be used to indicate that there may be a problem, but it is insufficient on its own to identify the cause of the problem. Identifying the cause requires use of the DMVs or of some of the automated reporting (discussed next). The main use of these counters is to establish a baseline level of activity for these events, so that we can establish "normal" behavior, and thus quickly spot abnormal behavior. The main counters of interest are `Avg Wait Time (ms)`, `Lock Waits/sec`, and `Number of Deadlocks/sec`, as shown in Figure 6.8.

The `Lock requests/sec` counter can also be traced, but since the acquisition of a large number of locks is quite normal behavior in SQL Server, it may not tell you anything of value.

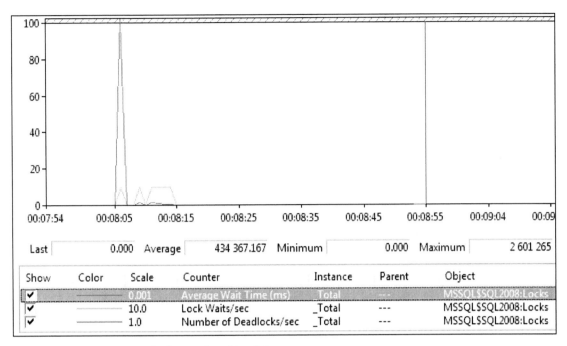

Figure 6.8: Monitoring locking-related PerfMon counters.

Automated Detection and Notification of Blocking

Automatic detection and notification requires some form of job or scheduled process that polls the server at regular intervals. While this is effective in detecting blocking, running a process against the server will consume processing resources and should be done strategically, to minimize the footprint of the process of gathering the information itself.

In SQL Server 2000 the only option in this area was the `sp_blocker_pss80` procedure, but things have improved significantly in SQL Server 2005 and later, with the emergence of the `Blocked Process Report` and `Lock Escalation` event classes, along with event notifications.

The sp_blocker_pss80 process

In SQL Server 2000, the only available option for automated detection and notification was to run the procedure sp_blocker_pss80 using either an infinite loop and WAITFOR DELAY, or a job or scheduled task with a very short interval. The sp_blocker_pss80 procedure will log information about the blocking process and blocked process, along with gathering the batch statement, and lock and wait statistics during the time of the blocking event.

The Sp_blocker_pss80 *process*

Sp_blocker_pss80 *is a Microsoft-provided solution for investigating blocking on SQL Server 7.0 and 2000 and is well documented. To learn more about setting up and utilizing this process, refer to KB article 271509 at* HTTP://SUPPORT.MICROSOFT.COM/KB/271509/.

If the sp_blocker_pss80 is not used, a custom script can be written using sysprocesses or sp_who2 to do much the same thing.

SQL Trace

SQL Trace is a powerful feature that allows for the creation of event traces within SQL Server, using a set of stored procedures. These procedures are the same ones that SQL Profiler uses to run its traces. The events that SQL Trace collects range from deadlock events, to ALTER commands, security or blocking, to complete SQL Batch events. SQL Trace should be utilized only when there is a need to capture events for troubleshooting. Events such as SP:Stmt* or Lock* will occur very frequently on a busy server and traces that capture these events will consume a great deal of resources in order to log all the events.

Troubleshooting blocking with SQL Trace can be extremely effective when used strategically to capture both the queries that are blocked and those that are causing the blocking. While the blocked process report (discussed in the next section) was only introduced in SQL Server 2005, monitoring of locks and query statistics from SQL Trace in SQL Server 2000 is still a powerful tool in finding and resolving blocking and other events.

The best, least resource-intensive way to capture traces is to run a server-side trace, with output directed to a file on a fast, local drive. The easiest way to create a server-side script is to use Profiler to set up the initial trace and the export it (all the details for how to do this are in *Chapter 5*). For automatic detection of blocking, the most likely event to trace is the blocked process report, although tracing for statement or batch completion, lock escalation or lock timeouts may also be of use. Again, be very careful when tracing frequently occurring events, such as `Lock Acquired`, as those may result in a trace that has a severe impact on the server.

The blocked process report

The blocked process report is implemented as an event that fires when a non-system task has been blocked by a deadlock detectable lock. An event is fired every time blocking occurs that exceeds in duration the threshold value, configured by the "blocked process threshold" `sp_configure` option. The limitation that it must be a deadlock detectable lock stems from the implementation of the event in the database engine, which uses the background deadlock monitor (covered in the next chapter) to walk through the list of waiting tasks that exceed the defined threshold limit.

The default value for the "blocked process threshold" is zero, meaning that the database engine doesn't perform the additional checks of waiting tasks and won't generate the blocked process reports. The value for the option is an integer between 0 and 86,400, and determines the number of seconds that a task must have been waiting for a locked resource before the report generates. Multiple reports can be generated for the same blocking chain if the value for the threshold is exceeded multiple times. So for example, if we set the threshold to 5 seconds and a task is blocked for 18 seconds then three blocked process reports would be generated. For further information on setting up and using the blocked process report event, see HTTP://WWW.SIMPLE-TALK.COM/CONTENT/ARTICLE. ASPX?ARTICLE=671 or HTTP://BIT.LY/QC6ZZ3.

Listing 6.9 shows how to enable the blocked process report, and sets the threshold to 2 seconds, using the sp_configure procedure (this would generally be considered rather low for most systems, but I've set it there just for demo purposes).

```
sp_configure 'show advanced options', 1
go
RECONFIGURE
go
sp_configure 'blocked process threshold', 2
go
RECONFIGURE
go
```

Listing 6.9: Enabling the blocked process report and setting the threshold.

The blocked process report can be captured in a number of ways. SQL Server Profiler can be used to actively capture the Blocked Process Report event class, or alternatively you can create a server-side SQL Trace script, using the sp_trace_* stored procedures as explained earlier.

When the blocked process threshold is met, the trace will log the event in the trace file. The fn_trace_gettable function can be used to read the file into a tabular format in SSMS, as shown in Figure 6.9.

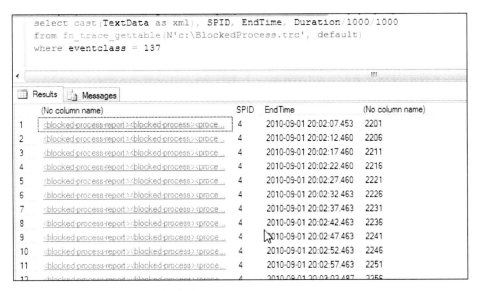

```
select cast(TextData as xml), SPID, EndTime, Duration/1000/1000
from fn_trace_gettable(N'c:\BlockedProcess.trc', default)
where eventclass = 137
```

	(No column name)	SPID	EndTime	(No column name)
1	<blocked-process-report><blocked-process><proce...	4	2010-09-01 20:02:07.453	2201
2	<blocked-process-report><blocked-process><proce...	4	2010-09-01 20:02:12.460	2206
3	<blocked-process-report><blocked-process><proce...	4	2010-09-01 20:02:17.460	2211
4	<blocked-process-report><blocked-process><proce...	4	2010-09-01 20:02:22.460	2216
5	<blocked-process-report><blocked-process><proce...	4	2010-09-01 20:02:27.460	2221
6	<blocked-process-report><blocked-process><proce...	4	2010-09-01 20:02:32.463	2226
7	<blocked-process-report><blocked-process><proce...	4	2010-09-01 20:02:37.463	2231
8	<blocked-process-report><blocked-process><proce...	4	2010-09-01 20:02:42.463	2236
9	<blocked-process-report><blocked-process><proce...	4	2010-09-01 20:02:47.463	2241
10	<blocked-process-report><blocked-process><proce...	4	2010-09-01 20:02:52.463	2246
11	<blocked-process-report><blocked-process><proce...	4	2010-09-01 20:02:57.463	2251
12	<blocked-process-report><blocked-process><proce...	4	2010-09-01 20:03:02.487	2256

Figure 6.9: Reading the blocked process report using `fn_trace_gettable`.

Each event is logged with the session ID, end time and, as shown in Figure 6.9, the duration of blocking. The session ID is of little interest, as it is the ID of the system task that is checking the waiting tasks, not that of the blocked or blocking sessions. In SSMS, clicking on the XML will open a new window with the XML nicely formatted. In the first row from Figure 6.9, the results logged are from the blocking simulation performed earlier in this chapter, and are shown in Listing 6.10.

```xml
<blocked-process-report>
 <blocked-process>
  <process id="process5a4f708" taskpriority="0" logused="0" waitresource="PAGE:
5:1:1961" waittime="2143" ownerId="94338" transactionname="SELECT"
lasttranstarted="2011-08-24T18:43:59.553" XDES="0x84fbf1e0" lockMode="S"
schedulerid="8" kpid="2588" status="suspended" spid="53" sbid="0" ecid="0"
priority="0" trancount="0" lastbatchstarted="2011-08-24T18:43:59.543"
lastbatchcompleted="2011-08-24T18:43:57.873" clientapp="Microsoft SQL Server
Management Studio - Query" hostname="AMachine" hostpid="4344" loginname="SomeLogin"
isolationlevel="read committed (2)" xactid="94338" currentdb="5"
lockTimeout="4294967295" clientoption1="671090784" clientoption2="390200">
   <executionStack>
    <frame line="1" sqlhandle="0x02000000314f4a04e43e9f09208ee7f0f3b4ddd93bd13
```

```
3f8"/>
   </executionStack>
   <inputbuf>
SELECT FirstName, LastName,
    SUM(soh.TotalDue) AS TotalDue, MAX(OrderDate) AS LastOrder
  FROM Sales.SalesOrderHeader AS soh
    INNER JOIN Sales.Customer AS c ON soh.CustomerID = c.CustomerID     INNER JOIN
Person.Person AS p ON c.PersonID = p.BusinessEntityID  WHERE soh.OrderDate &gt;=
&apos;2011/01/01&apos;
  GROUP BY c.CustomerID, FirstName, LastName
   </inputbuf>
   </process>
 </blocked-process>
 <blocking-process>
  <process status="sleeping" spid="52" sbid="0" ecid="0" priority="0" trancount="1"
lastbatchstarted="2011-08-24T18:43:43.493" lastbatchcompleted="2011-08-
24T18:43:44.817" clientapp="Microsoft SQL Server Management Studio - Query"
hostname=" AMachine " hostpid="4344" loginname="SomeLogin" isolationlevel="read
committed (2)" xactid="93835" currentdb="5" lockTimeout="4294967295"
clientoption1="671090784" clientoption2="390200">
   <executionStack/>
   <inputbuf>
DECLARE @SalesOrderHeaderID INT

BEGIN TRANSACTION

INSERT INTO Sales.SalesOrderHeader
    (RevisionNumber, OrderDate, DueDate, ShipDate, Status,
      OnlineOrderFlag, PurchaseOrderNumber, AccountNumber, CustomerID,
      SalesPersonID, TerritoryID, BillToAddressID, ShipToAddressID,
      ShipMethodID, CreditCardID, CreditCardApprovalCode, CurrencyRateID,
      Comment, rowguid, ModifiedDate)
VALUES
    (5, &apos;2011/06/20&apos;, &apos;2011/06/25&apos;, &apos;2011/06/30&apos;, 5,
0, NULL,
      &apos;10-4030-018749&apos;, 18749, NULL, 6, 28374, 28374, 1, 8925,
      &apos;929849Vi46003&apos;, NULL, NULL, NEWID(), GETDATE()
    )

SET @SalesOrderHeaderID = @@IDENTITY

INSERT INTO Sales.SalesOrderDetail
    (SalesOrderID, CarrierTrackingNumber, OrderQty, ProductID,
      SpecialOfferID, UnitPrice, UnitPriceDiscount, rowguid,
```

```
        ModifiedDate)
VALUES
    (@SalesOrderHeaderID, &apos;4911-403C-98&apos;, 15, 722, 1, 2039.994, 0,
        NEWID(), GETDATE()),
    (@SalesOrderHeaderID, &apos;4911-403C-98&apos;, 4, 709, 1, 5.70, 0,
        NEWID(), GETD    </inputbuf>
  </process>
 </blocking-process>
</blocked-process-report>
```

Listing 6.10: Output of the blocked process report.

The blocked process is shown as the **SELECT** statement while the blocking process is the open transaction with uncommitted **INSERT**s.

Some blocking events may happen only periodically throughout a normal day or week of operations in SQL Server. The blocked process report, captured by a server-side trace, can be used to log these events automatically. The trace information can later be imported into SQL and used in Reporting Services or other reporting containers for analysis and resolution of these types of performance problems.

Event notifications

Event notifications have been available since SQL Server 2005 and offer the ability to capture, in real-time, most DDL events and trace events in SQL Server. Event notifications use Service Broker queues in order to capture log the events that you wish to monitor. When used in conjunction with the **BLOCKED_PROCESS_REPORT** event and the **LOCK_ESCALATION** event (SQL 2008 only), this would allow for instances of both events to be logged, asynchronously, as they happen. This asynchronous model means that event logging has a lower impact on overall server performance than when using SQL Trace or Profiler.

To set up event notifications we need to first configure and enable Service Broker in the database that we wish to monitor. Once Service Broker is ready, a queue and a service, based on the queue, are created. Finally, we can create the event notification that will use the service. If you haven't done so already, enable the **BLOCKED_PROCESS_REPORT** event as was shown in Listing 6.9. Next, ensure Service Broker is enabled as shown in Listing 6.11.

```
ALTER DATABASE AdventureWorks SET ENABLE_BROKER
GO
```

Listing 6.11: Enable Service Broker.

Set up the queue:

```
CREATE QUEUE systemeventqueue
GO
```

Listing 6.12: Create the Service Broker queue.

Set up the service:

```
CREATE SERVICE systemeventservice
ON QUEUE systemeventqueue ( [http://schemas.microsoft.com/SQL/Notifications/
PostEventNotification] )
GO
```

Listing 6.13: Create the Service Broker service.

Create the event notification on the service:

```
CREATE EVENT NOTIFICATION notification_blocking
ON SERVER
WITH FAN_IN
FOR blocked_process_report
TO SERVICE 'systemeventservice', 'current database' ;
GO
```

Listing 6.14: Create the event notification for blocking events.

All that's left now is to receive any blocked event messages that are logged in the queue, converting the **MESSAGE_BODY** column to XML format as shown in Listing 6.15.

```
RECEIVE CAST(message_body AS XML), * FROM systemeventqueue
```

Listing 6.15: Retrieving messages from the Service Broker queue.

The output of this query, for the blocking example that we've used throughout the chapter, is shown in Figure 6.10.

XMLFormattedEvent	status	priority	queuing_order	conversation_group_id	conversation_handle	message_sequence_number	service_name
1	EVENT_INSTANCE...EventType>BLOCKED_PROCESS_REPOR...	1	5	59	1712E19F-73CE-E011-912F-080027004459	1812E19F-73CE-E011-912F-080027004459	59	systemeventservice
2	EVENT_INSTANCE...EventType>BLOCKED_PROCESS_REPOR...	1	5	60	1712E19F-73CE-E011-912F-080027004459	1812E19F-73CE-E011-912F-080027004459	60	systemeventservice
3	EVENT_INSTANCE...EventType>BLOCKED_PROCESS_REPOR...	1	5	61	1712E19F-73CE-E011-912F-080027004459	1812E19F-73CE-E011-912F-080027004459	61	systemeventservice
4	EVENT_INSTANCE...EventType>BLOCKED_PROCESS_REPOR...	1	5	62	1712E19F-73CE-E011-912F-080027004459	1812E19F-73CE-E011-912F-080027004459	62	systemeventservice
5	EVENT_INSTANCE...EventType>BLOCKED_PROCESS_REPOR...	1	5	63	1712E19F-73CE-E011-912F-080027004459	1812E19F-73CE-E011-912F-080027004459	63	systemeventservice
6	EVENT_INSTANCE...EventType>BLOCKED_PROCESS_REPOR...	1	5	64	1712E19F-73CE-E011-912F-080027004459	1812E19F-73CE-E011-912F-080027004459	64	systemeventservice

Figure 6.10: Event notification for the blocked process report.

Notice that multiple entries have been inserted into the queue, due to the fact that we set the threshold for the event to two seconds. So, if a blocking event lasted for ten seconds, five unique rows would be logged in the **systemeventqueue**.

Creating an event notification session for the **LOCK_ESCALATION** event is done in exactly the same manner, as shown in Listing 6.16.

```
CREATE EVENT NOTIFICATION notification_lockescalation
ON SERVER
WITH FAN_IN
FOR lock_escalation
TO SERVICE 'systemeventservice', 'current database' ;
GO
```

Listing 6.16: Create an event notification for lock escalation events.

Extended Events

In SQL Server 2008 there are no Extended Events for detecting blocking. However, in Denali (the next major version of SQL Server), the `sqlserver.blocked_process_report` event has been added. This, like the blocked process trace event and the blocked process event notification, require that the server configuration setting `blocked process threshold` be set using `sp_configure`.

The Extended Event session can be set up with the Denali Extended Events wizard, as shown in Figure 6.11.

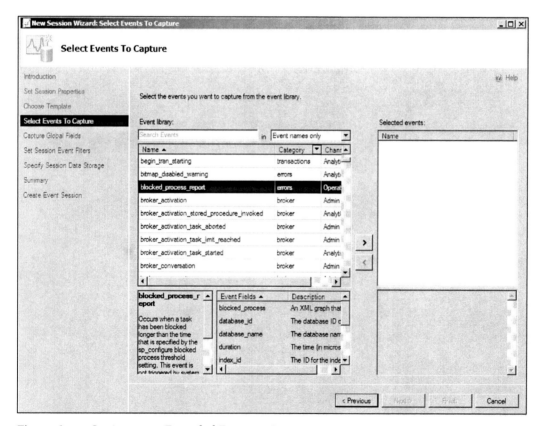

Figure 6.11: Setting up an Extended Event session.

The events can be sent to a memory buffer, as in this example, but in a production environment would more likely be sent to disk, as we did when using SQL Trace. For quick monitoring, the data can also be viewed live, as shown in Figure 6.12.

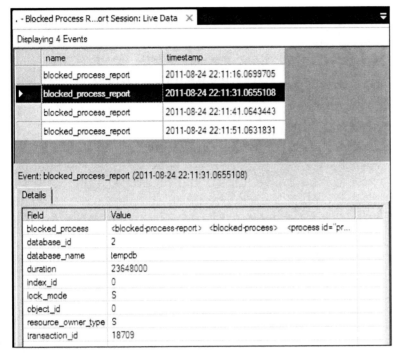

Figure 6.12: Viewing Extended Event data.

For more information on Extended Events, Jonathan's *An XEvent a day* series is well worth reading: HTTP://WWW.SQLSKILLS.COM/BLOGS/JONATHAN/CATEGORY/XEVENT-A-DAY-SERIES. ASPX.

Resolving Blocking

The manner in which we resolve blocking will vary depending on the particular reason for the block and, in some cases, the version and edition of SQL Server that is being used. As noted earlier in this chapter, blocking is most often caused by long-running queries that hold certain locks on a row, table, page, or even database. In cases where T-SQL statements are causing locks to be set and held for long periods, the only real answer to the problem is to tune the queries to ensure they run as fast as possible. This may not eradicate blocking completely, but your goal is certainly to see, for example, a significant reduction in the number of recorded blocked process report events, as locks are acquired and released faster, and fewer instances of blocking reach the configured threshold for the event.

To all databases, and the applications that use them, are attached a specific set of requirements and expected response times. What's considered "normal" for one application may be considered very worrying in another. For example, one application may trigger a lengthy process that requires an exclusive lock on a table for its entire duration, and still be considered an acceptable part of normal business operating procedures. Conversely, another process, one that never holds locks for more than a few seconds, may be cause for concern.

In short, before you go in and start tuning, you need to know what's normal and expected behavior, and how this is reflected in execution times and locking periods. It may be that your blocking threshold is set at a level that is catching blocking events for processes that are behaving perfectly normally; make sure this threshold is set appropriately for your system (see Listing 6.9).

Bad database design

A database that is poorly normalized, such that data changes have to be made in a number of places instead of one, will result in transactions that run for longer than necessary. Modification transactions acquire exclusive locks, and the the risk of blocking rises the more that are acquired, and the longer they are held.

This is not something that is easily fixed after the database is in production; proper normalization is an issue that should be kept in mind during the design phase.

Denormalization and OLTP systems

People often claim that denormalizing a database improves performance. The real story is that denormalization can improve read performance at the expense of write performance. This is why denormalization may be useful for data warehouse or decision-support systems, but is seldom appropriate for OLTP-type systems.

Inappropriate isolation level

A fairly common cause of severe blocking is the use of an inappropriately high isolation level, often without the knowledge of the application developer. I've seen more than one data access library that, by default, requests an isolation level of SERIALIZABLE when connecting to SQL Server. This results in a huge number of rows being locked for long periods, for just about any operation. In many cases, the degree of transaction isolation needed by the application does not warrant the use of SERIALIZABLE; if it is causing issues then the application needs to be examined to see if the level can be lowered to REPEATABLE READ or even READ COMMITTED, or whether one of the SNAPSHOT isolation levels can be used. This is something that needs to be evaluated on a case-by-case basis; there is no single isolation level that's appropriate for all applications.

One of the most effective ways, on SQL Server 2005 or above, to deal with applications and databases that are highly prone to blocking is to either use **READ COMMITTED SNAPSHOT** isolation on the entire database, or to enable **SNAPSHOT** isolation and use it in the most affected areas. The overhead of maintaining the row version store in **TempDB** is often not severe, especially in light of the considerable advantages of having read queries that don't block writers and vice versa.

Of course, testing needs to be done before making a change as radical as switching the entire database over to **READ COMMITTED SNAPSHOT**, but it should be a serious consideration if dealing with an application prone to severe blocking.

Poorly written queries

Queries that are written inefficiently will hold locks for longer than necessary. When there are multiple such queries running concurrently there is a good chance that severe blocking will occur. Full coverage of how to write efficient queries would require at least one book on its own; two good ones are: *Inside SQL Server 2005 Query Tuning and Optimization* (HTTP://WWW.AMAZON.COM/INSIDE-MICROSOFT®-SQL-SERVER-2005/DP/0735621969) and *SQL Server 2008 Query Performance Tuning Distilled* (HTTP://WWW.AMAZON.COM/ SERVER-PERFORMANCE-TUNING-DISTILLED-EXPERTS/DP/1430219025). Here, we'll stick to a few general principles:

- Keep transactions as short as possible (but no shorter). For example, if a select does not need to be run within the transaction, put it outside.

- Ensure that columns that are compared/joined have the same data type to avoid implicit conversion problems.

- Keep queries as simple as possible. Test whether splitting a complex query up and using temp tables to hold intermediate results will be faster or not.

- Use set-based methods as much as possible. They are faster than row-by-row processing in the vast majority of cases.

Missing indexes

If SQL is missing an index that would be useful to the query, then that query will take longer to run than necessary, holding locks longer than necessary, and it will read more data than is necessary, in this way taking and releasing many more locks than it would in the presence of the index. This increases the chances of the query either blocking another query or being blocked itself. For more on preventing, finding and fixing duplicate and missing indexes, refer to *Chapter 5*.

Poor application design

Often, poor application design imposes on the database a process flow that can hugely increase the prevalence of blocking events in the database. Fixing problems caused by application design is never easy, as it usually demands close cooperation between DBAs, developers and vendors. Nevertheless, if the application is really the source of the problem, it has to be done.

Some of the classic application design malpractices that can cause blocking are: user input within transactions; applications that read far more information than they need; and overly-chatty applications. I'll spend a couple of paragraphs on each.

User input within transactions

This happens when an application starts a transaction, does some work and then waits for the user to confirm an action, or to input data, or similar. This is a potentially serious problem, because the transaction is open and the locks are held until the user acts. Tales are rife of users going to lunch or leaving for the day with transactions left open and locks held in the database, causing severe blocking problems.

The solution is to never allow any form of user interaction within a database transaction. A database transaction should be started and committed (or rolled back) in a single trip to the database.

Reading too much data

A few years ago, I saw an application that, in order to get a filtered set of matching rows from two tables, fetched to the front end the entire contents of both tables, looped through them to get the rows that matched, and then filtered out the ones it didn't need. It would read several hundred thousand rows from the database server in order to get the ten rows it needed.

This caused huge problems, not least of which was the huge numbers of locks that it took as a result. The general rule here is that an application should read just what is necessary and no more. Let the database do the work of joining and filtering; that's what it's good at.

Chatty applications

If an application repeatedly and frequently queries the database for data that it either already has or doesn't really need, this can cause serious difficulties, including huge locking problems on the database. An example of this would be an application that, on a search screen, fires off a database query for each key pressed, rather than when the user has completed entering details of the required search.

Outdated hardware

In rare cases, outdated hardware, with insufficient CPU, memory and disk I/O capacity, will be the cause of the blocking problems. If all other avenues have been investigated, and blocking issues remain, it may simply be that the application has outgrown its hardware and you'll need to upgrade.

Hints, Trace Flags and Other Last Resorts

If nothing else works, there are hints and Trace Flags that influence SQL Server's locking behavior. These should be used only as short-term, temporary measures while more permanent solutions are investigated.

Locking hints

There are a number of hints that affect in various ways how SQL Server takes locks. They can be divided into three main groups, as follows:

- isolation level hints

- lock mode hints

- lock granularity hints.

Isolation level hints

The isolation level hints change the effective isolation level used for locks on a table that is being accessed within a query. These hints are per table, not for the entire query. The available isolation level hints are as follows:

- **ReadUncommitted/Nolock** – the READ UNCOMMITTED isolation level.

- **ReadCommitted** – the READ COMMITTED isolation level using locks or row versions, depending on the READ_COMMITTED_SNAPSHOT setting in the database.

- **ReadCommittedLock** – the READ COMMITTED isolation level, using locks.

- **RepeatableRead** – the REPEATABLE READ isolation level.

- **Serializable** – the SERIALIZABLE isolation level.

Lock mode hints

The lock mode table hints dictate a mode (e.g. shared, update, exclusive) for the locks taken on table during processing of a query. There are only two lock mode hints:

- UPDLOCK – takes locks on that table as Update (U) locks.

- XLOCK – takes locks on that table as Exclusive (X) locks.

One very important point to note is that this hint just specifies the lowest (i.e. least restrictive) mode that can be used; SQL can and will take a higher lock mode if necessary. For example, if a table in a DELETE query is given the UPDLOCK hint and that is the table from which the rows are being deleted, SQL will still take exclusive locks, as an update lock is not sufficient for a delete.

The main use for these hints is to take more restrictive locks on read queries to reduce the chance of deadlocks later in a transaction.

Lock granularity hints

The lock granularity hints dictate to SQL Server the granularity of the lock that should initially be taken on a given table. SQL is still free to escalate locks if necessary. The lock granularity hints are as follows:

- ROWLOCK – locks on that table start as row locks.

- PAGLOCK – locks on that table start as page locks.

- TABLOCK – locks on that table start as table locks.

There is also a TABLOCKX hint which is equivalent to a combination of TABLOCK and XLOCK.

Index locking options

There are two lock-related options that can be set on indexes and they are both ON by default.

- ALLOW_ROW_LOCKS

- ALLOW_PAGE_LOCKS

These two control whether or not the particular granularities of lock may be taken on the index. If ALLOW_ROW_LOCKS is OFF, SQL Server can only take page and table-level locks on that index. If ALLOW_PAGE_LOCKS is OFF, SQL Server can only take row and table-level locks on that index. If both are OFF, SQL can only take table-level locks.

There are few valid reasons for messing with these options and they should never be changed without significant testing, as there will be side effects. For example, an index that has ALLOW_PAGE_LOCKS set to OFF cannot be reorganized, it can only be rebuilt.

Sometimes disabling row locks on indexes can resolve deadlocks caused by key lookups, but it is by no means a guaranteed fix. Another reason for disabling page locks is when there are very, very frequent single-row INSERTs on the table and there's contention on the lock manager, as described at HTTP://BLOG.KEJSER.ORG/2011/05/30/DIAGNOSING-AND-FIXING-SOS_OBJECT_STORE-SPINS-FOR-SINGLETON-INSERTS/.

Trace Flags 1211 and 1224

If lock escalation is persistent and problematic, the lock escalation process can be altered by using Trace Flags 1211 and 1224.

Trace Flag 1211 provides the ability to disable lock escalation altogether. This Trace Flag should only be used if all other attempts to troubleshoot lock escalation have failed. Disabling lock escalation itself can cause an impact on SQL Server by allowing for many low-level locks and causing long-holding locks. If lock memory grows to 60% of total dynamically allocated memory, further lock requests will fail.

Trace Flag 1224 is more flexible than 1211, since it restricts lock escalation at the statement level, and based only on the number of locks that are being held. However, SQL Server still has the flexibility to escalate locks if locked memory exceeds 40% of total memory. These Trace Flags should be enabled only after careful consideration and testing, and any instances with them enabled needs to be carefully monitored. With Trace Flag 1211, in particular, it is possible for SQL Server to run out of lock memory because it is not allowed to escalate locks. If that happens, no more locks can be taken and every single query against that SQL instance will fail, with the following message, until some lock memory becomes available.

```
Server: Msg 1204, Level 19, State 1, Line 1
The SQL Server cannot obtain a LOCK resource at this time. Rerun your statement
when there are fewer active users or ask the system administrator to check the SQL
Server lock and memory configuration.
```

For more information on setting these and other Trace Flags, refer to: HTTP://MSDN. MICROSOFT.COM/EN-US/LIBRARY/MS188396.ASPX.

Summary

Blocking is one of the most common performance problems in SQL Server. Given the tools and monitoring steps covered, blocking can be quickly identified and resolved. DBAs should always actively monitor for blocking, especially as and when new queries and applications are added to SQL Server in response to new business requirements.

Chapter 7: Handling Deadlocks

A deadlock is defined in the dictionary as "a standstill resulting from the action of equal and opposed forces," and this turns out to be a reasonable description of a deadlock in SQL Server: two or more sessions inside of the database engine end up waiting for access to locked resources held by each other. In a deadlock situation, none of the sessions can continue to execute until one of those sessions releases its locks, so allowing the other session(s) access to the locked resource. Multiple processes persistently blocking each other, in an irresolvable state, will eventually result in a halt to processing inside the database engine.

A common misconception is that DBAs need to intervene to "kill" one of the processes involved in a deadlock. In fact, SQL Server is designed to detect and resolve deadlocks automatically, through the use the **Lock Monitor**, a background process that is initiated when the SQL Server instance starts, and that constantly monitors the system for deadlocked sessions. However, when deadlocks are reported, the DBA must investigate their cause immediately. Many of the same issues that cause severe blocking in the database, such as poor database design, lack of indexing, poorly designed queries, inappropriate isolation level and so on (all discussed in *Chapter 6*), are also common causes of deadlocking. This chapter will provide the tools, techniques and tweaks you need to diagnose and prevent deadlocks, and to ensure that they are handled gracefully if they ever do occur. Specifically, it will cover:

- how to capture deadlock graphs using a variety of techniques, including Trace Flags, the Profiler deadlock graph event, and service broker event notifications

- how to read deadlock graphs to locate the sessions, queries and resources that are involved

- common types of deadlock and how to prevent them

- using server- or client-side `TRY...CATCH` error handling for deadlocks, to avoid `UnhandledException` errors in the application.

The Lock Monitor

When the Lock Monitor performs a deadlock search and detects that one or more sessions are embraced in a deadlock, one of the sessions is selected as a deadlock victim and its current transaction is rolled back. When this occurs, all of the locks held by the victim's session are released, allowing any previously blocked other sessions to continue processing. Once the rollback completes, the victim's session is terminated, returning a 1205 error message to the originating client.

SQL Server selects the deadlock victim based on the following criteria:

1. **Deadlock priority** – the assigned DEADLOCK_PRIORITY of a given session determines the relative importance of it completing its transactions, if that session is involved in a deadlock. The session with the lowest priority will always be chosen as the deadlock victim. Deadlock priority is covered in more detail later in this chapter.

2. **Rollback cost** – if two or more sessions involved in a deadlock have the same deadlock priority, then SQL Server will choose as the deadlock victim the session that has lowest estimated cost to roll back.

Capturing Deadlock Graphs

When 1205 errors are reported, it is important that the DBA finds out why the deadlock happened and takes steps to prevent its recurrence. The first step in troubleshooting and resolving a deadlocking problem is to capture the **deadlock graph** information.

A deadlock graph is an output of information regarding the sessions and resources that were involved in a deadlock. The means by which you can capture a deadlock graph have diversified and improved over recent versions of SQL Server. If you are still running SQL Server 2000, then you are stuck with a single, somewhat limited, Trace Flag (**1204**). SQL Server 2005 added a new Trace Flag (**1222**), provided the **XML Deadlock Graph** event in

SQL Server Profiler, and enabled deadlock graph capture via Service Broker event notifications, and the WMI (Windows Management Instrumentation) Provider for Server Events. In each case, the deadlock graph contains significantly more information about the nature of the deadlock than is available through Trace Flag 1204. This minimizes the need to gather, manually, additional information from SQL Server in order to understand why the deadlock occurred; for example, resolving the `pageid` for the locks being held to the `objectid` and `indexid`, using `DBCC PAGE`, and using SQL Trace to walk the deadlock chain and find out which currently executing statements are causing the problem. SQL Server 2008 provides all of these facilities, plus the **system_health** Extended Events Session.

To allow you to work through each section, and generate the same deadlock graphs that are presented and described in the text, the resource materials for this book (HTTP:// WWW.SIMPLE-TALK.COM/REDGATEBOOKS/JONATHANKEHAYIAS/TROUBLESHOOTINGSQL-SERVER_CODE.ZIP) include example code to generate a deadlock in SQL Server.

Trace Flag 1204

Trace Flags in SQL Server enable alternate "code paths" at key points inside the database engine, allowing additional code to execute when necessary. If you are seeing queries failing with deadlock errors on a SQL Server instance, Trace Flags can be enabled for a single session or for all of the sessions on that instance. When Trace Flag 1204 is enabled for all sessions on a SQL Server instance, any deadlock detected by the deadlock monitor will cause a deadlock graph to be written to the SQL Server error log.

In SQL Server 2000, this Trace Flag is the only means by which to capture a deadlock graph, which makes troubleshooting deadlocking in SQL Server 2000 quite challenging, though still possible. In later SQL Server versions, this Trace Flag is still available although superseded by Trace Flag 1222.

Trace Flag 1204, like all Trace Flags, can be enabled and disabled on an ad hoc basic using the **DBCC TRACEON** and **DBCC TRACEOFF** database console commands. Listing 7.1 shows how to enable Trace Flag 1204, for a short term, at the server-level (specified by the –1 argument) so that all subsequent statements run with this Trace Flag enabled.

```
DBCC TRACEON(1204, -1)
```

Listing 7.1:   Turning on Trace Flag 1204 for all sessions.

Alternatively, Trace Flags can be turned on automatically, using the –T startup parameter. To add a startup parameter to SQL Server, right-click on the Server Node in **Enterprise Manager** and open the **Server Properties** page. Under the **General** tab, click the **Startup Parameters** button, and then add the startup parameter to the server as shown in Figure 7.1.

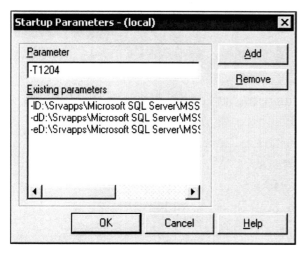

Figure 7.1:   Using the –T startup parameter.

In cases where it is possible to perform an instance restart, using a startup parameter can be helpful when you want to capture every deadlock that occurs from the server, over a long period of time. However, once deadlock troubleshooting has been completed, the

Trace Flag should be removed from the startup parameters. Since the Trace Flag enables the instance to write the deadlock graph to the SQL Server error log, the only way to retrieve the graph is to read the error log file and then extract the events from the log file for analysis.

Trace Flag 1222

SQL Server 2005 added Trace Flag 1222 to capture the deadlock graphs in an easier-to-read and more comprehensive format than was available with the 1204 flag. It captures and presents the information in a manner that makes it much easier to identify the deadlock victim, as well as the resources and processes involved in the deadlock (covered in detail in the *Reading Deadlock Graphs* section).

Trace Flag 1204 is still available, for backwards compatibility reasons, but when using Trace Flags to capture deadlock graphs in SQL Server 2005 or later, you should always use Trace Flag 1222 in preference to Trace Flag 1204. Trace Flag 1222 is enabled in the same manner as 1204, using `DBCC TRACEON()`, as shown in Listing 7.1 or the –T startup parameter, as shown in Figure 7.1.

SQL Profiler XML Deadlock Graph event

New to SQL Server 2005, the `Deadlock Graph` event in SQL Trace captures the deadlock graph information, without writing it to the SQL Server Error Log. The `Deadlock Graph` event is part of the **Locks** event category and can be added to a SQL Server Profiler trace by selecting the event in Profiler's **Trace Properties** dialog, as shown in Figure 7.2.

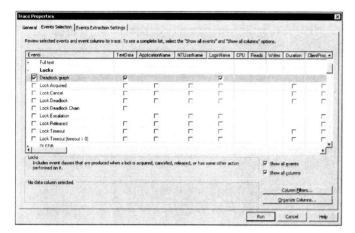

Figure 7.2: Selecting `Deadlock Graph` event in the Trace Properties dialog.

SQL Profiler can be configured to save the deadlock graphs separately, into XDL files, as shown in Figure 7.3.

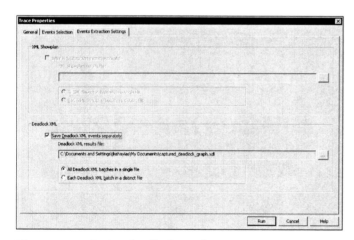

Figure 7.3: Saving deadlock graphs.

An XDL file is a standard XML file. Management Studio recognizes the file extension when opening the file and displays the deadlock information graphically, rather than as XML.

If you prefer to work directly with server-side traces, removing the overhead of the Profiler client, then you can capture the deadlock graph information directly from your scripts, using the `SP_TRACE_*` set of system stored procedures. The captured graphs will be written to a SQL Trace file on the SQL Server. The easiest way to generate a script for a server-side trace is to first create the trace in SQL Profiler, and then export it to a script using **File | Export | Script Trace Definition**, as described in detail in *Chapter 5*.

A server-side trace file can be read using the system function `fn_trace_gettable`, or by opening it inside of SQL Profiler. When using SQL Profiler to view the trace file contents, the deadlock events can be exported to individual XDL files that can be opened up graphically using SQL Server Management Studio, through the **File | Export | Extract SQL Server Events | Extract deadlock Events** menu item.

Service Broker event notifications

Also new in SQL Server 2005, event notifications allow the capture of deadlock graph information using SQL Server Service Broker, by creating a **service** and **queue** for the `DEADLOCK_GRAPH` trace event. The information contained in the deadlock graph captured by event notifications is no different than the information contained in the deadlock graph captured by SQL Trace; the only difference is the mechanism of capture.

Setting up an event notification to capture deadlock graph information requires three Service Broker objects:

- A **QUEUE** to hold the `DEADLOCK_GRAPH` event messages

- A **SERVICE** to route the messages to the queue

- An **EVENT NOTIFICATION** to capture the deadlock graph and package it in a message that is sent to the Service.

Listing 7.2 shows how to create these objects using T-SQL. Note that you need to create the objects in a broker-enabled database, like **msdb**. The **Master** database is not enabled for broker, by default.

```
USE msdb;

--   Create a service broker queue to hold the events
CREATE QUEUE DeadlockQueue
GO

--   Create a service broker service receive the events
CREATE SERVICE DeadlockService
ON QUEUE DeadlockQueue ([http://schemas.microsoft.com/SQL/Notifications/
PostEventNotification])
GO

-- Create the event notification for deadlock graphs on the service
CREATE EVENT NOTIFICATION CaptureDeadlocks
ON SERVER
WITH FAN_IN
FOR DEADLOCK_GRAPH
TO SERVICE 'DeadlockService', 'current database' ;
GO
```

Listing 7.2:   Creating the Service Broker service, queue, and event notification objects.

With the objects created, deadlock graphs will be collected in the queue, as deadlocks occur on the server. While the queue can be queried using a **SELECT** statement, just as if it were a table, the contents remain in the queue until they are processed using the **RECEIVE** command, as demonstrated in Listing 7.3.

```
USE msdb ;
-- Cast message_body to XML and query deadlock graph from TextData
SELECT   message_body.valuequery('(/EVENT_INSTANCE/TextData/
                                deadlock-list)[1]', 'varchar(128)')
                            AS DeadlockGraph
FROM     ( SELECT    CAST(message_body AS XML) AS message_body
           FROM      DeadlockQueue
         ) AS sub ;
```

```
GO

-- Receive the next available message FROM the queue
DECLARE @message_body XML ;

RECEIVE TOP(1) -- just handle one message at a time
 @message_body=message_body
 FROM DeadlockQueue ;

-- Query deadlock graph from TextData
SELECT   @message_body.valuequery('(/EVENT_INSTANCE/TextData/
                        deadlock-list)[1]','varchar(128)')
                              AS DeadlockGraph
GO
```

Listing 7.3:   Query and processing DEADLOCK_GRAPH event messages in the queue.

Since Event Notifications utilize a service broker queue for processing, additional actions can be performed when the deadlock event fires. When a deadlock event occurs, Service Broker can "activate" a stored procedure that processes the message and responds appropriately, for example, by sending an email notification using Database Mail, logging the event in a table, or gathering additional information, like the execution plans for both statements, from SQL Server, based on the information contained inside of the deadlock graph. Full coverage of this topic is beyond the scope of this chapter. However, a full example of how to use queue activation to completely automate deadlock collection can be found in the code download file for this book.

WMI Provider for server events

Also new to SQL Server 2005, the WMI Provider for Server Events allows WMI to be used to monitor SQL Server events as they occur. Any event that can be captured through event notifications has a corresponding **WMI Event Object**, and any WMI management application can subscribe to these event objects.

SQL Server Agent was updated to manage WMI events, through the use of WMI Query Language (WQL), a query language similar to T-SQL that is used with WMI and Agent Alerts for WMI events.

A full example of how to create a SQL Agent alert to capture and store deadlock graphs is out of scope for this chapter, and can be found in the Books Online Sample, *Creating a SQL Server Agent Alert by Using the WMI Provider for Server Events* (HTTP://MSDN. MICROSOFT.COM/EN-US/LIBRARY/MS186385.ASPX). However, in essence, it involves creating, via the WMI Event Provider, a SQL Agent alert to monitor deadlock graph events. The alert queries for events using WQL, and when it receive notification that one has occurred, it fires a job that captures the deadlock graph in a designated SQL Server table.

To capture deadlock graphs using the WMI Event Provider and a SQL Agent alert in this manner requires that the "Replace tokens for all job responses to alerts" in SQL Server Agent Alert System properties must be enabled. It also requires that Service Broker (which processes the notification messages) is enabled in `msdb` as well as the database in which the deadlock graphs are stored.

WMI event provider bug

It is worth noting that there is a known bug in the WMI Event Provider for server names that exceed fourteen characters; this was fixed in Cumulative Update 5 for SQL Server 2005 Service Pack 2.

Extended Events

Prior to SQL Server 2008, there was no way to retroactively find deadlock information. Obtaining deadlock graphs required that a SQL Trace was actively running, or that Trace Flag 1222 or 1205 was turned on for the instance. Since tracing deadlocks by either of these methods can be resource intensive, this usually meant that a series of deadlocks had to occur to prompt starting a trace or enabling the Trace Flags.

SQL Server 2008 includes all of the previously discussed techniques for capturing deadlock graphs, and adds one new one, namely collecting the deadlock information through the `system_health` default event session in Extended Events. This default event session (akin, in concept, to the default trace) is running by default on all installations of SQL Server 2008 and collects a range of useful troubleshooting information for errors that occur in SQL Server, including deadlocks. Deadlock graphs captured by Extended Events in SQL Server 2008 have the unique ability to contain information about multi-victim deadlocks (deadlocks where more than session was killed by the Lock Monitor to resolve the conflict).

More on Extended Events

We can't cover Extended Events in detail in this book but, for a good overview of the topic, read Paul Randal's article, "SQL 2008: Advanced Troubleshooting with Extended Events" (HTTP://TECHNET. MICROSOFT.COM/EN-US/MAGAZINE/2009.01.SQL2008.ASPX).

The `system_health` session uses a `ring_buffer` target which stores the information collected by events firing in memory as an XML document in the `sys.dm_xe_session_targets` DMV. This DMV can be joined to the `sys.dm_xe_sessions` DMV to get the session information along with the data stored in the `ring_buffer` target, as shown in Listing 7.4.

```
SELECT   CAST(target_data AS XML) AS TargetData
FROM     sys.dm_xe_session_targets st
         JOIN sys.dm_xe_sessions s ON s.address = st.event_session_address
WHERE    name = 'system_health'
```

Listing 7.4: Retrieving `system_health` session information.

The query in Listing 7.5 shows how to retrieve a valid XML deadlock graph from the default `system_health` session using XQuery, the `target_data` column, and a `CROSS APPLY` to get the individual event nodes. Note that, due to changes in the deadlock graph to support multi-victim deadlocks, and to minimize the size of the event data, the resulting XML cannot be saved as an XDL file for graphical representation.

```sql
SELECT   CAST(event_data.value('(event/data/value)[1]',
                       'varchar(max)') AS XML) AS DeadlockGraph
FROM     ( SELECT    XEvent.query('.') AS event_data
           FROM      (     -- Cast the target_data to XML
                     SELECT    CAST(target_data AS XML) AS TargetData
                     FROM      sys.dm_xe_session_targets st
                     JOIN sys.dm_xe_sessions s
                       ON s.address = st.event_session_address
                     WHERE     name = 'system_health'
                               AND target_name = 'ring_buffer'
                     ) AS Data -- Split out the Event Nodes
                     CROSS APPLY TargetData.nodes('RingBufferTarget/
                               event[@name="xml_deadlock_report"]')
                     AS XEventData ( XEvent )
           ) AS tab ( event_data )
```

Listing 7.5:   Retrieving an XML deadlock graph.

Note, also, that there is a bug in the RTM release of SQL Server 2008 that causes deadlock graphs not to be captured and retained in an Extended Events session. This bug was fixed in Cumulative Update 1 for SQL Server 2008 and is also included in the latest Service Pack. An additional bug exists for malformed XML in the deadlock graph generated by Extended Events, which was corrected in Cumulative Update Package 6 for SQL Server 2008 Service Pack 1. It is still possible to generate a valid XML document in these earlier builds, by hacking the deadlock graph being output by Extended Events. However, since the fix to SQL Server has already been released, the specifics of the work-around will not be covered in this chapter.

> **Changes to Extended Events in SQL Server Denali**
>
> *At the time of the final edits of this chapter, SQL Server Denali CTP3 was released, with changes associated to how the Extended Events targets store XML data inside of the* `value` *element of the Event XML output. Listing 7.5 shows the use of the* `.value()` *method from XML in SQL Server, but in Denali CTP3, a* `.query()` *method has to be used to retrieve the deadlock graph from the Event XML output.*

Reading Deadlock Graphs

The precise format of the deadlock graph in SQL Server has changed from version to version, and mainly for the better. In general, it now contains better information in an easier-to-digest format, such as the graphical display provided in SQL Server Management Studio and SQL Profiler, so allowing us to more easily troubleshoot deadlocks.

Even with the changes to the deadlock graph XML that is output by Extended Events, in SQL Server 2008, the fundamentals of how to interpret the graph are the same as for any other XML deadlock graph.

Interpreting Trace Flag 1204 deadlock graphs

Perhaps one of the most difficult aspects of troubleshooting deadlocks in SQL Server 2000 is interpreting the output of Trace Flag 1204. The process is complicated by the need to query the `sysobjects` and `sysindexes` system tables to find out exactly what objects are involved in the deadlock.

Listing 7.6 shows an example deadlock graph that was generated by enabling Trace Flag 1204, and then creating a deadlock situation (the code to do this is provided as part of the code download for this book).

```
Deadlock encountered .... Printing deadlock information

Wait-for graph

Node:1
KEY: 13:1993058136:2 (08009d1c9ab1) CleanCnt:2 Mode: S Flags: 0x0
 Grant List 0::
   Owner:0x567e7660 Mode: S        Flg:0x0 Ref:1 Life:00000000 SPID:54 ECID:0
   SPID:54 ECID: 0 Statement Type: SELECT Line #:3
   Input Buf: Language Event: WHILE (1=1)
BEGIN
   INSERT INTO #t1 EXEC BookmarkLookupSelect 4
   TRUNCATE TABLE #t1
END

 Requested By:
   ResType:LockOwner Stype:'OR' Mode: X SPID:55 ECID:0 Ec:(0x26F7DBD8)
Value:0x58f80880 Cost:(0/3C)

Node:2
KEY: 13:1993058136:1 (040022ae5dcc) CleanCnt:2 Mode: X Flags: 0x0
 Grant List 1::
   Owner:0x58f80940 Mode: X        Flg:0x0 Ref:0 Life:02000000 SPID:55 ECID:0
   SPID: 55 ECID: 0 Statement Type: UPDATE Line #: 4
   Input Buf: Language Event: SET NOCOUNT ON
WHILE (1=1)
BEGIN
   EXEC BookmarkLookupUpdate 4
END

 Requested By:
   ResType:LockOwner Stype:'OR' Mode: S SPID:54 ECID:0 Ec:(0x2F881BD8)
Value:0x567e76c0 Cost:(0/0)

Victim Resource Owner:
 ResType:LockOwner Stype:'OR' Mode: S SPID:54 ECID:0 Ec:(0x2F881BD8)
Value:0x567e76c0 Cost:(0/0)
```

Listing 7.6: Sample deadlock graph from Trace Flag 1204, involving KEY locks.

The first thing to pay attention to in the graph output is that there are two **nodes**, each node representing a locked resource. The first line of output for each node shows the resource on which the lock is held, and then the **Grant List** section provides details of the deadlocking situation, including:

- `Mode` of the lock being held on the resource

- `SPID` of the associated process

- `Statement Type` the `SPID` is currently running

- `Line #` (line number) that marks the start of the currently executing statement

- `Input Buf`, the contents of the input buffer for that `SPID` (the last statement sent).

So, for Node 1, we can see that a shared read (S) lock is being held by `SPID` 54 on an index `KEY` of a non-clustered index (`:2`) on an object with ID 1993058136. Node 2 shows that an exclusive (X) lock is being held by `SPID` 55 on an index key of the clustered index (`:1`) of the same object.

Further down, for each node, is the **Requested By** section, which details any resource requests that cannot be granted, due to blocking. For Node 1, we can see that that `SPID` 55 is waiting for an exclusive lock on the non-clustered index key (it is blocked by the S lock held by `SPID` 54). For Node 2, we can see that `SPID` 54 is waiting to acquire a shared read lock on the clustered index key (it is blocked by the exclusive lock held by `SPID` 55).

Furthermore, back in the **Grant List** section, we can see that `SPID` 54 has issued the `SELECT` statement on Line # 3 of the `BookmarkLookupSelect` stored procedure (but is unable to acquire a shared read lock) and `SPID` 55 has issued the `UPDATE` statement on Line # 4 of the `BookmarkLookupUpdate` stored procedure (but is unable to acquire an exclusive lock).

This is a classic deadlock situation, and happens to be one of the more common types of deadlock, covered in more detail later in this chapter, in the section titled *Bookmark lookup deadlock*.

Finally, in the **Victim Resource Owner** section we can find out which `SPID` was chosen as the deadlock victim, in this case, `SPID` 54. Alternatively, we can identify the deadlock victim by matching the binary information in the `Value` to the binary information in the `Owner` portion of the Grant List.

We've discussed a lot about the deadlocking incident, but so far we know only that it occurred on an object with an ID of 1993058136. In order to identify properly the object(s) involved in the deadlock, the information in the `KEY` entry for each node needs to be used to query `sysobjects` and `sysindexes`. The `KEY` entry is formatted as `databaseid:objected:indexid`. So, in this example, `SPID` 54 was holding a Shared (S) lock on `index id` 2, a non-clustered index, with `objectID` 1993058136. The query in Listing 7.7 shows how to determine the table and index names associated with the deadlock.

```
SELECT    o.name AS TableName ,
          i.name AS IndexName
FROM      sysobjects AS o
          JOIN sysindexes AS i ON o.id = i.id
WHERE     o.id = 1993058136
          AND i.indid IN ( 1, 2 )
```

Listing 7.7: Finding the names of the objects associated with the deadlock.

If a deadlock involves a `PAG` lock instead of a `KEY` lock, the deadlock graph might look as shown in Listing 7.8.

```
Wait-for graph

Node:1
PAG: 8:1:96                     CleanCnt:2 Mode: X Flags: 0x2
 Grant List 0::
   Owner:0x195fb2e0 Mode: X        Flg:0x0 Ref:1 Life:02000000
   SPID: 56 ECID: 0 Statement Type: UPDATE Line #: 4
   Input Buf: Language Event: SET NOCOUNT ON
WHILE (1=1)
BEGIN
```

```
    EXEC BookmarkLookupUpdate 4
END

 Requested By:
    ResType:LockOwner Stype:'OR' Mode: S SPID:55 ECID:0 Ec:(0x1A5E1560)
Value:0x1960dba0 Cost:(0/0)
```

Listing 7.8: Page lock example, generated by Trace Flag 1204.

Notice now that the lock reference is of the form `databaseid:fileid:pageid`. In order to identify the object to which this page belongs, we need to enable Trace Flag 3604, dump the page header information to the client message box `DBCC PAGE()`, and then disable the Trace Flag, as shown in Listing 7.9.

```
DBCC TRACEON(3604)
DBCC PAGE(8,1,96,1)
DBCC TRACEOFF(3604)
```

Listing 7.9: Identifying the objects involved in a deadlock involving page locks.

The output of the `DBCC PAGE()` command will include a `PAGE HEADER` section, shown in Listing 7.10, which contains the IDs of the object (`m_objId` field) and index (`m_indexId`) to which the page belongs.

```
Page @0x1A5EC000
-----------------
m_pageId = (1:96)          m_headerVersion = 1        m_type = 1
m_typeFlagBits = 0x0       m_level = 0                m_flagBits = 0x4
m_objId = 1977058079       m_indexId = 0             m_prevPage = (0:0)
m_nextPage = (1:98)        pminlen = 116              m_slotCnt = 66
m_freeCnt = 110            m_freeData = 7950          m_reservedCnt = 0
m_lsn = (912:41:3)         m_xactReserved = 0         m_xdesId = (0:0)
m_ghostRecCnt = 0          m_tornBits = 2
```

Listing 7.10: Page Header section from the output of the `DBCC PAGE()`.

Understanding the statements that are being executed along with the indexes and objects involved in the deadlock is critical to troubleshooting the problem. However, there are situations where the currently executing statement may not be the actual statement that caused the deadlock. Multi-statement stored procedures and batches that enlist an explicit transaction will hold all of the locks acquired under the transaction scope until the transaction is either committed or rolled back. In this situation, the deadlock may involve locks that were acquired by a previous statement that was executed inside the same transaction block. To completely troubleshoot the deadlock it is necessary to look at the executing batch from the `Input Buf` as a whole, and understand when locks are being acquired and released.

Bart Duncan is the definitive source for interpreting SQL Server deadlock graphs. For additional information on reading the output of Trace Flag 1204, see his blog post *Interpreting Trace Flag 1204 Output* (HTTP://BLOGS.MSDN.COM/B/BARTD/ARCHIVE/2006/09/09/DEADLOCK-TROUBLESHOOTING_2C00_-PART-1.ASPX).

Interpreting Trace Flag 1222 deadlock graphs

The format of the information, as well as the amount of information, returned by Trace Flag 1222 is very different than the output from Trace Flag 1204. Listing 7.11 shows the Trace Flag 1222 output, in SQL Server 2005, for an identical deadlock to the one previously seen for the Trace Flag 1204 output, from SQL Server 2000.

```
deadlock-list
 deadlock victim=process8d8c58

  process-list
    process id=process84b108 taskpriority=0 logused=220 waitresource=KEY:
34:72057594038452224 (0c006459e83f) waittime=5000 ownerId=899067977
transactionname=UPDATE lasttranstarted=2009-12-13T00:22:46.357 XDES=0x157be250
lockMode=X schedulerid=1 kpid=4340 status=suspended spid=102 sbid=0
ecid=0 priority=0 transcount=2 lastbatchstarted=2009-12-13T00:13:37.510
lastbatchcompleted=2009-12-13T00:13:37.507 clientapp=Microsoft SQL Server
Management Studio - Query hostname=SQL2K5TEST hostpid=5516 loginname=sa
```

```
isolationlevel=read committed (2) xactid=899067977 currentdb=34
lockTimeout=4294967295 clientoption1=673187936 clientoption2=390200
    executionStack
      frame procname=DeadlockDemo.dbo.BookmarkLookupUpdate line=4 stmtstart=260
stmtend=394 sqlhandle=0x03002200e7a4787d08a10300de9c00000100000000000000
UPDATE BookmarkLookupDeadlock SET col2 = col2-1 WHERE col1 = @col2
      frame procname=adhoc line=4 stmtstart=82 stmtend=138 sqlhandle=0x020000002a709
3322fbd674049d04f1dc0f3257646c4514b
EXEC BookmarkLookupUpdate 4
    inputbuf
SET NOCOUNT ON
WHILE (1=1)
BEGIN
    EXEC BookmarkLookupUpdate 4
END
   process id=process8d8c58 taskpriority=0 logused=0 waitresource=KEY:
34:72057594038386688 (0500b49e5abb) waittime=5000 ownerId=899067972
transactionname=INSERT EXEC lasttranstarted=2009-12-13T00:22:46.357
XDES=0x2aebba08 lockMode=S schedulerid=2 kpid=5864 status=suspended
spid=61 sbid=0 ecid=0 priority=0 transcount=1 lastbatchstarted=2009-12-
13T00:22:46.347 lastbatchcompleted=2009-12-13T00:22:46.343 clientapp=Microsoft
SQL Server Management Studio - Query hostname=SQL2K5TEST hostpid=5516
loginname=sa isolationlevel=read committed (2) xactid=899067972 currentdb=34
lockTimeout=4294967295 clientoption1=673187936 clientoption2=390200
    executionStack
      frame procname=DeadlockDemo.dbo.BookmarkLookupSelect line=3 stmtstart=118
stmtend=284 sqlhandle=0x03002200ae80847c07a10300de9c00000100000000000000
SELECT col2, col3 FROM BookmarkLookupDeadlock WHERE col2 BETWEEN @col2 AND @col2+1
      frame procname=adhoc line=3 stmtstart=50 stmtend=146 sqlhandle=0x02000000e00b6
6366c680fabe2322acbad592a896dcab9cb
INSERT INTO #t1 EXEC BookmarkLookupSelect 4
    inputbuf
WHILE (1=1)
BEGIN
    INSERT INTO #t1 EXEC BookmarkLookupSelect 4
    TRUNCATE TABLE #t1
END

  resource-list
    keylock hobtid=72057594038386688 dbid=34 objectname=DeadlockDemo.dbo.
BookmarkLookupDeadlock indexname=cidx_BookmarkLookupDeadlock id=lock137d65c0 mode=X
associatedObjectId=72057594038386688
    owner-list
      owner id=process84b108 mode=X
```

```
     waiter-list
       waiter id=process8d8c58 mode=S requestType=wait
     keylock hobtid=72057594038452224 dbid=34 objectname=DeadlockDemo.dbo.
BookmarkLookupDeadlock indexname=idx_BookmarkLookupDeadlock_col2 id=lock320d5900
mode=S associatedObjectId=72057594038452224
       owner-list
         owner id=process8d8c58 mode=S
       waiter-list
         waiter id=process84b108 mode=X requestType=wait
```

Listing 7.11: Sample deadlock graph, generated by Trace Flag 1222.

The new format breaks a deadlock down into sections that define the deadlock victim, the processes involved in the deadlock (**process-list**), and the resources involved in the deadlock (**resource-list**). Each process has an assigned **process id** that is used to uniquely identify it in the deadlock graph. The deadlock victim lists the process that was selected as the victim and killed by the deadlock monitor. Each process includes the **SPID** as well as the **hostname** and **loginname** that originated the request, and the isolation level under which the session was running when the deadlock occurred. The **execution stack** section, for each process, displays the entire execution stack, starting from the most recently executed (deadlocked) statement backwards to the start of the call stack. This eliminates the need to perform additional steps to identify the statement being executed.

The **resource-list** contains all of the information about the resources involved in the deadlock and is generally the starting point for reading a deadlock graph. The index names are included in the output and each resource displays the owner process and the type of locks being held, as well as the waiting process and the type of locks being requested.

As with the Trace Flag 1204 output, the definitive source for understanding the output from Trace Flag 1222 is Bart Duncan. He has a three-part series on troubleshooting deadlocks with the output from Trace Flag 1222 on his blog, starting with *Deadlock Troubleshooting, Part 1* (HTTP://BLOGS.MSDN.COM/BARTD/ARCHIVE/2006/09/09/747119.ASPX).

Using the same technique employed in these posts, we can construct a description of the deadlock described, as shown in Listing 7.12.

```
SPID 102 (process84b108) is running this query (line 4 of the BookmarkLookupUpdate
sproc):
   UPDATE BookmarkLookupDeadlock SET col2 = col2-1 WHERE col1 = @col2

SPID 61 (process8d8c58 )is running this query (line 3 of BookmarkLookupSelect
sproc):
   SELECT col2, col3 FROM BookmarkLookupDeadlock WHERE col2
                                         BETWEEN @col2 AND @col2+1

SPID 102 is waiting for an Exclusive KEY lock on the idx_BookmarkLookupDeadlock_
col2 index (on the BookmarkLookupDeadlock table).
   (SPID 61 holds a conflicting S lock)

SPID 61 is waiting for a Shared KEY lock on the index cidx_BookmarkLookupDeadlock
(on the BookmarkLookupDeadlock table)..
   (SPID 102 holds a conflicting X lock)
```

Listing 7.12: Deadlock analysis, constructed from the Trace Flag 1222 deadlock graph.

As we can see from the deadlock list section of Listing 7.11, SPID 61, attempting to run the SELECT statement against cidx_BookmarkLookupDeadlock, is chosen as the deadlock victim.

Interpreting XML deadlock graphs

The information contained in XML deadlock graph, obtained from SQL Profiler, or Service Broker Event notifications, and so on, is essentially the same as that obtained from the output of Trace Flag 1222, and it is interpreted in exactly the same way. However, the format in which the information is presented is very different. The XML deadlock graph can be displayed graphically in Management Studio by saving the XML to a file with a .XDL extension and then opening the file in Management Studio (although, as discussed earlier, the XML generated by Extended Events can't be displayed graphically, in this manner).

Figure 7.4 displays graphically the same deadlock graph that we saw for the two Trace Flags.

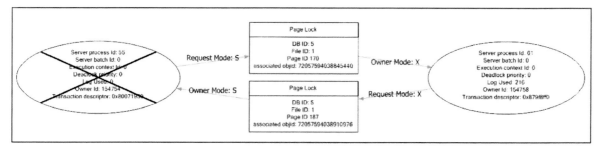

Figure 7.4: SSMS graphical deadlock graph.

In the graphical display, the deadlock processes are displayed as ovals. The process information is displayed inside of the oval, and includes a tooltip, which pops up when the mouse hovers over the process, and displays the statement being executed, as shown in Figure 7.5. The deadlock victim process is shown crossed out.

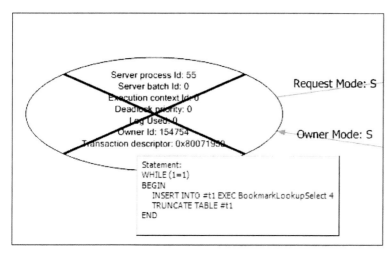

Figure 7.5: SSMS graphical deadlock graph: the victim process.

The resources contributing to the deadlock are displayed in rectangular boxes in the center of the graphical display. The locks, and their respective modes, are displayed by arrows between the processes and the resources. Locks owned by a process are shown with the arrow pointed towards the process, while locks being requested are shown with the arrow pointed towards the resource as shown in Figure 7.6.

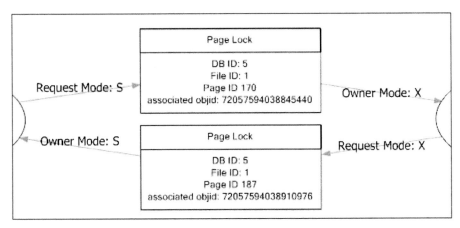

Figure 7.6:   SSMS graphical deadlock graph: processes and resources.

A visual display like this makes it much easier to understand the circular blocking that caused the deadlock to occur.

Common types of deadlock and how to eliminate them

When troubleshooting any type of problem in SQL Server, you learn with experience how to recognize, from a distance, the particular varieties of problem that tend to crop up on a regular basis. The same is true of deadlocks; the same types of deadlock tend to appear with predictable regularity and, once you understand what patterns to look for, resolving the deadlock becomes much more straightforward.

This section assumes knowledge of basic locking mechanisms inside SQL Server (see *Chapter 6*) and examines how to resolve the most common types of deadlock, namely the **bookmark lookup** deadlock, the **serializable range scan** deadlock, the **cascading constraint** deadlock, the **intra-query parallelism** deadlock and the **accessing objects in different orders** deadlock.

Bookmark lookup deadlock

Bookmark lookup deadlocks are one of the most common deadlocks in SQL Server. Fortunately, although they have a habit of appearing randomly, without any changes to the database or the code inside of it, they are also one of the easiest types of deadlock to troubleshoot.

Bookmark lookup deadlocks generally have a `SELECT` statement as the victim, and an `INSERT`, `UPDATE`, or `DELETE` statement as the other contributing process to the deadlock. They occur partly as a general consequence of SQL Server's pessimistic locking mechanisms for concurrency, but mainly due to the lack of an appropriate covering index for the `SELECT` operation.

When a column is used in the `WHERE` clause to filter the `SELECT` statement and a non-clustered index exists on that column, then the database engine takes a shared lock on the required rows or pages in the non-clustered index. In order to return any additional columns from the table, not covered by the non-clustered index, the database engine performs an operation known as KEY, or RID, lookup (in SQL Server 2000, the term "bookmark lookup" was used). This operation uses either the Clustered Index Key or RID (in the case of a heap) to look up the row in the table data and retrieve the additional columns.

When a lookup operation occurs, the database engine takes additional shared locks on the rows or pages needed from the table. These locks are held for the duration of the

`SELECT` operation, or until lock escalation is triggered to increase the lock granularity from row or page to table.

The deadlock occurs, as we have seen in previous sections, when an operation that changes the data in a table (for example, an `INSERT`, `UPDATE`, or `DELETE` operation) occurs simultaneously with the `SELECT`. When the data-changing session executes, it acquires an exclusive lock on the row or page of the clustered index or table, and performs the data change operation. At the same time the `SELECT` operation acquires a shared lock on the non-clustered index. The data-changing operation requires an exclusive lock on the non-clustered index to complete the modification, and the `SELECT` operation requires a shared lock on the clustered index, or table, to perform the bookmark lookup. Shared locks and exclusive locks are incompatible, so if the data-changing operation and the `SELECT` operation affect the same rows then the data-changing operation will be blocked by the `SELECT`, and the `SELECT` will be blocked by the data change, resulting in a deadlock.

One of the most common online recommendations for curing this type of deadlock is to use a `NOLOCK` table hint in the `SELECT` statement, to prevent it from acquiring shared locks. This is bad advice. While it might prevent the deadlock, it can have unwanted side effects, such as allowing operations to read uncommitted changes to the database data, and so return inaccurate results.

The correct fix for this type of deadlock is to change the definition of the non-clustered index so that it contains, either as additional key columns or as `INCLUDE` columns (see *Chapter 5*), all the columns it needs to cover the query. Columns returned by the query that are not used in a `JOIN`, `WHERE`, or `GROUP BY` clause, can be added to the index as `INCLUDE` columns. Any column used in a `JOIN`, the `WHERE` clause, or in a `GROUP BY` should ideally be a part of the index key but, in circumstances where this exceeds the 900-byte limit, addition as an `INCLUDE` column may work as well. Implementing the covering index will resolve the deadlock without the unexpected side effects of using `NOLOCK`.

A shortcut to finding the appropriate covering index for a query is to run it through the Database Engine Tuning Advisor (DTA). However, as discussed in *Chapter 5*, the DTA recommendations are only as good as the supplied workload, and repeated single-query evaluations against the same database can result in an excessive number of indexes, which often overlap. Manual review of any index recommendation made by the DTA should be made to determine if modification of an existing index can cover the query without creating a new index. A good video example, *Using the DTA to Assist in Performance Tuning*, can be found on the SQL Share website (HTTP://WWW.SQLSHARE.COM/USING-THE-DTA-TO-ASSIST-IN-PERFORMANCE-TUNING_599.ASPX).

Range scans caused by SERIALIZABLE isolation

The `SERIALIZABLE` isolation level is the most restrictive isolation level in SQL Server for concurrency control, ensuring that every transaction is completely isolated from the effects of any other transaction.

To accomplish this level of transactional isolation, **range locks** are used when reading data, in place of the row or page level locking used under `READ COMMITTED` isolation. These range locks ensure that no data changes can occur that affect the result set, allowing the operation to be repeated inside the same transaction with the same result. While the default isolation level for SQL Server is `READ COMMITTED`, certain providers, like COM+ and BizTalk, change the isolation to `SERIALIZABLE` when connections are made.

Range locks have two components associated with their names, the lock type used to lock the range and then the lock type used for locking the individual rows within the range. The four most common range locks are shared-shared (`RangeS-S`), shared-update (`RangeS-U`), insert-null (`RangeI-N`), and exclusive (`RangeX-X`). Deadlocks associated with `SERIALIZABLE` isolation are generally caused by lock conversion, where a lock of higher compatibility, such as a `RangeS-S` or `RangeS-U` lock, needs to be converted to a lock of lower compatibility, such as a `RangeI-N` or `RangeX-X` lock.

A common deadlock that occurs under SERIALIZABLE isolation has a pattern that involves a transaction that checks if a row exists in a table before inserting or updating the data in the table. A reproducible example of this deadlock is included in the code examples for this chapter. This type of deadlock will generally produce a deadlock graph with a resource-list similar to the one shown in Listing 7.13.

```
<resource-list>
  <keylock hobtid="72057594050969600" dbid="5" objectname="AdventureWorks.
Sales.SalesOrderHeader" indexname="IX_SalesOrderHeader_CustomerID" id="lock35bcc80"
mode="RangeS-U" associatedObjectId="72057594050969600">
    <owner-list>
      <owner id="processad4d2e8" mode="RangeS-U" />
      <owner id="process9595b8" mode="RangeS-S" />
    </owner-list>
    <waiter-list>
      <waiter id="processad4d2e8" mode="RangeI-N" requestType="convert" />
      <waiter id="process9595b8" mode="RangeI-N" requestType="convert" />
    </waiter-list>
  </keylock>
</resource-list>
```

Listing 7.13: Extract from a deadlock graph for a SERIALIZABLE range scan deadlock.

In this example, two processes have acquired compatible shared locks, RangeS-S and RangeS-U, on the SalesOrderHeader table. When one of the processes requires a lock conversion to a lock type that is incompatible with the lock being held by the other process, in this case a RangeI-N, it is blocked. If both processes require a lock conversion to RangeI-N locks, the result is a deadlock since each session is waiting on the other to release its high compatibility lock.

There are several possible solutions to this type of deadlock and the most appropriate one depends on the database and the application it supports. If it is not necessary for the database to maintain the range locks acquired during the SELECT operation that checks for row existence and the SELECT operation can be moved outside of the transaction that performs the data change, then the deadlock can be prevented.

If the operation doesn't require the use of **SERIALIZABLE** isolation, then changing the isolation level to a less restrictive isolation level, for example **READ COMMITTED**, will prevent the deadlock and allow a greater degree of concurrency.

If neither of these solutions is appropriate, the deadlock can be resolved by forcing the **SELECT** statement to use a lower-compatibility lock, through the use of an **UPDLOCK** or **XLOCK** table hint. This will block any other transactions attempting to acquire locks of higher compatibility. This fix is specific to this particular type of deadlock due to the usage of **SERIALIZABLE** isolation. Using **UPDLOCK** hints under **READ COMMITTED** may result in deadlocks occurring more frequently under certain circumstances.

Cascading constraint deadlocks

Cascading constraint deadlocks are generally very similar to a Serializable Range Scan deadlock, even though the isolation level under which the victim transaction was running isn't **SERIALIZABLE**. To enforce cascading constraints, SQL Server has to traverse the **FOREIGN KEY** hierarchy to ensure that orphaned child records are not left behind, as the result of an **UPDATE** or **DELETE** operation to a parent table. To do this requires that the transaction that modifies the parent table be isolated from the effects of other transactions, in order to prevent a change that would violate **FOREIGN KEY** constraints, when the cascade operation subsequently completes.

Under the default **READ COMMITTED** isolation, the database engine would acquire and hold, for the duration of the transaction, Exclusive locks on all rows that had to be changed. This blocks users from reading or changing the affected rows, but it doesn't prevent another session from adding a new row into a child table for the parent key being deleted. To prevent this from occurring, the database engine acquires and holds range locks, which block the addition of new rows into the range affected by the cascading operation. This is essentially an under-the-cover use of **SERIALIZABLE** isolation, during the enforcement of the cascading constraint, but the isolation level for the batch is not actually changed; only the type of locks used for the cascading operation are changed.

When a deadlock occurs during a cascading operation, the first thing to look for is whether or not non-clustered indexes exist for the FOREIGN KEY columns that are used (see *Chapter 5* for more on Indexing Foreign Keys). If appropriate indexes on the FOREIGN KEY columns do not exist, the locks being taken to enforce the constraints will be held for longer periods of time, increasing the likelihood of a deadlock between two operations, if a lock conversion occurs.

Intra-query parallelism deadlocks

An intra-query parallelism deadlock occurs when a single session executes a query that runs with parallelism, and deadlocks itself. Unlike other deadlocks in SQL Server, these deadlocks may actually be caused by a bug in the SQL Server parallelism synchronization code, rather than any problem with the database or application design. Since there are risks associated with fixing some bugs, it may be that the bug is known and won't be fixed, since it is possible to work around it by reducing the degree of parallelism for that the query, using the MAXDOP query hint, or by adding or changing indexes to reduce the cost of the query or make it more efficient.

The deadlock graph for a parallelism deadlock will have the same SPID for all of the processes, and will have more than two processes in the process-list. The resource-list will have **threadpool**, **exchangeEvent**, or both, listed as resources, but it won't have lock resources associated with it. In addition, the deadlock graph for this type of deadlock will be significantly longer than any other type of deadlock, depending on the degree of parallelism and the number of nodes that existed in the execution plan.

Additional information about this specific type of deadlock can be found on Bart Duncan's blog post, *Today's Annoyingly-Unwieldy Term: "Intra-Query Parallel Thread Deadlocks"* (HTTP://BLOGS.MSDN.COM/BARTD/ARCHIVE/2008/09/24/TODAY-S-ANNOYINGLY-UNWIELDY-TERM-INTRA-QUERY-PARALLEL-THREAD-DEADLOCKS.ASPX).

267

Accessing objects in different orders

One of the easiest deadlocks to create, and consequently one of the easiest to prevent, is caused by accessing objects in a database in different operation orders inside of T-SQL code, inside of transactions, as shown in Listings 7.14 and 7.15.

```
BEGIN TRANSACTION

UPDATE    TableA
SET       Column1 = 1

SELECT    Column2
FROM      TableB
```

Listing 7.14: Transaction1 updates `TableA` then reads `TableB`.

```
BEGIN TRANSACTION

UPDATE    TableB
SET       Column2 = 1

SELECT    Column1
FROM      TableA
```

Listing 7.15: Transaction2 updates `TableB` then reads `TableA`.

Transaction1's **UPDATE** against `TableA` will result in an exclusive lock being held on the table until the transaction completes. At the same time, Transaction2 runs an **UPDATE** against `TableB`, which also results in an exclusive lock being held until the transaction completes. After completing the **UPDATE** to `TableA`, Transaction1 tries to read `TableB` but is blocked and unable to acquire the necessary shared lock, due to the exclusive lock being held by Transaction2. After completing its **UPDATE** to `TableB`, Transaction2 reads `TableA` and is also blocked, unable to acquire a shared lock due to the exclusive lock held by Transaction1. Since the two transactions are both blocking each other, the result is a

268

deadlock and the Lock Monitor will kill one of the two sessions, rolling back its trans-action to allow the other to complete.

When using explicit transactions in code, it is important that objects are always accessed in the same order, to prevent this type of deadlock from occurring.

Handling Deadlocks to Prevent Errors

In most cases, the same issues that cause severe blocking in the database, such as poor database design, lack of indexing, poorly designed queries, inappropriate isolation level and so on (all discussed in *Chapter 6*), are also the common causes of deadlocking. In most cases, by fixing such issues, we can prevent deadlocks from occurring. Unfortunately, by the time deadlocks become a problem, it may not be possible to make the necessary design changes to correct them.

Therefore, an important part of application and database design is defensive programming; a technique that anticipates and handles exceptions as a part of the general code base for an application or database. Defensive programming to handle deadlock exceptions can be implemented in two different ways:

* database-side, through the use of T-SQL **TRY...CATCH** blocks
* application-side, through the use of application **TRY...CATCH** blocks.

In either case, proper handling of the 1205 exception raised by SQL Server for the deadlock victim can help avoid `UnhandledException` errors in the application and the ensuing end-user phone calls to Help Desk or Support.

T-SQL TRY…CATCH blocks

Depending on how an application is designed, and whether there is separation between application code and database code, the simplest implementation of deadlock error handling could be via the use of **BEGIN TRY/CATCH** blocks inside of the T-SQL being executed.

This technique is most applicable in cases where an application calls stored procedures for all of its data access. In such cases, changing the code in a stored procedure so that it handles the deadlock exception doesn't require changes to application code, or recompiling and redistribution of the application. This greatly simplifies the implementation of such changes.

The best way to deal with a deadlock, within your error handling code, will depend on your application and its expected behavior in the event of a deadlock. One way of handling the deadlock would be to retry the transaction a set number of times before actually raising an exception back to the application for handling. The cross-locking situation associated with a deadlock generally only lasts a very short duration, usually timed in milliseconds so, more often than not, a subsequent attempt at executing the T-SQL code selected as a victim will succeed, and there will be no need to raise any exceptions to the application.

However, it is possible that the deadlock will continue to occur, and we need to avoid getting into an infinite loop, attempting repeatedly to execute the same failing code. To prevent this, a variable is used to count down from a maximum number of retry attempts; when zero is reached, an exception will be raised back to the application. This technique is demonstrated in Listing 7.16.

```
DECLARE @retries INT ;
SET @retries = 4 ;

WHILE ( @retries > 0 )
    BEGIN
```

```
        BEGIN TRY
            BEGIN TRANSACTION ;

       -- place sql code here
            SET @retries = 0 ;

            COMMIT TRANSACTION ;
        END TRY
        BEGIN CATCH
        -- Error is a deadlock
            IF ( ERROR_NUMBER() = 1205 )
                SET @retries = @retries - 1 ;

        -- Error is not a deadlock
            ELSE
                BEGIN
                    DECLARE @ErrorMessage NVARCHAR(4000) ;
                    DECLARE @ErrorSeverity INT ;
                    DECLARE @ErrorState INT ;

                    SELECT  @ErrorMessage = ERROR_MESSAGE() ,
                            @ErrorSeverity = ERROR_SEVERITY() ,
                            @ErrorState = ERROR_STATE() ;

                    -- Re-Raise the Error that caused the problem
                    RAISERROR (@ErrorMessage, -- Message text.
                       @ErrorSeverity, -- Severity.
                       @ErrorState -- State.
                       ) ;
                    SET @retries = 0 ;
                END

            IF XACT_STATE() <> 0
                ROLLBACK TRANSACTION ;
        END CATCH ;
    END ;
GO
```

Listing 7.16: TRY...CATCH handling of deadlock exceptions, in T-SQL.

271

Handling ADO.NET SqlExceptions in .NET code

While it is possible to handle deadlocks in SQL Server 2005 and 2008, using BEGIN TRY and BEGIN CATCH blocks, the same functionality doesn't exist in SQL Server 2000, and in any event it may not be acceptable to have the database engine retry the operation automatically. In either case, the client application should be coded to handle the deadlock exception that is raised by SQL Server.

There isn't much difference between the error handling in .NET and the error handling in T-SQL. A TRY...CATCH block is used to execute the SQL call from the application and catch any resulting exception raised by SQL Server. If the code should reattempt the operation in the event of a deadlock, a maximum number of retries should be set by a member variable that is decremented each time a deadlock is encountered.

The example in Listing 7.17 shows how to catch the SqlException in C#, but can be used as a model to handle deadlocks in other languages as well.

```
int retries = 4;
while (retries > 0)
{
  try
  {
    // place sql code here
    retries = 0;
  }
  catch (SqlException exception)
  {
    // exception is a deadlock
    if (exception.Number == 1205)
    {
        // Delay processing to allow retry.
        Thread.Sleep(500);
        retries --;
    }
    // exception is not a deadlock
    else
    {
```

```
            throw;
        }
    }
}
```

Listing 7.17: TRY...CATCH handling of deadlock exceptions, in C#.

Rather than retrying the operation, it may be desirable to log the exception in the Windows Application Event Log, or perhaps display a MessageBox dialog and determine whether or not to retry the operation, based on user input. These are two examples of how handling the deadlock exception in the application code allows for more flexibility over handling the deadlock in the database engine.

Controlling Deadlock Behavior with Deadlock Priority

There are circumstances (for example, a critical report that performs a long running SELECT that must complete even if it is the ideal deadlock victim) where it may be preferable to specify which process will be chosen as the deadlock victim in the event of a deadlock, rather than let SQL Server decide based purely on the cost of rollback. As demonstrated in Listing 7.18, SQL Server offers the ability to set, at the session or batch level, a deadlock priority using the SET DEADLOCK PRIORITY option.

```
-- Set a Low deadlock priority
SET DEADLOCK_PRIORITY LOW ;
GO

-- Set a High deadlock priority
SET DEADLOCK_PRIORITY HIGH ;
GO

-- Set a numeric deadlock priority
SET DEADLOCK_PRIORITY 2 ;
```

Listing 7.18: Setting deadlock priority.

A process running in a batch or session with a low deadlock priority will be chosen as the deadlock victim over one that is running with a higher deadlock priority. Like all other `SET` options in SQL Server, the **`DEADLOCK PRIORITY`** is only in effect for the current execution scope. If it is set inside of a stored procedure, then when the stored procedure execution completes, the priority returns to the original priority of the calling execution scope.

Note that SQL Server 2000 offers only two deadlock priorities; `Low` and `Normal`. This allows the victim to be determined by setting its priority to `Low`. SQL Server 2005 and 2008 however, have three named deadlock priorities; `Low`, `Normal`, and `High`, as well as a numeric range from -10 to +10, for fine-tuning the deadlock priority of different operations.

The deadlock priority is set at execution time, and all users have the permission to set a deadlock priority. This can be a problem if users have ad hoc query access to SQL Server, and set their deadlock priority higher than other processes, in order to prevent their own process from being selected as a victim.

Summary

This chapter has covered how to capture and interpret deadlock graph information in SQL Server to troubleshoot deadlocking. The most common deadlocks have also been covered to provide a foundation for troubleshooting other types of deadlocks that might occur. Most often, deadlocks are the result of a design problem in the database or code that can be fixed to prevent the deadlock from occurring. However, when changes to the database are not possible to resolve the deadlock, adding appropriate error handling in the application code reduces the impact caused by a deadlock occurring. The information included in this chapter should allow rapid and efficient troubleshooting of most deadlocks in SQL Server.

Chapter 8: Large or Full Transaction Log

A transaction log is a physical file in which SQL Server stores a record of all the transactions and data modifications performed on the database with which the log file is associated. It is arguably the single most important component of a SQL Server database, since the SQL Server engine uses it to ensure transaction durability (all valid, committed data will be preserved) and transaction rollback (the effects of any partial, uncommitted transactions, in the data file, can be "undone"), and the SQL Server DBA can use it to restore a database to a previous point in time, in the event of a disaster.

Unfortunately, however, it is also one of the most misunderstood and mismanaged components of SQL Server and the resulting problems are a frequent source of questions and pleas for help in the online technical forums. This chapter will examine, briefly, how the transaction log works, and then discuss the most common problems and forms of mismanagement that lead to runaway growth of the transaction log, including:

- performing index maintenance
- operating a database in FULL recovery mode, without taking log backups
- long-running or uncommitted transactions that prevent space in the transaction log from being reused.

Of course, if runaway growth is left unchecked your log file may expand until it eats up all of your disk space, at which point you'll receive the infamous 9002 (transaction log full) error, and the database will become read-only. We'll cover the correct ways to respond to runaway log growth and the 9002 error, and also explain why commonly given advice to truncate the log and shrink it is often dangerous.

Finally, we'll cover strategies for ensuring smooth and predictable growth of your log file, while minimizing problems associated with log fragmentation. In a busy database, a large transaction log may be a simple fact of life and, managed properly, this is not necessarily a bad thing, even if the log file space is unused a majority of the time.

Note that in order to focus on the topic of diagnosing and curing a runaway or full transaction log, we assume prior knowledge of related topics such as database recovery models. If you need a refresher, a good source is Gail Shaw's *Recovery Models* article, at HTTP://WWW.SQLSERVERCENTRAL.COM/ARTICLES/ADMINISTRATION/75461/.

How the Transaction Log Works

Whenever a change is made to a database object or the data it contains, not only is the data or object updated in the data file, but also details of the change are recorded as a sequence of log records in the transaction log. Each log record contains the details of a specific change that has been made to the database, allowing that change to be performed again as a part of REDO, or undone as a part of UNDO, during crash recovery. Other log records contain details regarding the ID of the transaction that performed the change, when that transaction started and ended, which pages were changed, the data changes that were made, and so on.

SQL Server, like most transactional relational database systems, utilizes the Write-Ahead Logging (WAL) protocol for all data modifications that occur in all databases.

> ### *The WAL protocol*
>
> *This is described by Chunder Mohan in the paper, "ARIES: A Transaction Recovery Method Supporting Fine-Granularity Locking and Partial Rollbacks Using Write-Ahead Logging"* (HTTP://WWW.CS.BERKELEY.EDU/~BREWER/CS262/ARIES.PDF).

The WAL protocol dictates that before a data page is changed in non-volatile storage, the information describing the change to the data page must first be written to stable storage, allowing the change to be redone or undone in the event of a failure. SQL Server implements this protocol by logging the information describing changes to database objects and data pages using log records in the transaction log. Before a transaction that changes data in the database completes, the log records describing the changes must first be hardened to disk. Changes made to the data pages in the buffer cache are then subsequently written out to permanent storage in the database files at checkpoint, or by the Lazy Writer process when the instance is under memory pressure in the buffer pool. Uncommitted changes can also be written to the data file by the CHECKPOINT or Lazy Writer processes, as long as the log records describing those changes have been first written to the transaction log file.

By always writing changes to the log file first, SQL Server has the basis for a mechanism that can guarantee that the effects of all committed transactions will ultimately be reflected in the data files, and that any data modifications on disk that originate from incomplete transactions, i.e. those for which neither a COMMIT nor a ROLLBACK have been issued, are ultimately *not* reflected in the data files.

This process of reconciling the contents of the data and log files occurs during the **database recovery process** (sometimes called crash recovery), which is initiated automatically whenever SQL Server restarts, or as part of the RESTORE command.

Any transactions that were committed, and therefore recorded in the transaction log, before the service was interrupted, or before the time to which the database is being manually restored, but are not reflected in the data files, will be "rolled forward" (redone). Likewise, any data changes in the database that are associated with uncommitted transactions will be "rolled back" (undone), by reading the relevant operations from the log file, and performing the reverse physical operation on the data.

In these ways, SQL Server ensures that either all the actions associated with a transaction succeed as a unit, or that they all fail, allowing SQL Server to return the database to a consistent state with regard to a particular point in time. As such, the transaction log represents one of the fundamental means by which SQL Server ensures data consistency and integrity during normal operation.

How SQL Server writes to the transaction log

The way in which SQL Server writes to the transaction log is basically different from the way it writes to data files. Writes to **data files** occur in a random fashion, since data changes affect random pages stored in the database. As such, the disk on which a data file is stored is regularly subject to multiple seek operations, which reposition the head to the correct disk cylinder in order to write the changes. Write performance can be improved by writing to the data files in a striped fashion utilizing a proportional fill methodology, where the amount of data written to a specific file is proportionate to the amount of free space in the file, compared to the amount of free space in other files in the filegroup.

By contrast, SQL Server writes to the **transaction log** sequentially, one record after another, and so a disk storing only a transaction log will rarely need to perform random seek operations. Certain operations, such as transaction log backups, Change Data Capture jobs and the replication log reader agent, will read the transaction log in a "random" fashion, but writing operations are generally sequential and can be much faster. This is why the recommended best practice is to segregate the log file from the data files and store the former on physical disks that are configured for high-speed sequential writes, as discussed in *Chapter 2, Disk I/O Configuration*.

The fact that writes are always sequential also means that SQL Server will only ever write to one transaction log file at a time. There is therefore no advantage, in terms of log writing performance, to having multiple transaction log files. The only reason to have more than one log file is if space considerations dictate the need for multiple log files, on different disks, in order to achieve the necessary log size for a database.

Understanding log truncation

Log truncation is the mechanism through which SQL Server marks the space inside of the transaction log as available for reuse by the database. The allocated space inside of a transaction log file is internally divided into smaller segments known as virtual log files (VLFs), and the process of log truncation is simply the act of marking a VLF as "inactive" and so making the space in that VLF available for reuse. It does not, as the term "truncation" might suggest, reduce the physical size of the transaction log.

A VLF can only be considered inactive if it contains no part of what is termed the **active log**. A full discussion of transaction log architecture is out of scope but, briefly, any log record relating to an open transaction is required for possible rollback and so must be part of the active log. In addition, there are various other activities in the database, including replication, mirroring and CDC (Change Data Capture) that use the transaction log and need transaction log records to remain around until they have been processed. These records will also be part of the active log.

As discussed previously, transaction log files are **sequential** files and each log record inserted into the log file is stamped with a **Logical Sequence Number (LSN)**. The log record with the lowest LSN (`MinLSN`) is defined as the oldest log record that may still be required for some database operation or activity, and this record marks the start of the active log. The log record with the highest LSN (i.e. the most recent record added) marks the end of the active log.

A log record is no longer part of the active log if each of the following three conditions is met:

1. It relates to a transaction that is committed, and so is no longer required for rollback.

2. It is no longer required by any other database process, including a transaction log backup when using `FULL` or `BULK LOGGED` recovery models.

3. It is older (i.e. has a lower LSN) than the `MinLSN` record.

Any VLF that contains no part of the active log is inactive and can be truncated, although the point at which this truncation occurs depends on the recovery model in use. In the `SIMPLE` recovery model, truncation can occur immediately upon `CHECKPOINT`; cached data pages are flushed to disk (after first writing the transaction details) and any VLFs that contain no part of the active log are truncated.

In the `FULL` (or `BULK LOGGED`) recovery model, once a full backup of the database has been taken, the inactive portion of the log is not marked as reusable on `CHECKPOINT`, because it is necessary to maintain a complete LSN chain, and so allow point-in-time recovery of the database. Truncation can only occur upon a `BACKUP LOG` operation. In this case, once the log backup has backed up the log, it marks any VLFs that are no longer necessary as inactive and hence reusable.

Later in the chapter, in the section entitled *Lack of log space reuse*, we'll discuss factors, such as uncommitted or long-running transactions, which can prevent space reuse and cause the log file to grow rapidly in size.

Sizing and growing the log

Whenever a log file needs to grow, and additional space is allocated, this space is divided evenly into VLFs, based on the amount of space that is being allocated. When additional space is allocated in small blocks, for example using a default ten percent auto-growth setting, the resulting transaction log may have a large number of small VLFs. When additional space is allocated in larger sizes, for example when initially sizing the log to 16 GB in a single operation, the resulting transaction log has a small number of larger VLFs.

> ### Transaction Log VLFs – too many or too few?
>
> *SQL Server MVP Kimberly Tripp discusses the impact of VLF sizes and provides guidance for how to properly manage VLF size in her blog post, "Transaction Log VLFs – too many or too few?"* (HTTP:// WWW.SQLSKILLS.COM/BLOGS/KIMBERLY/POST/TRANSACTION-LOG-VLFS-TOO-MANY-OR-TOO-FEW. ASPX).

A very high number of small VLFs, known as log file fragmentation, can have a considerable impact on performance, especially for crash recovery, restores and backups, particularly log backups; in other words, operations that read the log file. Conversely, if the database has only a few VLFs which are large in size, this can lead to problems related to rapid log growth in cases where truncation is delayed, for some reason (see the *Lack of log space reuse* section). For example, let's assume that each VLF is 1 GB in size. If all VLFs within the log file contain some part of the active log then the log file will grow in 1 GB steps until some of the existing VLFs cease to contain any part of the active log, at which point it can be truncated by the next log backup if using FULL recovery, or the next CHECKPOINT operation in SIMPLE recovery. As such, it's important that the log is sized appropriately initially, and grown in appropriately-sized steps, to minimize fragmentation but also avoid tying up large portions of the log for long periods.

There is also a second reason why it is very important to size the log appropriately and grow it in a very controlled fashion: for log files, each growth event is a relatively expensive operation. It is natural that both data and log files will grow in size over time, but whereas the process of adding new data files and expanding existing data files can be optimized to some degree by enabling instant file initialization, the same is not true for log files. When a data file is created or grows, the space allocated on disk has to be initialized, or zeroed out, by SQL Server to remove the remnants of any previous data. SQL Server 2005 introduced a new feature, **instant file initialization**, to allow the data files to allocate space on disk without having to fill the space with zeros. This feature however, does not apply to log files, which still require initialization and zeroing whenever space is allocated.

The transaction log, when properly managed, works in a circular fashion, and the starting point of the transactions that must be processed as a part of crash recovery is maintained in the database boot page. However, nothing tracks the position of the last log record requiring processing during crash recovery, so the log records are stamped with a parity bit that gets flipped when the transaction log reaches the end of the file and wraps back around to the beginning of the file. To prevent the possibility of introducing corruption by processing random data that existed previously on disk and matches the parity bit for the existing log records, the space being allocated must be zeroed out whenever the log file grows.

Why can't the transaction log use instant initialization?

*For further information about transaction log zeroing, see Paul Randal's blog post, "Search Engine Q&A #24: Why can't the transaction log use instant initialization?" (*HTTP://SQLSKILLS.COM/BLOGS/PAUL/ POST/SEARCH-ENGINE-QA-24-WHY-CANT-THE-TRANSACTION-LOG-USE-INSTANT-INITIALIZATION. ASPX*).*

Diagnosing a Runaway Transaction Log

If you are experiencing uncontrolled growth of the transaction log, it is due either to an incredibly high rate of log activity, or to factors that are preventing space in the log file from being reused, or both.

If the growth is due primarily to excessive log activity, you need to investigate whether there might be log activity that could be avoided, for example, by adjusting how you carry out bulk data and index maintenance operations, so that these operations are not fully logged (i.e. the BULK LOGGED recovery model is used for these operations). However, any bulk logged operation will immediately prevent point-in-time recovery to any point within a log file that contains records relating to the minimally logged operations. If this is not acceptable, you must simply accept a large log as a fact, and plan its growth and management (such as frequency of log backups) accordingly, as described in the *Proper Log Management* section later in this chapter.

If the growth is due to a lack of log space reuse, you need to find out what is preventing this reuse and take steps to correct the issue.

Excessive logging: index maintenance operations

Index maintenance operations are the second most common cause of transaction log usage and growth, especially in databases using the FULL recovery model. The amount of log space required to perform index maintenance depends on the following factors:

- **rebuild or reorganize** – index rebuilds generally use a lot more space in the log

- **recovery model** – if the risks to point-in-time recovery are understood and acceptable, then index rebuilds can be minimally logged by temporarily switching the database to run in BULK LOGGED recovery mode. Index reorganization, however, is always fully logged.

Index rebuilds

Rebuilding an index offline, using ALTER INDEX REBUILD (or the deprecated DBCC DBREINDEX in SQL Server 2000) drops the target index and rebuilds it from scratch (online index rebuilds do not drop the existing index until the end of the rebuild operation).

Logging and online index rebuilds

Online Index Rebuild is a fully-logged operation on SQL Server 2008 and later, whereas it is minimally logged in SQL Server 2005. Therefore, performing such operations in later SQL Server versions will require substantially more transaction log space. See: HTTP://SUPPORT.MICROSOFT.COM/KB/2407439.

In the FULL recovery model, index rebuilds can be a very resource intensive operation, requiring a lot of space in the transaction log. In the SIMPLE or BULK LOGGED recovery model, rebuilding an index is a minimally logged operation, meaning that only the allocations are logged, and not the actual pages changed, therefore reducing the amount of log space required by the operation.

If you switch to the SIMPLE model to perform an index rebuild, the LSN chain will be automatically broken. You'll only be able to recover your database to a point of time contained in the previous transaction log backup. To restart the chain, you'll need to switch back to the FULL model and immediately take a full or differential database backup.

If you switch to the BULK LOGGED model, the LSN chain is always maintained but there are still implications for your ability to perform point-in-time restores, since a log backup that contains a minimally logged operation can't be used to recover to a point in time. In other words, you won't be able to use the STOPAT option when restoring a log file that contains minimally logged operations. It is still possible to restore the entire transaction log backup to roll the database forward, and it is still possible to restore to a point in time in a subsequent log file, which doesn't contain any minimally logged operations. However, in the event of an application bug, or a user change that causes data to be deleted, around the same period as the minimally logged operation, it will not be possible to stop at a specific point in time in the log in which these changes are recorded, in order to recover the data that was deleted.

If the ability to perform a point-in-time recovery is paramount for a database, the BULK LOGGED recovery model should not be used for index rebuilds or any other minimally logged operation, unless it can be done at a time when there is no concurrent user activity in the database.

If the BULK LOGGED model is used, steps should be taken to minimize the time period where point-in-time restore is unavailable, and so minimize exposure to data loss. To do this, take a log backup in FULL mode, switch to BULK LOGGED, perform the index rebuild, then switch back to FULL and take another log backup.

A final important point to note is that an **ALTER INDEX REBUILD** operation occurs in a *single* transaction. If the index is large, this could represent a long-running transaction that will prevent space reuse in the log for its duration. This means that, even if you rebuild an index in **SIMPLE** mode, where you might think that the log should remain small since it is auto-truncated during a checkpoint operation, the log file can expand rapidly during the operation.

Index reorganization

In contrast to rebuilding an index, reorganizing (defragmenting) an index, using **ALTER INDEX REORGANIZE** (or the deprecated **DBCC INDEXDEFRAG** in SQL Server 2000) is always a fully-logged operation, regardless of the recovery model, and so the actual page changes are always logged. However, index reorganizations generally require less log space than an index rebuild, although this is a function of the amount of fragmentation that exists in the index; a heavily fragmented index will require more log space to reorganize than a minimally fragmented one.

Furthermore, the **ALTER INDEX REORGANIZE** operation is accomplished using multiple, shorter transactions. Therefore, when performed in conjunction with frequent log backups (or when working in **SIMPLE** mode), log space can be made available for reuse during the operation, so minimizing the size requirements for the transaction log during the operation.

For example, rebuilding a 20 GB index can require more than 20 GB of space for the rebuild operation because it occurs in a single transaction. However, reorganizing a 20 GB index requires much less log space because each page allocation change in the reorganization is a separate transaction, and so the log records can be truncated with frequent log backups, allowing the log space to be reused.

Strategies for controlling excessive logging

If your organization has zero tolerance to any potential data loss, then you'll have no choice but to perform index rebuild operations in the FULL recovery model, and plan your log size and growth appropriately. If your Service Level Agreements (SLAs) and Operational Level Agreements (OLAs) allow some potential for data loss, then switching to BULK LOGGED recovery at the start of index rebuild can minimize the amount of space required to rebuild the index. However, do so in a way that minimizes exposure to data loss, as discussed earlier.

If your database is in FULL recovery, and is subject to frequent index reorganization operations, then you might need to consider increasing the frequency with which you take log backups, especially during the time that the indexes are being rebuilt, in order to control the size of the log. Regardless of the frequency of log backups, the log will be at least as large as the largest index being rebuilt.

Regardless of the recovery model in use, one can minimize the impact of index maintenance operations on the transaction log by reorganizing rather than rebuilding, if possible, and by only maintaining those indexes that really need it.

Microsoft has provided guidelines that can be used for most, but not all, environments for determining when to rebuild an index versus when to reorganize it to minimize the impact of index maintenance operations. These guidelines can be found in the Books Online Topic, *Reorganizing and Rebuilding Indexes* (HTTP://TECHNET.MICROSOFT.COM/ EN-US/LIBRARY/MS189858.ASPX). They state that for fragmentation levels greater than 5 percent but less than or equal to 30 percent, you should reorganize the index, and for fragmentation levels greater than 30 percent, you should rebuild it.

It's also worth noting that rebuilding small indexes is generally not worthwhile. The commonly cited threshold is around 1,000 pages. These values are based on recommendations made by Paul Randal while he managed the storage engine development team at Microsoft, and which are documented in Books Online. Note, though, that this is guideline advice only and may not be appropriate for all environments, as discussed by

Paul in his blog post, *Where do the Books Online index fragmentation thresholds come from?* (HTTP://WWW.SQLSKILLS.COM/BLOGS/PAUL/POST/WHERE-DO-THE-BOOKS-ONLINE-INDEX-FRAGMENTATION-THRESHOLDS-COME-FROM.ASPX).

If you use the SSMS Maintenance Plans Wizard for index maintenance, it is an all-or-nothing process: you either rebuild or reorganize all indexes in your database (and all databases in the maintenance plan) or you rebuild none of them. A better approach may be to use the `sys.dm_db_index_physical_stats` DMV to investigate fragmentation and so determine a rebuild/reorganize strategy based on need.

Ola Hallengren's free maintenance scripts

A comprehensive set of free maintenance scripts is made available online by Ola Hallengren. Ola's scripts demonstrate how to use `sys.dm_db_index_physical_stats` *to perform index analysis for intelligent maintenance, and can be used as a replacement for Database Maintenance Plans created by the wizards in SSMS* (HTTP://OLA.HALLENGREN.COM).

Lack of log space reuse

If you suspect log growth is being caused by the log space not being reused, your first job is to find out what's preventing reuse. Start by querying `sys.databases`, as shown in Listing 8.1, and see what the value of the column `log_reuse_wait_desc` is for the database mentioned in the error message.

```
DECLARE @DatabaseName VARCHAR(50) ;
  SET @DatabaseName = 'VeryImportant'

  SELECT name ,
         recovery_model_desc ,
         log_reuse_wait_desc
  FROM   sys.databases
  WHERE  name = @DatabaseName
```

Listing 8.1: Examining the value of the `log_reuse_wait_desc` column.

The value of the `log_reuse_wait_desc` column will show the current reason why log space cannot be reused. It is possible more than one thing is preventing log reuse. The `sys.databases` view will only show one of the reasons. It is therefore possible to resolve one problem, query `sys.databases` again and see a different `log_reuse_wait` reason.

The possible values for `log_reuse_wait_desc` are listed in Books Online (HTTP:// MSDN.MICROSOFT.COM/EN-US/LIBRARY/MSI78534.ASPX), but we'll cover the most common causes here, and explain how to safely ensure that space can start to get reused.

FULL recovery model without log backups

If the value returned for `log_reuse_wait_desc`, from the previous `sys.databases` query, is `Log Backup`, then you are suffering from one of the most common causes of a full or large transaction log, namely operating a database in the `FULL` recovery model (or less common, but still possible, the `BULK_LOGGED` recovery model), without taking transaction log backups.

It varies, depending on the edition of SQL Server that is installed, but the `model` database is configured in `FULL` recovery mode at installation, for many editions. Since the `model` database is a template database that is used to create new databases in SQL Server, this configuration is inherited from `model`, by the new database.

Using the `FULL` recovery model is a recommended practice for most production database environments, since it allows for point-in-time recovery of the database, minimizing data loss in the event of a disaster. However, a common mistake is then to adopt a backup strategy consisting entirely of full (and possibly differential) database backups without taking frequent transaction log backups. There are two big problems with this strategy:

I. **Taking full database backups only protects the contents of the data file, not the log file.** The only way to properly protect the data that has changed since the last full or differential backup, which will be required for point-in-time restores, is to perform a log backup.

2. **Full database backups do not truncate the transaction log.** Only a log backup will cause the log file to be truncated. Without the latter, space in the log file will never be marked for reuse, and the log file will constantly grow in size.

In order to perform a point-in-time recovery **and** control the size of the log, transaction log backups must be taken in conjunction with full and/or differential database backups.

If you do discover that a lack of log backups is the cause of your log growth problems, the first thing to do is to verify that the database in question really does need the ability to recover to a point in time during a restore, and therefore needs to be operating in FULL recovery. If it doesn't, then switch to using the SIMPLE recovery model, where the inactive portion of the transaction log is automatically marked as reusable, at checkpoint.

If the database does need to operate in the FULL recovery model, then start taking log backups. The frequency of the transaction log backups depends on a number of factors such as the frequency of data changes, and on SLAs for acceptable data loss in the event of a crash. Also, you should take steps to ensure that the log growth is controlled and predictable in future, as described in the *Proper Log Management* section, later in the chapter.

Active transactions

If the value returned for log_reuse_wait_desc is ACTIVE_TRANSACTION, then you are suffering from the second most common cause of a full or large transaction log in SQL Server: long-running or uncommitted transactions. As discussed in the Understanding log truncation section of this chapter, a VLF inside the transaction log can only be truncated when it contains no part of the active log, and if the database is using the FULL or BULK LOGGED recovery models, this truncation only occurs when the transactions contained in the VLF have been committed and backed up. Long-running transactions in a database delay truncation of the VLFs that contain the log records generated after the start of the transaction, including the log records generated by changes to data in the database by other sessions, even when those changes have been committed. Additionally, the amount of space required by a long-running transaction will be increased by space reservations for "compensation log records," which are the log records that would be generated if the transaction were rolled back in the system. This reservation is required to ensure that the transaction can be reverted successfully without running out of log space during the rollback.

Another common cause of the `Active Transaction` value for `log_reuse_wait_desc` is the presence of "orphaned" explicit transactions that somehow never got committed. Applications that allow for user input inside a transaction are especially prone to this kind of problem.

Long-running transactions

One of the most common operations that results in a long-running transaction, which also generates large numbers of log records in a database is archiving or purging of data from a database. Data retention tends to be an afterthought in database design, usually being considered after the database has been active for a period of time and is approaching the capacity limits of the available storage on a server.

Usually, when the need to archive data arises, the first reaction is to remove the unneeded data from the database using a single `DELETE` statement, as shown in Listing 8.2.

```
DELETE   ExampleTable
WHERE    DateTimeCol < GETDATE() - 60
```

Listing 8.2: Bulk data deletion.

Depending on the number of rows that exist in the date range to be deleted, this can easily become a long-running transaction that will cause transaction log growth issues, even when the database is using the `SIMPLE` recovery model. The problem can be exacerbated by the presence of cascading `FOREIGN KEY` constraints or auditing triggers. If the table from which data is being deleted is referenced by other tables, using `FOREIGN KEY` constraints that are designed to CASCADE ON DELETE, then details of the rows that are deleted through the cascading constraint will also be logged. If the table has a DELETE trigger on it, for auditing data changes, the operations being performed during the triggers execution will also be logged.

To minimize the impact on the transaction log, the data purge operation should be broken down into a number of shorter, individual transactions. There are a number of ways to break a long-running transaction down into smaller batches. If cascading constraints or a DELETE trigger exist for a table, we can perform the DELETE operation inside of a loop, to delete one day of data at a time, as shown in Listing 8.3.

```
DECLARE @StopDate DATETIME ,
    @PurgeDate DATETIME
SELECT @PurgeDate = DATEADD(DAY, DATEDIFF(DAY, 0, MIN(DateTimeCol)), 0) ,
       @StopDate = DATEADD(DAY, DATEDIFF(DAY, 0, GETDATE()) - 60, 0)
FROM    ExampleTable

WHILE @PurgeDate < @StopDate
    BEGIN
        DELETE   ExampleTable
        WHERE    DateTimeCol < @PurgeDate
        SELECT   @PurgeDate = DATEADD(DAY, 1, @PurgeDate)
    END
```

Listing 8.3: Breaking down data purges into smaller transactions.

Using this model for purging data, the duration of each DELETE transaction is only the time required to delete a single day's data from the table, plus the time required for any triggers or cascading constraints to perform their operations. If the database uses the SIMPLE recovery model, the log records generated by each daily purge will be truncated the next time checkpoint occurs. If the database uses the FULL or BULK LOGGED recovery model, the log records generated by each daily purge will be truncated after the next log backup that occurs for the database, if no part of the active log exists inside the VLFs affected by the purge.

When cascading constraints or auditing triggers are not a factor in the process, a different method can be used to purge the data from the table while minimizing the transaction duration. Instead of performing a single day DELETE operation, which can affect more or less data depending on the number of rows that exist for a specific date, the TOP operator can be used inside the DELETE statement to limit the number of rows affected by each loop of the operation. By capturing into a variable the number of rows affected by the DELETE operation, using @@ROWCOUNT, the operation can continue to purge data from the table in small batches, until the value of @@ROWCOUNT is less than the number of rows specified in the TOP clause of the DELETE statement, as shown in Listing 8.4.

This method only works when triggers and cascading constraints aren't being used because, when they are, the result of @@ROWCOUNT will not be the actual rows deleted from the base table, but instead the number of rows that are affected by the trigger execution or through enforcing the cascading constraint.

```
DECLARE @Criteria DATETIME ,
    @RowCount INT
SELECT  @Criteria = GETDATE() - 60 ,
        @RowCount = 10000
WHILE @RowCount = 10000
    BEGIN
        DELETE TOP ( 10000 )
        FROM    ExampleTable
        WHERE   DateTimeCol < @Criteria
        SELECT  @RowCount = @@ROWCOUNT
    END
```

Listing 8.4: Using the TOP operator inside the DELETE statement for data purges.

These methods can be used in any edition of SQL Server 2000, 2005, and 2008 to minimize transaction duration during data purge operations.

However, if the database is SQL Server 2005 or 2008 **Enterprise Edition**, and the data purging process will be run regularly, then an even better way to purge the data is to partition the table using a sliding window partition on the column being used to delete the data. This will have even less impact on the transaction log, since the partition containing the data can be switched out of the table and truncated, which is a metadata-only operation.

Managing archiving

It is well outside the scope of this chapter to delve into full, automated archiving scheme, but a possible archiving process could involve partitioning, and duplicate schemas between tables, allowing a partition to be switched out of one table and into another one, minimizing the active portion of data in the main OLTP table, but reducing the archiving process to being metadata changes only. Kimberley Tripp has produced a detailed white paper called "Partitioned Tables and Indexes in SQL Server 2005," which also covers the sliding window technique, (see HTTP://MSDN.MICROSOFT.COM/EN-US/LIBRARY/ MS345146(V=SQL.90).ASPX).

Uncommitted transactions

By default, SQL Server wraps any data modification statement in an implicit transaction to ensure that, in the event of a failure, the changes already made at the point of failure can all be rolled back, returning the data to a consistent state. If the changes succeed, the implicit transaction is committed to the database. In contrast to implicit transactions, which occur automatically, explicit transactions are created in code to wrap multiple changes into a single transaction, ensuring that all the changes can be undone by issuing a ROLLBACK command, or persisted by issuing a COMMIT for the transaction.

When used properly, explicit transactions can ensure that data modifications that span multiple tables complete successfully as a unit, or not at all. When used incorrectly, however, orphaned transactions can be left active in the database, preventing truncation of the transaction log, and so resulting in the transaction log growing or filling up. There are a number of cases that can result in an orphaned transaction in SQL Server, and it's beyond the scope of this chapter to investigate them in full detail.

However, some of the most common causes are:

- application timeouts caused by a long-running transaction

- incorrect error handling in TSQL or application code

- failure during trigger execution

- linked server failures resulting in orphaned distributed transactions

- no corresponding **COMMIT/ROLLBACK** statement to a **BEGIN TRANSACTION** command.

Once a transaction is created it will continue to remain active until a **COMMIT** or **ROLLBACK** statement is issued on the connection that created the transaction, or the connection disconnects from the SQL Server. It is critical that you understand this last point when troubleshooting orphaned transactions, since modern applications generally utilize connection pooling, keeping connections to the SQL Server in a pool for reuse by the application, even when the application code calls the **Close()** method on the connection. Even though the connection is reset before being added or returned to the application's connection pool, open transactions continue to exist in the database if they have not been properly terminated.

Identifying the active transaction

The fastest way to identify whether transaction log growth is being caused by an orphaned (or just long-running) transaction is to use **DBCC OPENTRAN**. This command can accept the database name as an input parameter in the format **DBCC OPENTRAN(DatabaseName)** where **DatabaseName** is the name of the database to check for open transactions.

If an active transaction exists in the database, this command will output information similar to the following:

```
Transaction information for database 'TestDatabase'.

Oldest active transaction:
    SPID (server process ID): 105
    UID (user ID) : -1
    Name          : user_transaction
    LSN           : (4212:44992:2)
    Start time    : Mar 26 2010  2:37:31:907AM
    SID           : 0x0105000000000000515000000c5dc918918d95a068b7acf204f730000
DBCC execution completed. If DBCC printed error messages, contact your system
administrator.
```

Only the oldest active transaction is reported by DBCC OPENTRAN, and the primary indicator of whether or not the active transaction is problematic is the Start Time. Generally, uncommitted transactions that become problematic with regard to transaction log growth have been open for a long period of time.

The other important piece of information is the SPID (server process ID), which is the session that created the open transaction. We can use the SPID to determine whether the transaction is actually an orphaned transaction or just a long-running one, by querying the sysprocesses view (in SQL Server 2000) or the sys.dm_exec_sessions and sys.dm_exec_connections DMVs in SQL Server 2005 and 2008, as shown in Listing 8.5. Note that the sysprocesses view is still available in SQL Server 2005 and 2008 for backwards compatibility.

```
-- SQL 2000 sysprocess query
SELECT  spid ,
        status ,
        hostname ,
        program_name ,
        loginame ,
        login_time ,
        last_batch ,
        ( SELECT    text
```

```
            FROM        ::
                        fn_get_sql(sql_handle)
            ) AS [sql_text]
    FROM    sysprocesses
    WHERE spid = <SPID>

    -- SQL 2005/2008 DMV query
    SELECT  s.session_id ,
            s.status ,
            s.host_name ,
            s.program_name ,
            s.login_name ,
            s.login_time ,
            s.last_request_start_time ,
            s.last_request_end_time ,
            t.text
    FROM    sys.dm_exec_sessions s
            JOIN sys.dm_exec_connections c ON s.session_id = c.session_id
            CROSS APPLY sys.dm_exec_sql_text(c.most_recent_sql_handle) t
    WHERE s.session_id = <SPID>
```

Listing 8.5: Identifying orphaned or long-running transactions using the DMVs.

If the SPID is in a runnable, running, or suspended status, then it is likely that the source of the problem is a long-running, rather than orphaned, transaction. However, further investigation of the command text will be needed to make the final determination. It is possible that an earlier transaction failed and the connection was reset, for use under connection pooling, and that the currently executing statement is not associated with the open transaction.

In SQL Server 2005 and 2008, the sys.dm_tran_session_transactions and sys. dm_tran_database_transactions DMVs can be used to gather information specific to the open transaction including the transaction start time, number of log records used by the open transaction, as well as the bytes of log space used, as shown in Listing 8.6.

```
SELECT   st.session_id ,
         st.is_user_transaction ,
         dt.database_transaction_begin_time ,
         dt.database_transaction_log_record_count ,
         dt.database_transaction_log_bytes_used
FROM     sys.dm_tran_session_transactions st
         JOIN sys.dm_tran_database_transactions dt
                  ON st.transaction_id = dt.transaction_id
                     AND dt.database_id = DB_ID('master')
WHERE  st.session_id = <SPID>
```

Listing 8.6: Gathering information about the open transaction.

If the open transaction was created before the last request start time, it is likely to be an orphaned transaction.

Unless the application was specifically designed to check for, and handle, orphaned transactions, the only way to clear the transaction is to KILL the session which will cause the transaction to roll back as the connection terminates, allowing the space in the log be made available for reuse, during the next log backup. However, the ramifications of performing the rollback must be understood.

Other possible causes of log growth

In addition to those previously identified, there are a few other problems that may prevent reuse of space in the log, and so lead to excessive log growth.

Why is my transaction log full?

For further discussion on these issues, please see Gail Shaw's article, "Why is my transaction log full?" at HTTP://WWW.SQLSERVERCENTRAL.COM/ARTICLES/TRANSACTION+LOG/72488/.

Replication

During transactional replication, it is the job of the log reader agent to read the transaction log, looking for log records that are associated with changes that need to be replicated to subscribers (i.e. are "pending replication"). Once the changes are replicated, it marks the log entry as "replicated." Slow or delayed log reader activity can lead to records being left as "pending replication" for long periods, during which time they will remain part of the active log, and so the parent VLF cannot be truncated. A similar problem exists for log records required by the Change Data Capture (CDC) feature.

In either case, the `log_reuse_wait_desc` column of `sys.databases` will show `REPLICATION` as the root cause of the problem. The problem will also reveal itself in the form of bottlenecks in the throughput performance of the transaction log disk array, specifically, delayed read operations under concurrent write loads. As explained in *Chapter 2*, writes to the log file occur sequentially, but read operations associated with the log reader agent and log backups read the file sequentially as well. Having sequential reads and writes occurring at the same time can, depending on the level of activity in the system and the size of the active portion of the log, result in random I/O activity as the disk heads have to change position to read from the beginning of the active log and then write to the end of the active log. The disk latency counters, explained in *Chapter 2*, can be used to troubleshoot this type of problem.

The first step in troubleshooting these `REPLICATION` wait issues is to verify that the log reader SQL Agent jobs are actually running. If they are not, attempt to start them. If this fails, you'll need to find out why.

If the jobs are running but the `REPLICATION` waits persist, and the transaction log is growing rapidly, you need to find some way to get the relevant log entries marked as "replicated" so that space in their parent VLFs can be reused. Unfortunately, there is no perfect solution that will avoid side effects to replication or CDC in the environment, but you could try one of the solutions below.

- In the case of transactional replication, the `sp_repldone` command can be used to mark all of the log records currently waiting on the log reader to process them as processed, but this will require re-initialization of the subscribers, using a snapshot, to resynchronize the replication topology. With CDC, this command will not resolve the problem with transaction log growth.

- Disabling CDC or replication and performing a manual resynchronization of the data. Once CDC or replication has been removed, the pending replication log records in the transaction log will no longer be pending and can be cleared by the next log backup in **FULL** or **BULK LOGGED** recovery or **CHECKPOINT** operation in **SIMPLE** recovery. However, the trade-off is that the environment will require manual synchronization of the data for CDC, or it will require re-initialization of the subscribers for replication, if these features are added back to the database.

Remember that simply switching to the **SIMPLE** recovery model, in the hope of truncating the log, will not work since replication and CDC are both supported using **SIMPLE** recovery, and the log records will continue to be required until the log reader SQL Agent process harvests them.

Snapshot Replication schema change issue

There is a known issue with Snapshot Replication in SQL Server 2005 that causes log entries that are marked for replication of schema changes not to be unmarked when the changes are replicated. This problem is explained in the following blog post that also explains how to work around the issue by using `sp_repldone`: *"Size of the Transaction Log Increasing and cannot be truncated or Shrinked due to Snapshot Replication"* (HTTP://BLOGS.MSDN.COM/B/SQLSERVERFAQ/ARCHIVE/2009/06/01/SIZE-OF-THE-TRANSACTION-LOG-INCREASING-AND-CANNOT-BE-TRUNCATED-OR-SHRINKED-DUE-TO-SNAPSHOT-REPLICATION.ASPX).

ACTIVE_BACKUP_OR_RESTORE

When the `log_reuse_wait_desc` column shows `ACTIVE_BACKUP_OR_RESTORE` as the current wait description, a long-running full or differential backup of the database is the most likely cause of the log reuse problems. During a full or differential backup of the database, the backup process delays log truncation so that the active portion of the transaction log can be included as a part of the full backup. This allows changes made to database pages during the backup operation to be undone when the backup is restored `WITH RECOVERY`, to bring the database to a consistent state. If such waits are causing persistent problems, you'll need to investigate ways to optimize the backup process, such as by improving the performance of the backups (via backup compression) or improving the performance of the underlying disk I/O system.

DATABASE_MIRRORING

When the `log_reuse_wait_desc` column shows `DATABASE_MIRRORING`, as the current wait description, synchronous database mirroring operations may be the cause of the log reuse issues.

In synchronous mirroring, transactions on the principal are only committed once their related log records have been transferred to the mirror database. If the connection to the mirror is slow or broken, or the mirroring session is suspended, then a large number of log records on the principal will remain part of the active log, preventing log space reuse, until they are copied over to the mirror.

In such cases, I would first check the status of the mirroring session for the affected database(s). If they are not synchronizing correctly, then you will need to troubleshoot the cause of the failed connection between the principal and the mirror. One of the most common problems with database mirroring, when certificates are used to secure the endpoints, is the expiration of the certificates, requiring that they be recreated. A full discussion of troubleshooting mirroring connectivity problems is outside of the scope of this chapter but, unless the databases are properly synchronizing so that the log records are being sent to the mirror, the active portion of the transaction log on the principal will continue to grow and not be able to be truncated without breaking the mirroring setup.

If the transaction rate on the principal greatly exceeds the rate at which log records can be transferred to the mirror, then the log on the principal can grow rapidly. If the mirror server is being used for reporting, by creating snapshots, verify that the disk I/O configuration for the mirror is not saturated, by using the latency counters as explained in *Chapter 2*. If this is where the problem is, eliminating use of the mirror server for reporting may provide temporary relief of the problem. If the problem is strictly the sheer volume of transactions and the database is not running on SQL Server 2008 or higher, then upgrading may be able to resolve the problem due to the use of log stream compression in SQL Server 2008 and beyond.

The best approach is to determine the cause of the mirroring issue and resolve it. For example, tuning operations that produce a significant number of log records, such as bulk loading data, or reorganizing indexes, may reduce the impact to the system overall during the operation.

Handling a "Transaction Log Full" Error

In the worst case, transaction log mismanagement or sudden, rapid, log growth can cause a transaction log to grow and grow and eventually eat up all available space on its drive. At this point it can grow no more, you'll encounter Error 9002, the **transaction log full** error, and the database will become read-only.

Despite the urgency of this problem, it's important to react calmly, and avoid the sort of "spontaneous" solutions that are covered in the following section, *Mismanagement or What Not To Do*. Obviously the pressing concern is to allow SQL Server to continue to write to the log, by making more space available. The first port of call is to establish if the cause is a lack of log backups. Run the query in Listing 8.1 and if the value for the `log_reuse_wait_desc` column is `Log Backup` then this is the likely cause of the issue.

A query to the backupset table (HTTP://MSDN.MICROSOFT.COM/EN-US/LIBRARY/MS186299. ASPX) in the MSDB database, as shown in Listing 8.7, will confirm whether or not log backups are being taken on the database, and when the last one was taken.

```
USE msdb ;
SELECT    backup_set_id ,
          backup_start_date ,
          backup_finish_date ,
          backup_size ,
          recovery_model ,
          [type]
FROM      dbo.backupset
WHERE     database_name = 'DatabaseName'
```

Listing 8.7:   Determine when the last log backup was taken.

In the type column, a D represents a database backup, L a log backup and I a differential backup. If log backups aren't being taken, or are being taken very infrequently, then your best course of action is to take a log backup (assuming the database is operating in FULL or BULK LOGGED recovery model). Hopefully, this will free up substantial space within the log and you can then implement an appropriate log backup scheme, and log file growth management strategy.

If, for some reason, it is not possible to perform a log backup due to a lack of disk space, or the time it would take to perform a log backup exceeds the acceptable time to resolve the problem, then it might, depending on the disaster recovery policy for the database in question, be acceptable to force a truncation of the log by temporarily switching the database to the SIMPLE recovery model in order that inactive VLFs in the log can be truncated on CHECKPOINT. You can then switch the recovery model back to FULL and perform a new full database backup (or a differential backup, assuming a full backup was taken at some previous time) to restart the log chain for point-in-time recovery. Of course, you'll still need to investigate the problem fully, in order to make sure that the space isn't simply eaten up again.

Bear in mind also that, as discussed previously, if the problem preventing space reuse is anything other than `Log Backup`, then this technique won't work, since those records will simply remain part of the active log, preventing truncation.

If a lack of log backups isn't the problem, or taking a log backup doesn't solve the problem, then investigating the cause will require a little more time. If you can easily and quickly make extra space on the log drive, by shifting off other files, or adding capacity to the current log drive, or adding an addition log file on a different disk array, then this will buy you the bit of breathing space you need to get the database out of read-only mode, and perform a log backup.

If a log backup fails to free up space, you need to find out what is preventing space reuse in the log. Interrogate `sys.databases` (Listing 8.1) to find out if anything is preventing reuse of space in the log, and take appropriate action, as described throughout the previous *Lack of log space reuse* section.

If this reveals nothing, you'll need to investigate further and find out which operations are causing the excessive logging that led to the log growth, as described in the *Diagnosing a Runaway Transaction Log* section.

Ultimately, having resolved any space reuse issue, you may still be left with a log file that is consuming the vast majority of the space on the drive. As a one-off measure, i.e. assuming steps will be taken to ensure proper management of log growth in the future (see the *Proper Log Management* section, shortly), it is acceptable to use DBCC SHRINKFILE (see HTTP://MSDN.MICROSOFT.COM/EN-US/LIBRARY/MS189493.ASPX) to reclaim the space used by a bloated transaction log file.

You can either specify a `target_size` to which to shrink the log file, or you can specify 0 (zero) as the target size and shrink the log to its smallest possible size, and then immediately resize it to a sensible size using ALTER DATABASE. The latter is the recommended way, as it minimizes fragmentation of the log file. This fragmentation issue is the main reason why you should *never* schedule regular DBCC SHRINKFILE tasks as a means of controlling the size of the log; this is discussed in more detail in the next section.

Mismanagement or What Not To Do

Unfortunately, a quick search of the Internet for "Transaction Log Full" will return a number of forums threads, blog posts, and even articles published on seemingly reputable SQL Server sites, which recommend remedial action that is, frankly, dangerous. We'll cover a few of the more popular suggestions here.

Detach database, delete log file

The idea here is that you clear all users off the database, detach the database (or shut it down), delete the log file (or rename it) and then re-attach the database, causing a new log file to be created at whatever size is dictated by the `model` database. This is arguably the most appalling of all the terrible ways to handle a full transaction log. It can result in the database failing to start, leaving it in the `RECOVERY_PENDING` state.

Depending on whether or not the database had been cleanly shut down at the time of the log deletion, the database may not be able to perform the `UNDO` and `REDO` operations that are a normal part of the database recovery process, because the transaction log is missing, and so can't return the database to a consistent state. When the log file is missing, and the database requires the transaction log to perform crash recovery, the database will fail to start up properly and the only recourse will be to restore the database from the most recent backup available, which will most likely result in data loss.

Creating, detaching, re-attaching, and fixing a suspect database

Under specific circumstances, it may be possible to hack the existing database into a configuration that allows the transaction log to be rebuilt, although it may compromise the integrity of the data contained in the database. This type of operation is, at best, a last-ditch effort that may be used when there is absolutely no other way of recovering the database data, and it is not a recommended practice of the authors, technical editors, or anyone else involved in the authoring of this book. For an explanation of how to attempt hacking a database back into SQL Server where the transaction log file has been deleted, see Paul Randal's blog post, "Creating, detaching, re-attaching, and fixing a suspect database"

(HTTP://WWW.SQLSKILLS.COM/BLOGS/PAUL/POST/TECHED-DEMO-CREATING-DETACHING-RE-ATTACH-ING-AND-FIXING-A-SUSPECT-DATABASE.ASPX).

Forcing log file truncation

In SQL Server 2000, `BACKUP LOG WITH TRUNCATE_ONLY` was a supported way of forcing SQL Server to truncate the transaction log, while the database was operating in the `FULL` or `BULK LOGGED` model, without actually making a backup copy of the contents of the log; the records in the truncated VLFs are simply discarded. So, unlike with a normal log backup, you're destroying your LSN chain and will only be able to restore to a point in time in any previous log backup files. Also, even though the database is set to `FULL` (or `BULK LOGGED`) recovery, it will actually, from that point on, operate in an auto-truncate mode, continuing to truncate inactive VLFs on checkpoint. In order to get the database operating in `FULL` recovery again, and restart the LSN chain, you'd need to perform a full (or differential) backup.

This command was often used without people realizing the implications it had for disaster recovery, and it was deprecated in SQL Server 2005 and removed from SQL Server 2008. Unfortunately, an even more insidious variation of this technique, which continues to be supported, has crept up to take its place, and that is `BACKUP LOG TO DISK='NUL'`, where `NUL` is a "virtual file" that discards any data that is written to it. The really nasty twist to this technique is that, unlike with `BACKUP LOG WITH`

TRUNCATE_ONLY, SQL Server is unaware that the log records have simply been discarded. As far as SQL Server is concerned, a log backup has been performed, the log records are safely stored in a backup file so the LSN chain is intact, and any inactive VLFs in the live log can safely be truncated. Any subsequent, conventional log backups will succeed but will be entirely useless from the point of view of disaster recovery since a log backup file is "missing" and so the database can only be restored to some point in time covered by the last standard log backup that was taken before BACKUP LOG TO DISK='NUL' was issued.

Do not use either of these techniques. The right way to "force" log truncation is to temporarily switch the database into the SIMPLE recovery model, as discussed earlier.

Scheduled shrinking of the transaction log

As discussed in the *Handling a "Transaction Log Full" error* section, in rare circumstances where transaction log growth has occurred due to a lack of management, and where the log growth is currently being actively managed, using DBCC SHRINKFILE to reclaim the space used by the transaction log file is an acceptable operation.

However, the transaction log should never be shrunk using DBCC SHRINKFILE, or a database maintenance plan step to shrink the database, as part of normal, scheduled maintenance operations. The reason for this is that every time you shrink the log, it will need to immediately grow again to store log records for subsequent transactions and every log. If auto-growth is being relied upon solely for transaction log growth (see the next section for a fuller discussion), excessive VLFs can accumulate in the log file and this log fragmentation will impact the performance of any process that needs to read the log file and, if fragmentation gets really bad, possibly even the performance of data modifications. Also, as discussed previously in the *Sizing and growing the log* section, the transaction log cannot take advantage of instant file initialization, so all log growths incur the cost to zero-byte the storage space being allocated.

The best practice for the transaction log file continues to be to size it appropriately up front so it does not have to grow under normal operations, and then to monitor its usage periodically to determine if the need to grow it manually occurs, allowing you to determine the appropriate growth size and determine the number and size of VLFs that will be added to the log file.

Proper Log Management

In the absence of any unexpected operations or problems that have resulted in unusual log growth (replication problems, uncommitted transactions, and so on, as discussed earlier), if the transaction log associated with a FULL recovery model database fills up, and is forced to grow, there are really only two causes:

- the size of the log file was too small to support the volume of data changes that were occurring in the database
- the frequency of log backups was insufficient to allow rapid reuse of space within the log file.

The best thing to do, if you can't increase the frequency of the log backups by decreasing the amount of time between log backups, is to manually grow the log file to a size that prevents it from having to grow using auto-growth when under load, and then leave the log file that size. Having a large transaction log file that has been properly grown to minimize the number of VLFs is not a bad thing, even if the log file has free space a majority of the time.

When configuring the initial size of the transaction log for a database, it is important to take into account the size of the largest table in the database, and whether or not index maintenance operations will be performed. As a rule of thumb, the transaction log should be sized to 1.5 times the size of the largest index or table in the database, to allow for logging requirements to rebuild the index under FULL recovery.

In addition to the initial sizing requirements, it is important to monitor and adjust the size of the transaction log periodically to fit the size of the database as it grows. There are a couple of problems with the auto-growth settings that a database will inherit from `model`, which is currently to grow in steps of 10% of the current transaction log size:

- initially, when the log file is small, the incremental growth will be small, resulting in the creation of a large number of small VLFs in the log, causing the fragmentation issues discussed earlier

- when the log file is very large, the growth increments will be correspondingly large; since the transaction log has to be zeroed out during initialization, large growth events can take time, and if the log can't be grown fast enough this can result in 9002 (transaction log full) errors and even in the auto-growth timing out and being rolled back.

The auto-growth settings should be configured explicitly to a fixed size that allows the log file to grow quickly, if necessary, while also minimizing the number of VLFs being added to the log file for each growth event.

To minimize the chances of a timeout occurring during normal transaction log growth, you should measure how long it takes to grow the transaction log by a variety of set sizes while the database is operating under normal workload, and based on the current I/O subsystem configuration. In cases where the necessary zero-initialization performance characteristics are not known for a database, I recommend, as a general rule, a fixed auto-growth size of 512 MB.

Ultimately, though, remember that auto-growth should be configured as a security net only, allowing the system to automatically grow the log file when you are unable to respond manually. Auto-growth is not a replacement for appropriate monitoring and management of the transaction log file size.

Summary

The transaction log for a SQL Server database is critical to the operation of the database and the ability to minimize data loss in the event of a disaster. Proper management of log backups and sizing of the transaction log is crucial to managing a database in SQL Server. This chapter covered the most common causes for log growth in SQL Server, and how to properly handle those scenarios to minimize log usage, or troubleshoot the problem to prevent further issues with the transaction log.

Chapter 9: Truncated Tables, Dropped Objects and Other Accidents Waiting to Happen

The sudden disappearance of an important object in a database, or of all the data in a table, can test the nerves of even the most imperturbable DBA. In the best case, the data or object can be recovered in a matter of minutes. Sometimes it can take several days. In the worst case, it can never be recovered and might even mean the end of business for a company.

Regardless of how strictly you control write access to your databases, such accidents, whether user initiated or due to a bug in application code or to hardware problems, can and will happen, and will bring with them a real risk of data loss. The primary responsibility of any database administrator is to ensure the ability to recover a database and its data quickly, and with no, or minimum acceptable, loss. Without a complete, secure set of database and log backups, the chances of achieving this are slim.

This chapter covers the following strategies, tools, and tweaks for ensuring an adequate response to accidental data loss, and minimizing the risk of it happening in the first place.

- Recovering the database from backup, to a marked transaction, or particular point in time.

- **Last ditch attempts to save your data**, in the absence of backups – including use of log recovery tools, source control, or High Availability solutions, such as replication or log shipping.

- **Using the default trace** to obtain details of what happened and who did it.

- **Minimizing risk of data loss** through:

    - a well-planned and tested backup and recovery strategy

    - a strict change control process

    - a well-designed permissions architecture based on "minimum required rights."

- **Using DML and DDL triggers** to prevent or log changes. These access control tweaks are especially useful in cases where you can't implement as tight a security model as you would like.

Example Case: The Missing Sales Order Data

A manager is running the usual series of "end of business day" reports, when he or she notices that the numbers seems a lot lower than usual. The manager decides to run the same reports for the current month and finds that the month-to-date totals exactly match today's daily totals. You, as the DBA, hear your phone ring just as you are walking out the office. The manager demands, angrily, to know why the numbers are all wrong.

Some quick research reveals that the `SalesOrderDetail` table contains data only for the last three hours of the business day! You know that the Sales application was implemented almost a year ago, and so the `SalesOrderDetail` table should have entries dating back to the day that the application was implemented. It is now up to you to determine what happened, and recover the data that is missing from the database.

Recovering Lost Data

All too often, in the face of such a problem, people's first instinct is to focus on who caused the problem, and how to prove it. Of course, this will need to be established, but it's a secondary objective. The paramount concern is that a critical object or data is missing from a database, and the very first step is to recover the object or data in the most efficient manner possible.

In truth, there is only one sure way to recover all, or very nearly all, of the lost data, and that's to perform a RESTORE operation, using the last full database backup, and the sequence of log backups that succeeded it. In this way, it should be possible to recover the database to a point immediately before the data was lost. This will only be possible if the database has been operating in FULL recovery model, and if you have been taking, and retaining in a safe location, regular full database backups and transaction log backups. We'll examine, first, the case where full and log backups are available, and then the "damage limitation" strategies that you might consider in the absence of such backup files.

Recovering from backup

As discussed, the extent of your exposure to data loss as a result of events such as this will be determined to a large degree by the recovery model selected for the database, and by your backup strategy.

In this section, we'll assume the database in question in using the FULL recovery model and that full and transaction log backups, representing an unbroken LSN chain (see *Chapter 8*) are available; then we'll demonstrate how to restore a database to a specific point within a log file.

The RESTORE LOG command supports three different options for restoring a database to a particular point within a log file, each of which is described in Books Online.

- **Recovering to a marked transaction** (HTTP://MSDN.MICROSOFT.COM/EN-US/LIBRARY/MS188623.ASPX).

- **Recovering to a specific point in time** (HTTP://MSDN.MICROSOFT.COM/EN-US/LIBRARY/MS178143.ASPX).

- **Recovering to a Log Sequence Number** (HTTP://MSDN.MICROSOFT.COM/EN-US/LIBRARY/MS191459.ASPX).

In the first instance, we'll demonstrate restoring to a point represented by a marked transaction. We'll then discuss general issues regarding restores to a specific point in time within a log file.

Restore to a marked transaction

Marked transactions can be used to create a known recovery point for significant changes to a database, or multiple databases when the same transaction mark is used in multiple databases, to establish a common recovery point for all of the affected databases. It is rare that a user who mistakenly drops, truncates, or deletes a table will have been kind enough to use a marked transaction. However, a wise DBA can use them to create an easy recovery point, prior to deploying a large set of changes to a database, in cases where the potential for problems exists.

To simulate this type of restore, we'll use the AdventureWorks database. The first step is to put the database into FULL recovery and take a full backup of the database to begin the LSN chain, as shown in Listing 9.1.

```
USE [master]
GO
ALTER DATABASE [AdventureWorks] SET RECOVERY FULL
 GO
BACKUP DATABASE [AdventureWorks]
TO  DISK = N'D:\SQLBackups\AdventureWorks.bak'
WITH NOFORMAT,
    INIT,
    NAME = N'AdventureWorks-Full Database Backup',
    SKIP,
    STATS = 10,
    CHECKSUM
GO
```

Listing 9.1: Setting AdventureWorks to use FULL recovery model.

With a full backup taken, we have a known point in time where the database is in a known, good state. Next, we simulate transactional work on the database by modifying rows in the ErrorLog table of the database. After that, we take a log backup to capture those changes.

```
USE [AdventureWorks]
GO
SELECT  ErrorTime ,UserName ,ErrorNumber ,
        ErrorSeverity ,ErrorState ,ErrorProcedure ,
        ErrorMessage
FROM    dbo.ErrorLog
GO
INSERT  INTO dbo.ErrorLog
        ( ErrorTime ,UserName ,ErrorNumber ,
          ErrorSeverity ,ErrorState ,ErrorProcedure ,
          ErrorMessage
        )
        SELECT  GETDATE() ,
                SYSTEM_USER ,
                100 ,
                12 ,
                1 ,
                'SomeProcedure' ,
                'Failed'
GO
```

```
SELECT    ErrorTime ,UserName ,ErrorNumber ,
          ErrorSeverity ,ErrorState ,ErrorProcedure ,
          ErrorMessage
FROM      dbo.ErrorLog
GO
BACKUP LOG [AdventureWorks]
TO   DISK = N'D:\SQLBackups\AdventureWorks_Log1.bak'
WITH NOFORMAT,
     INIT,
     NAME = N'AdventureWorks-Transaction Log  Backup',
     SKIP,
     STATS = 10
GO
```

Listing 9.2: Insert data into `ErrorLog`; back up the `AdventureWorks` log.

Now, we simulate our lost data issue, by issuing a `DELETE` against the `Sales.SalesOrderDetail` table, without a `WHERE` clause filter. The subsequent `SELECT` operation will return zero rows.

```
BEGIN TRANSACTION Delete_Bad_SalesOrderDetail WITH MARK
DELETE   Sales.SalesOrderDetail
-- Forgotten WHERE clause = Oops
COMMIT TRANSACTION
GO
SELECT    SalesOrderID ,
          SalesOrderDetailID ,
          CarrierTrackingNumber ,
          OrderQty ,
          ProductID ,
          SpecialOfferID ,
          UnitPrice ,
          UnitPriceDiscount ,
          rowguid ,
          ModifiedDate
FROM      Sales.SalesOrderDetail
GO
```

Listing 9.3: An erroneous (marked) transaction deletes the `SaleOrderDetail` table.

Even though the data in the table has been deleted, the database is still online. It isn't until 5 p.m., when the end-of-day report is run that the boss discovers the problem. Now our focus shifts immediately to recovering the data, if possible. Since the database is in FULL recovery model, it is generally safe to assume that, as long as the entire LSN chain (see *Chapter 8*) is intact, the data can be recovered without data loss.

It is important to first know the extent of the data loss, and its impact on the overall operational environment for your server (hopefully, via your auditing tool, as we'll discuss later in the chapter). In this case, the SalesOrderDetail information has been lost, which affects the ability to view the details of past orders, but doesn't stop new orders from being entered, or stop application changes to other data inside the database, for example, updating a customer's contact information.

We can't afford to lose any changes or additions to the sales order data made after the data loss occurred so, in such cases, the quickest method of recovery may be to restore a *copy* of the database to a point in time before the data loss occurred, and then transfer the missing data back into the table in the live database. Preferably, we'll restore this copy to a different server but if only one SQL Server exists in the environment, the database can be restored with a different name side-by-side with the existing database.

The first step, shown in Listing 9.4, is to back up the existing database transaction log using BACKUP LOG.

```
USE [master]
GO
BACKUP LOG [AdventureWorks]
TO   DISK = N'D:\SQLBackups\AdventureWorks_Log2.bak'
WITH NOFORMAT,
    INIT,
    NAME = N'AdventureWorks-Transaction Log  Backup',
    SKIP,
    STATS = 10
GO
```

Listing 9.4:   Final log backup of the live transaction log.

317

At this stage, i.e. before we actually begin restoring and recovering the copy database, and then copying the lost data back to the live database, it is generally a recommended practice to take a separate full backup of the "damaged" database, as shown in Listing 9.5. This will secure the existing state before making any changes, protecting against further loss from another mistake during the data recovery process. It is extremely important that this backup be made to a different location than the existing full database backup, since this would overwrite the backup set, making recovery impossible.

```
BACKUP DATABASE [AdventureWorks]
TO   DISK = N'D:\SQLBackups\AdventureWorks_Damaged.bak'
WITH NOFORMAT,
    INIT,
    NAME = N'AdventureWorks-Damaged Full DB Backup',
    SKIP,
    STATS = 10,
    CHECKSUM
GO
```

Listing 9.5:   Full backup of the damaged database.

We now begin the **RESTORE** operations, starting by restoring our good full backup, from Listing 9.1. Note that, because we're restoring to a copy of the database rather than restoring to the live database, we specify the **MOVE** option to create new database files for the database, as shown in Listing 9.6. We also specify the **NORECOVERY** option, which puts the copy database into a restoring state and allows us to continue the restore operation by applying additional backups.

```
--Begin Recovery Process
RESTORE DATABASE [AdventureWorks_Copy]
FROM   DISK = N'D:\SQLBackups\AdventureWorks.bak'
WITH   FILE = 1,
       MOVE N'AdventureWorks_Data' TO N'D:\SQLDATA\AdventureWorks_Copy.mdf',
       MOVE N'AdventureWorks_Log' TO N'D:\SQLDATA\AdventureWorks_Copy_1.ldf',
       NORECOVERY,
       STATS = 10
GO
```

Listing 9.6:   Restoring a copy of **AdventureWorks** from a full backup.

In our example, the rogue **DELETE** statement was a marked transaction, and so we can recover the database to the point that this marked transaction began. To do this, all of the transaction log backups up to the one containing the marked transaction are restored using the **RESTORE LOG** command, specifying the **STOPBEFOREMARK** option with the marked transaction name, as well as the **NORECOVERY** option to allow subsequent log backups to be applied to the database, as shown in Listing 9.7.

```
RESTORE LOG [AdventureWorks_Copy]
FROM  DISK = N'D:\SQLBackups\AdventureWorks_Log1.bak'
WITH  FILE = 1,
   NORECOVERY,
   STATS = 10,
   STOPBEFOREMARK = N'Delete_Bad_SalesOrderDetail'
GO
```

Listing 9.7: Restoring the first log backup.

When applying log backups, the output information will contain the following statement until the log backup containing the marked transaction is restored.

```
This log file contains records logged before the designated mark. The database is
being left in the Restoring state so you can apply another log file.
```

When this message appears, subsequent log backups must continue to be applied, to roll the database forward in time to the marked transaction. The first log backup to be restored that does not contain this message is the log backup that contains the marked transaction, and no further log backups need to be applied to the database to recover the lost data. In this example, the second log backup contains the marked transaction, and so needs to be restored.

```
RESTORE LOG [AdventureWorks_Copy]
FROM  DISK = N'D:\SQLBackups\AdventureWorks_Log2bak'
WITH  FILE = 1,
      NORECOVERY,
      STATS = 10,
      STOPBEFOREMARK = N'Delete_Bad_SalesOrderDetail'
GO
```

Listing 9.8: Restoring the second log backup, containing the marked transaction.

Restoring this log file will not output the message, meaning that the database can be recovered using the **RESTORE DATABASE** command and the **WITH RECOVERY** option. The database will enter the recovery process, which will roll back the marked transaction, as well as any changes that occurred after, or were uncommitted when the marked transaction began.

```
RESTORE DATABASE [AdventureWorks_Copy]
WITH   RECOVERY
GO
```

Listing 9.9: Recovering the AdventureWorks_Copy database.

A simple query will validate that the copy database has the missing data, and this data can now be copied back into the production database using an **INSERT** statement, or the Import/Export wizard, or a SSIS Package.

When inserting the data back into the original Sales.SalesOrderDetail table, it is necessary to turn on **IDENTITY_INSERT** for the table, in order to preserve the SalesOrderDetailID values as they exist in the restored copy, and prevent new identity values from being generated as the rows are reinserted into the live database, as shown in Listing 9.10.

```
USE [AdventureWorks]
GO
SET IDENTITY_INSERT Sales.SalesOrderDetail ON
INSERT   INTO Sales.SalesOrderDetail
        ( SalesOrderID , SalesOrderDetailID ,
          CarrierTrackingNumber , OrderQty ,
          ProductID , SpecialOfferID ,
          UnitPrice ,UnitPriceDiscount ,
          rowguid , ModifiedDate
        )
        SELECT   SalesOrderID , SalesOrderDetailID ,
                CarrierTrackingNumber , OrderQty ,
                ProductID , SpecialOfferID ,
                UnitPrice , UnitPriceDiscount ,
                rowguid , ModifiedDate
```

```
           FROM AdventureWorks_Copy.Sales.SalesOrderDetail
           WHERE NOT EXISTS ( SELECT SalesOrderDetailID
                                FROM Sales.SalesOrderDetail )
SET IDENTITY_INSERT Sales.SalesOrderDetail OFF
GO
```

Listing 9.10: Inserting the lost data back into AdventureWorks.

As a sanity check, it makes sense to validate that the data was "restored" to the live database in the same state as it existed in the copy database, either by manually reviewing the two datasets or, if the data sets are very large, using the **EXCEPT** operator to examine any data that is different between the two tables, as shown in Listing 9.11.

```
-- comparing both data sets
SELECT  *
FROM    Sales.SalesOrderDetail
GO
SELECT  *
FROM    AdventureWorks_Copy.Sales.SalesOrderDetail
GO

-- data differences
SELECT  *
FROM    Sales.SalesOrderDetail
EXCEPT
SELECT  *
FROM    AdventureWorks_Copy.Sales.SalesOrderDetail
GO
```

Listing 9.11: Checking the state of the reinserted data.

Restore to a point in time

This previous example used a marked transaction to establish the point of recovery but, in most cases, a point-in-time recovery will be used to apply the transaction logs up to a known point in time before the data loss occurred. Once the point in time is reached in the **RESTORE LOG** process, the database can be recovered.

If the exact time when the data loss occurred is unknown, one option is to restore a backup of the database in **STANDBY** mode. This allows further log backups to be restored but, unlike when using **NORECOVERY**, the database is still readable. So the scheme might be:

1. Restore a full backup of the database, in **STANDBY** mode, alongside the live database.

2. Gradually roll the database forward, by applying each log file to the standby database, till you reach the point when the bad transaction occurred, and data was lost.

3. Copy the lost data across to the live database and drop the restored copy.

Listing 9.12 restores a copy of **AdventureWorks** in **STANDBY** mode.

```
--Begin Recovery Process
RESTORE DATABASE [AdventureWorks_Copy]
FROM   DISK = N'D:\SQLBackups\AdventureWorks.bak'
WITH   FILE = 1,
       MOVE N'AdventureWorks_Data' TO
              N'D:\SQLDATA\AdventureWorks_Copy.mdf',
       MOVE N'AdventureWorks_Log' TO
              N'D:\SQLDATA\AdventureWorks_Copy_1.ldf',
       STANDBY =
          N'D:\SQLBackups\AdventureWorks_Copy_UNDO.bak',
       STATS = 10
GO
```

Listing 9.12: Restoring a full backup of **AdventureWorks** in **STANDBY**.

The **WITH STANDBY** option specifies an undo file to allow read-only access to the restoring database and allow continued **RESTORE LOG** operations to occur.

```
RESTORE LOG [AdventureWorks_Copy]
FROM   DISK = N'D:\SQLBackups\AdventureWorks_Log2.bak'
WITH   FILE = 1,
       STANDBY =
          N'D:\SQLBackups\AdventureWorks_Copy_UNDO.bak',
```

```
        STATS = 10,
        STOPAT = 'Jan 05, 2011 11:00 AM'
GO
```

Listing 9.13: Restoring log backups to the standby database.

This process is not necessarily straightforward, and can be quite time-consuming. Unless you've purchased a specialized log reading tool, and can interrogate the log backup directly, rolling the logs forward can mean a series of painstaking steps involving restoring a log, checking the data, restoring a bit further, and so on, to identify the point in the log chain where the data was lost.

Recovering without a backup

The depth of trouble in which you might find yourself, and the extent of potential data loss, will depend on which backups you do, and don't, have.

A valid full backup is the starting point for every recovery situation; without one there is little hope of recovering data lost due to a mistake. In short, if absolutely no full backup of the database exists, nothing anyone can do will help recover a missing object or data.

The first thing to do, in the event of a data loss incident, is to check the current recovery model of the database, as shown in Listing 9.14.

```
-- SQL Server 2000
SELECT  name ,
        DATABASEPROPERTYEX(name, 'Recovery')
FROM    sysdatabases

-- SQL Server 2005/2008
SELECT  name ,
        recovery_model_desc
FROM    sys.databases
```

Listing 9.14: Checking the recovery model.

If the database is in SIMPLE recovery, there is no real hope of recovering with zero data loss, since the only recovery point is the latest full or differential backup. It's not possible to take a log backup in this recovery model, and the transaction log records are truncated automatically at CHECKPOINT allowing the space to be reused (log truncation is discussed in full detail in *Chapter 8*). At this point, the only option is to confess the mistake to management and pray for clemency, which may not be forthcoming.

If the database is in FULL recovery but there has never been a full database backup, then the database is actually functioning as if it were in SIMPLE recovery and, again, it won't be possible to recover the lost data. When a database is changed from the SIMPLE recovery model to the FULL recovery model, the transaction log continues to be truncated at CHECKPOINT as it would under SIMPLE recovery until a full backup of the database is taken, which restarts the log chain. As of SQL Server 2005, the BACKUP LOG command will fail for a database using the FULL recovery model if an initial full backup has not been performed. This was a change from SQL Server 2000, which would allow the log backups to be taken even though they were useless, without a full backup to establish the start of the LSN chain.

If the database is in FULL recovery, and it has had a full backup since the database was switched to FULL recovery, but no log backups, then there may be some small hope. If you're fairly certain that the LSN chain is intact (e.g. no one ever took a log backup and deleted it), then it may be that you can simply take a log backup and proceed as described in the previous section.

However, if the LSN chain has been broken, by manual log truncation, a corrupt log backup, or a missing log backup (see *Chapter 8*), then this route will be closed. However, it may still be possible that the specific actions that resulted in data loss exist inside the transaction log and that a third-party tool may be able to read the log records and generate the INSERT, UPDATE or DELETE statements to reverse the operation. It's worth a try, but if the log records describing the change have been lost, then not even third-party tools will be able to help.

Log recovery tools

There are a couple of tools on the market that can attempt to recover the lost information or object from the transaction log. If you are on SQL Server 2000, Red Gate offers a free tool, SQL Log Rescue (HTTP://WWW.RED-GATE.COM/PRODUCTS/SQL_LOG_RESCUE/INDEX. HTM), which can be used to attempt recovery. For SQL Server 2005 and 2008, ApexSQL offers the ApexSQL Log tool (HTTP://WWW.APEXSQL.COM/SQL_TOOLS_LOG.ASP) which can potentially recover the information from the transaction log. It should be noted that, while these tools offer the potential for recovery, they do not guarantee it, and should not be relied upon. The only guaranteed method of recovery is a solid backup plan for the database.

Recovering objects from source control

If the loss is a database object and not data, for example, a stored procedure, trigger, function or view, the object should be recoverable without restoring a backup of the database. Any database code should be stored inside of a source control management system like Team Foundation Server, Visual Source Safe, Subversion, CVS, PVCS or one of the numerous other products available for source control. Recovery of an object from source control is generally as simple as checking the latest production revision out and redeploying the object back to the database.

If no source control management system is being used, the same steps used to recover lost data can be used to recover the missing database object. The only difference in the process is that the object can be scripted from the restored copy and then created on the production database from the script.

Recovering data from a secondary/replica database

When planning for disaster recovery it is imperative that you thoroughly understand the details of what specific configurations do or don't provide. SQL Server offers a lot of out-of-the-box high availability options, including database mirroring, log shipping, replication, and clustering. In addition to these, most hardware vendors offer high availability options, such as RAID, disk mirroring, and SAN mirroring and replication.

It is common to use a combination of hardware and SQL Server high availability options to protect against the impacts of hardware failures, but none of these options offers protection against changes to the database that occur inside of SQL Server. Most of these technologies, with the exception of clustering, which maintains a single copy of the database files on a shared SAN disk, are used to keep duplicate copies of the database, but the problem is that as changes occur in the principal database, they are made to the duplicated databases as well.

It is technically possible to recover from a loss when using log shipping or replication if the change is caught fast enough, but this can be complicated, and could require rebuilding the configuration after the recovery was performed.

In log shipping configurations, it may be possible to put the log-shipped copy database into read-only, standby mode, and then query out the deleted data, before the transaction log containing the change is applied to the log-shipped copy. However, if a point-in-time restore is required including the most recent log backup file, the log shipping configuration would have to be reinitialized after the data recovery was completed, since the point-in-time restore of the log would break the log shipping.

With replication configurations, depending on the topology, the process of inserting rows back into a publisher by querying a subscriber can cause conflicts to occur when the INSERT operations are replicated back down to the subscriber(s). In such cases, it may be necessary to split the replication, with the subscriber being used to reconstitute the data and then reinitialize the subscriber after the data recovery operation has been completed.

Finding the Culprit

After recovering the missing objects or data, your focus can turn towards finding out who made the fateful modification. This can be very hard, unless some form of auditing mechanism is already in place.

In SQL Server 2000, no auditing mechanisms are enabled by default. However, in SQL Server 2005 and 2008, the **default trace** is, as its name might suggest, active by default. It captures a number of important trace events that can be used to identify changes made to the database schema, and who made them. However, the default trace does not contain any information about data modification statements (`INSERT`, `UPDATE`, `DELETE`).

The default trace is configured to write its trace files to the `ErrorLog` path for the SQL Server instance. It uses file rollover when the current trace file reaches 20 MB in size, and it maintains a maximum of five trace files. Once the fifth file is full, the oldest file is deleted, meaning that the trace data is only retained for a certain period.

Details of the default trace, including rollover characteristics, the file to which the trace is writing, and so on, can be found through the `sys.traces` dynamic management view.

```
SELECT    *
FROM      sys.traces
WHERE     is_default = 1 ;
```

Listing 9.15: Querying `sys.traces` for the default trace characteristics.

Unlike user-defined traces, the default trace cannot be changed, but it can be disabled completely, using `sp_configure`. The full list of events that the default trace collects can be found by running the query in Listing 9.16.

```
SELECT DISTINCT
        e.trace_event_id ,
        e.name
FROM    sys.fn_trace_geteventinfo (1) t
        JOIN sys.trace_events e
            ON t.eventID = e.trace_event_id
```

Listing 9.16: Events collected by the default trace.

The `Object:Deleted` and `Object:Altered` trace events can be used to investigate accidental changes to, or removal of, any table or other object in the database.

The contents of a trace file can be read using the **sys.fn_trace_gettable** system function. If the trace is configured to use file rollover, as is the default trace, then the function will read the trace file provided, plus any subsequent rollover files. If you use the filename, `Log.trc`, then any file in that path with "`Log`" as its base name, will be read.

```
DECLARE @FileName NVARCHAR(260)

SELECT  @FileName = SUBSTRING(path, 0,
                                LEN(path) - CHARINDEX('\',
                                REVERSE(path)) + 1)
        + '\Log.trc'
FROM    sys.traces
WHERE   is_default = 1 ;

SELECT  loginname ,
        hostname ,
        applicationname ,
        databasename ,
        objectName ,
        starttime ,
        e.name AS EventName ,
        databaseid
FROM    sys.fn_trace_gettable(@FileName, DEFAULT) AS gt
        INNER JOIN sys.trace_events e
            ON gt.EventClass = e.trace_event_id
WHERE   ( gt.EventClass = 47    -- Object:Deleted Event
                                -- from sys.trace_events
          OR gt.EventClass = 164
```

```
    ) -- Object:Altered Event from sys.trace_events
    AND gt.EventSubClass = 0
    AND gt.DatabaseID = DB_ID('AdventureWorks')
```

Listing 9.17: Reading a trace file using **sys.fn_trace_gettable**.

As noted earlier, if the default trace has rolled over five times, or the SQL Service has been restarted five times, since the object was changed or dropped, the information about who made the change, and when, may not exist.

However, if the database is in the **FULL** recovery model then the information may still exist in the transaction log or transaction log backups. One of the third-party tools mentioned in the *Recovering without a backup* section of this chapter may be able to read the backups or log file to identify who made the change.

Prevention is Better than Cure

Benjamin Franklin once said, "An ounce of prevention is worth a pound of cure." This now-famous quote was made in reference to fire-fighting, in a time when people who suffered fire damage to their homes also suffered irreversible economic loss. In 1752, he helped establish the *Philadelphia Contribution for Insurance Against Loss by Fire* to help ensure that people with insurance policies were not financially drained by the damage caused by a house fire.

These days, the loss of data can be equally damaging economically, resulting in the loss of business, as well as fees, penalties, or even fines. Fortunately, a little bit of up-front work and planning will, in most cases, prevent the problem from occurring, or at least minimize the impact that a loss causes.

First, it's important to accept that, regardless of how strictly you control write-access to your databases, accidents can, and will, happen. At some point, a user or application with permission to modify objects and data in the database for perfectly legitimate reasons, will make a mistake, and cause data loss. As such, it's vitally important to have in place a recovery plan that will enable you to recover from such losses, as well as from other disasters, such as hardware failure.

Having said this, it's also important to realize that the cause of most data losses can be traced to inadequate change control, and to developers, analysts, or other employees who had "too many rights" inside of a production database. As such, steps must also be taken to tighten up the change control process, and to implement a strict security model for production environments, which should also be replicated in development and testing environments.

Plan for recovery from all data losses

Planning for recovery is not just about planning to recover from a crashed or corrupt database; it's planning to recover from any type of problem, including the accidental deletion or truncation of a table. The only way to protect against accidental data loss in every case that it could occur, including hardware failures, is to have a solid backup plan for the database. It is out of scope for this chapter to offer full coverage of configuring database backups in SQL Server. However, we will cover a couple of basics that must be understood, in the context of preventing data loss from user- or application-initiated changes to the database.

In most cases, it is a relatively easy task to restore an accidentally-dropped or truncated object, or to undo an unwanted data change, as long as the database is operating in the FULL recovery model, and regular full (and differential) database backups are being taken, along with transaction log backups.

While use of the FULL recovery model allows for point-in-time restoration of a database, its use also requires significantly more planning and resources. For example, when running in FULL, a database will require frequent backups of the transaction log throughout the day, in order to minimize log file growth and to support the agreed maximum data loss limits. For example, if the maximum acceptable data loss is 2 hours, then a viable backup plan might be to take weekly full backups, nightly differential backups, and transaction log backups every two hours. This scheme would restrict the number of restore operations required for a point-in-time recovery to a maximum of 13; the last full backup, the last differential backup, and a maximum of 11 transaction log backups in a given day. Of course, if the maximum acceptable data loss is 10 minutes instead of 2 hours, then you'll need to adapt the scheme appropriately.

If it isn't possible to run certain databases in FULL recovery, for example due to lack of resources, then the extent of data loss that is possible must be made clear to all concerned. In SIMPLE recovery, the transaction log is auto-truncated and so it is likely that you will only be able to restore an object to the time of the last full or differential backup. The exposure to risk of data loss can be minimized by taking more frequent full backups, and/or interspersing full backups with differential backups but, ultimately, some degree of data loss, equating to the time between the loss occurring and the time the last backup was taken, is inevitable. If data loss is unacceptable under any circumstance, the SIMPLE recovery model won't be sufficient to meet your business needs.

Even if measures are put in place to minimize the time it takes to discover the problem (e.g. change logging), it's likely that the problem will not be discovered and addressed before the log is truncated, rendering useless any log reading tools (assuming one is available in the first place).

Recovery of dropped or erroneously-modified database objects, such as stored procedures, is generally possible without losing any changes, even in SIMPLE model, unless the code changes occur more frequently than you have differential backups from which to recover. Unfortunately, it's still true that many developers have direct production access to the systems and change/deploy code all the time without any release process.

Regardless of the recovery model in use, it is important that the actual backup files be stored in a secure location that is separate from the actual disks that hold the database files. This protects the backups from corruption in the event of a critical disk failure that causes database corruption. The backup files would generally be stored on some form of tape media, or backup appliance using RAID storage.

It's also important, though often overlooked, that the backup files are retained for an adequate period of time. I've seen cases where backups were being taken, but point-in-time recovery of a dropped object wasn't possible because the retention period of the log backups was too low.

Implement a change control process

One of the biggest causes of accidentally-dropped objects or erroneously-deleted data in a production database is the lack of any established and documented change control process. Any change to a production database should be developed in a development environment, and then tested in a testing or staging environment that mimics the actual production environment. This includes mimicking, in the development and test systems, the minimal access rights that a user will (or at least should, as discussed shortly) have in the production database.

A common argument against this kind of configuration is that the hardware and management costs associated with maintaining three separate environments are too high. There are several counter-arguments to this. Firstly, the cost of setting up separate development and test systems isn't as high as you might think, especially with virtualization. Also, bear in mind that the development server doesn't need to match the configuration of the production server, since it won't see normal production load, and unless full regression tests using production loads are run against the testing or staging environment, it also doesn't require a matching configuration to production.

The most powerful counterargument, however, takes the form of a question: "How much, per minute, does a database outage cost the company?" If you allow development in production you greatly increase the risk of untested changes causing data loss or server outages. In most cases, a single outage caused by a deleted table or dropped object will exceed the cost of having a dedicated development and testing environments.

Implement an appropriate security model

In smaller IT environments, where a dedicated database administrator doesn't exist, security is an often overlooked aspect of database design and configuration. Generally, security lock-downs only occur as a knee-jerk reaction to a data loss incident.

In my first year as a database developer, I worked in an environment where every developer had `sysadmin` rights in SQL Server, just because it was easier to create a login and check the box for the `sysadmin` role, providing access to anything, than it was to define the specific objects to which each person required rights. I worked in Query Analyzer or Management Studio, where it is very easy to fire off a query to any connected server, occasionally the wrong server. This ability, coupled with the rights necessary to drop a table from a production database, make for a potentially lethal combination. I know, because I made this mistake and brought the operations of a multi-million dollar a year business to a halt for a number of hours while a table was recovered from backup. Years later, as a Senior DBA, I was connected to the wrong server at the wrong time, and dropped an 80 GB table from a production database.

The first instance was caused by human error coupled with database privileges that I simply should not have been granted. The second instance was just a really bad day at the office.

There are two lessons here: the first one is that we should do everything we can to control, tightly, access rights in our production databases, and so minimize the risk of accidental data loss. Such concerns should override any objections on the grounds of reduced developer productivity. We'll discuss ways to implement this access control in the very next section.

The second lesson is that accidents can, and will, still happen, even to the most experienced developer or DBA. Such mistakes can cost you your job, regardless of whether there are significant security problems in the environment. What might save you is the ability to recover the data very quickly, so make sure your recovery plan gives you the best possible chance of doing that.

Access control measures

A full discussion of access control mechanisms is out of scope for this book, but we'll cover a few of the key points to consider when devising your access control mechanisms. Some of the things I look out for, in particular, are:

- **Use of Windows logins** – modern application design should favor the use of Windows rather than SQL logins, with write permissions being granted only to those Windows logins that really need them. Individual users that are not members of the DBA team should not have write access to production databases.

- **Database changes through stored procedures** – changes to the database should be made through stored procedures, which offer far greater control over the level of damage a user can cause than is possible with direct, ad hoc access to the database. Under no circumstances should a non-DBA login have the ability to create, alter, or drop an object from a production database.

- **Strict regulation of membership of all database roles** – this includes not only the obvious, high-privilege users and roles such as `dbo` or `sysadmin`, but also any role that proffers database modification privileges on its members, such as the `db_owner`, `db_datawriter`, or `db_ddladmin` database roles.

- A particular problem is the application login that runs as the `dbo` user, or is a member of the `db_owner` role in SQL Server. The combination of a high-privilege role and application login details that are widely known by many users is a recipe for potential problems.

Permissions through stored procedures

One of the easiest ways to control what a user can or cannot do in a production database is to perform database modifications through stored procedures, and then restrict users to EXECUTE rights on those stored procedures.

This effectively reduces the risks associated with the user having production access, since the only code they can execute is code that has already been written. However, if a stored procedure has the ability to DELETE every row in a database table, even minimizing user permissions to EXECUTE only won't prevent a problem.

Using triggers to prevent or log changes

It is possible that, due to the architecture of an application, it is not possible to implement a tight security model that prevents database access to all non-DBA or application service account users. In cases where it is impossible to lock down database access sufficiently, or where this will require long-term redesign of the application as well as the database, database triggers are a useful option. They can be used to prevent, or even log, changes that occur to the database, for auditing purposes. Two types of trigger exist in SQL Server:

- **DML triggers** which fire when a change is made to the data in a table
- **DDL triggers** which fire when a change is made to one of the database schema objects.

DML triggers

DML triggers can be created on a table or view and execute code in response to any data manipulation language event (INSERT, UPDATE, or DELETE) on the parent object. DML triggers can be used to provide audit tracking of all changes in a table, by writing information about the changes to a secondary table.

Listing 9.18 shows how to create an audit table and auditing trigger to track changes to the `Sales.SalesOrderDetail` table in `AdventureWorks`.

```
USE AdventureWorks
GO
CREATE TABLE Sales.SalesOrderDetailAudit
    (
        AuditID INT IDENTITY ,
        SalesOrderID INT ,
        SalesOrderDetailID INT ,
        CarrierTrackingNumber NVARCHAR(25) ,
        OrderQty SMALLINT ,
        ProductID INT ,
        SpecialOfferID INT ,
        UnitPrice MONEY ,
        UnitPriceDiscount MONEY ,
        LineTotal MONEY ,
        rowguid UNIQUEIDENTIFIER ,
        ModifiedDate DATETIME ,
        AuditAction VARCHAR(30) ,
        ChangeDate DATETIME ,
        ChangedBy SYSNAME ,
        CONSTRAINT PK_Audit_SalesOrderDetail_AuditID
                            PRIMARY KEY CLUSTERED
        ( AuditID ASC )
    )
GO

CREATE TRIGGER SalesOrderDetail_AUDIT_TRIGGER ON Sales.SalesOrderDetail
    AFTER INSERT, UPDATE, DELETE
AS
    DECLARE @i_action VARCHAR(30) ,
        @d_action VARCHAR(30)
    SELECT   @i_action = 'INSERTED' ,
            @d_action = 'DELETED'

    IF EXISTS ( SELECT   1
                FROM    inserted )
        AND EXISTS ( SELECT 1
                    FROM    deleted )
--RECORD WAS UPDATED
        BEGIN
```

```
            SELECT   @i_action = 'UPDATED_TO' ,
                     @d_action = 'UPDATED_FROM'
       END

   INSERT   INTO Sales.SalesOrderDetailAudit
            ( SalesOrderID , SalesOrderDetailID ,
              CarrierTrackingNumber , OrderQty ,
              ProductID , SpecialOfferID ,
              UnitPrice , UnitPriceDiscount ,
              LineTotal , rowguid ,
              ModifiedDate , AuditAction ,
              ChangeDate , ChangedBy
            )
            SELECT   SalesOrderID , SalesOrderDetailID ,
                     CarrierTrackingNumber , OrderQty ,
                     ProductID , SpecialOfferID ,
                     UnitPrice , UnitPriceDiscount ,
                     LineTotal , rowguid ,
                     ModifiedDate , @i_action ,
                     GETDATE() , ORIGINAL_LOGIN
            FROM     INSERTED
            UNION ALL
            SELECT   SalesOrderID , SalesOrderDetailID ,
                     CarrierTrackingNumber , OrderQty ,
                     ProductID , SpecialOfferID ,
                     UnitPrice , UnitPriceDiscount ,
                     LineTotal , rowguid ,
                     ModifiedDate , @d_action ,
                     GETDATE() , SYSTEM_USER
            FROM     DELETED
GO
```

Listing 9.18: A DML trigger to log data changes to an audit table.

Any DML operation performed against the `Sales.SalesOrderDetail` table will be logged to the audit table, with the type of action performed, when it occurred, and who made the change. Auditing in this manner requires more space inside the database, since every operation is duplicated in the audit table. To demonstrate how this auditing works, we'll `UPDATE` the `OrderQty` for one of the rows (`WHERE SalesOrderDetailID =1`) and then `SELECT` the rows from the audit table, as shown in Listing 9.19.

```
UPDATE    Sales.SalesOrderDetail
SET       OrderQty = 10
WHERE     SalesOrderDetailID = 1
GO
SELECT    *
FROM      Sales.SalesOrderDetailAudit
GO
```

Listing 9.19: An audited UPDATE on the SalesOrderDetail table.

The **UPDATE** statement wrote to the audit table the original state of the data, as well as the state of the data after the **UPDATE**. Using this information, the operation can be undone by issuing another **UPDATE** with the original value, or by performing a JOIN to the audit table to correct multiple rows in a set based operation.

```
UPDATE    sod
SET       sod.OrderQty = soda.OrderQty
FROM      Sales.SalesOrderDetail sod
          JOIN Sales.SalesOrderDetailAudit soda
            ON sod.SalesOrderDetailID =
                  soda.SalesOrderDetailID
WHERE     soda.AuditAction = 'UPDATED FROM'
          AND soda.SalesOrderDetailID = 1
```

Listing 9.20: Reverting the UPDATE using the audit table.

In a production environment it is likely that, over time, a row will have been updated more than once, so you'll want to target the **WHERE** clause to changes from a specific date range, by placing an additional predicate on the **ChangeDate** column of the audit table.

Along with writing the changes to an audit table, a DML trigger can also be used to prevent changes, based on the number of rows being affected. This is accomplished by checking the number of rows in the **inserted** and **deleted** tables in the trigger and issuing a **ROLLBACK** if they exceed a set value, as shown in Listing 9.21.

```
CREATE TRIGGER SalesOrderDetail_Prevent ON Sales.SalesOrderDetail
    FOR UPDATE, DELETE
AS
    DECLARE @INS INTEGER ,
        @DEL INTEGER
    SELECT  @INS = COUNT(*)
    FROM    INSERTED
    SELECT  @DEL = COUNT(*)
    FROM    DELETED

    IF ( ( @INS > 1000
          AND @DEL > 1000
          )
        OR @DEL > 1000
      )
      BEGIN
          PRINT 'You must disable Trigger "Sales.SalesOrderDetail_Prevent" to
change more than 1000 rows.'
          ROLLBACK
      END
GO
```

Listing 9.21: Preventing any UPDATE that would affect more than 1,000 rows.

Attempting to UPDATE or DELETE more than 1,000 rows of data will cause the transaction to rollback and return the following error:

```
You must disable Trigger "Sales.SalesOrderDetail_Prevent" to change more than 1000
rows.
Msg 3609, Level 16, State 1, Line 1
The transaction ended in the trigger. The batch has been aborted.
```

If the operation is an intended operation, the trigger can be disabled using the DISABLE TRIGGER statement allowing the operation to complete, and then using ENABLE TRIGGER to turn the trigger back on once the operation completes.

```
DISABLE TRIGGER Sales.SalesOrderDetail_Prevent
ON Sales.SalesOrderDetail

-- Perform data changes

ENABLE TRIGGER Sales.SalesOrderDetail_Prevent
ON Sales.SalesOrderDetail
```

Listing 9.22: Disabling and enabling DML triggers.

DDL triggers

DDL triggers were added to SQL Server 2005 and are similar to DML triggers except that they fire in response to Data Definition Language events.

DDL triggers can be used to log database changes as well as prevent the changes from occurring at all. Unlike DML triggers, DDL triggers can be scoped to a specific database, or at the server level, and they can be configured to fire in response to a much larger set of events. DDL events are grouped into a hierarchy to allow a trigger to fire for multiple events while simplifying the trigger's definition.

A full list of the DDL Events and Groups can be found in the Books Online topic, *DDL Event Groups* (HTTP://MSDN.MICROSOFT.COM/EN-US/LIBRARY/BB510452.ASPX).

The Books Online topic, *Understanding DDL Triggers* (HTTP://MSDN.MICROSOFT.COM/EN-US/LIBRARY/MS175941.ASPX) has an example DDL trigger, named "safety," which prevents dropping or altering any table in a database. In a similar manner to the previous DML trigger, it does so by issuing a ROLLBACK to prevent the change. New tables can still be created with this trigger in place, or the trigger can be disabled to allow approved changes to occur, and then the trigger can be enabled to prevent further changes.

The `AdventureWorks` database also contains a DDL trigger, named `ddlDatabase-TriggerLog`, which logs DDL changes to the `DatabaseLog` table. The trigger is disabled by default but can be used as a template for creating an auditing trigger for DDL Events. DDL triggers do not have an `inserted` or `deleted` virtual table, as DML triggers do. Instead the `EVENTDATA()` system function has to be called, which returns an XML document containing the event information.

Summary

My philosophy with regard to recovering from data loss is that prevention is better than cure. The two key pillars of this philosophy are strict change control processes and appropriate security permissions.

I know from hard, personal experience that human error is the most prevalent cause of accidental data loss. I also know that the two biggest enabling factors for these accidents are development activity directly on production databases, and users with more rights than they need.

Of course, potential data loss due to hardware failure, power loss, or natural disaster, is harder to predict or control. The use of disaster recovery solutions such as failover clustering, database mirroring, log shipping, or transactional replication, will put you in a stronger position to handle such situations, but generally won't protect you from data loss due to changes directly to a SQL Server database. They are no substitute for a comprehensive, and tested, backup and recovery plan.

For each SQL Server database, a DBA must implement a backup strategy, consisting of full, differential and transaction log backups, as appropriate, that will allow data to be recovered to within what the business deems to be an acceptable level of data loss for that database. These backups must be stored securely, along with the documented recovery plan, which must be tested regularly to ensure that data can be recovered, and systems brought back online, within an acceptable time.

With this backup and recovery strategy in place, you can sleep sounder in the knowledge that if disaster strikes, you'll at least be working through the techniques covered in the *Recovering from backup* section of this chapter, rather than the ones in the *Recovering without a backup* section, which could equally as well been called *Last Ditch Efforts to Save your Job*.

Having safely recovered your data, attention can turn to the auditing techniques that will help identify the cause and to the change and access control measures that can help prevent it happening again.

Appendix: What to Do When All Else Fails

While this book attempts to cover the most commonly encountered SQL Server problems, others will, inevitably, arise which aren't covered. SQL Server is a complex product, and with each release more and more components are added to the product stack. It's simply impossible to cover in a single book every variety of problem that could occur somewhere in this stack, and affect the performance of SQL Server.

This appendix offers some advice on where to go for help with these problems, as well as for additional information on the problems that were covered.

While this appendix attempts to cover some of the most popular and useful SQL Server resources, there are others out there that aren't covered. SQL Server is a complex product and...you get the message.

Microsoft Customer Support Services

If you are faced with a production server that is down, your best chance of resolving the problem in the least amount of time is to contact the Microsoft Customer Support Team (CSS). The caveat here is that you will have to pay for this support on a case-by-case basis, unless the problem is due to an actual bug in the product, or a known bug that has an existing hot-fix or Service Pack available. Support cases are allocated based on their assigned status level, with Level A, production down, being the most important.

If you try to escalate a less critical support case to Level A, in order to jump forward in the queue, it will actually be de-escalated to at least a Level B during the early stages of support. Don't try to beat the system and escalate your case to a level that is not appropriate. This will only cause delay in the long run.

Before you call CSS, be aware of the following considerations. Firstly, if you are not using SQL Server in a supported configuration, then your problem will not be a priority case for Microsoft Support. For example, if you are running SQL Server on an unsupported Active Directory Domain Controller, your case may not receive Level A status. Depending on your existing support agreements with Microsoft, you may be required to reproduce the problem in a supported configuration before a support engineer continues to work the case, or before the case is escalated inside of Microsoft Support.

If your problem is partially covered by a chapter in this book, for example, you have a deleted table/missing object, but the recommendations in the chapter don't meet your needs or expectations, then you may decide to open a Microsoft Support case. However, you may be heading for disappointment. As far as was possible, this book covers the recommendations you're likely to get from Microsoft Support. If the information provided here doesn't already recommend that you contact Microsoft for a specific problem, then the chances are that you will be making an unnecessary support call that will cost you or your company money, and result in no new information.

Unless you have a Level A case, i.e. a true production down case, in a supported configuration, then you can expect the engineer to ask you to perform a process known as data collection, where you run the **PSSDiag** or **SQLDiag** tool, using a provided configuration file. This collects the necessary data for the support team to troubleshoot your specific problem. At this point, it is common for the support representative to end the call and wait for you to upload the results of the data collection to a private FTP or HTTPS web interface, where they can gather the results and parse through them offline.

This does not end your support case; it simply allows the engineer to multi-task, working on other customer cases, while you gather the necessary information they need to continue the analysis of your problem. You can expect to receive continued support and updates from your support engineer until they escalate your case internally at Microsoft, or they reassign your case to another support engineer, to continue working it while they are away or have time off. Rest assured that your case is being well documented by the support engineers, and the engineer receiving the case will continue where the last engineer left off.

If the problem you have is a known bug that is fixed in an existing hot-fix to the product, you may be required to apply that hot-fix and validate that the problem still exists, to continue receiving support. You may also have a problem that has a work-around available, and it may be recommended that you use the existing work-around until the problem is actually resolved in the product, which could take weeks, months, or years, depending on the specific problem, and the potential impact of the problem on other customers.

While CSS is a great asset for troubleshooting critical situation (Crit-Sit) problems with SQL Server, it may not be the best first stop for your specific problem. Keep in mind that opening a CSS case for the problem doesn't preclude the use of the other available methods covered in this chapter. It is still possible that you may receive assistance faster through one of the other methods provided here.

Nevertheless, in a true production-down scenario, CSS is the fastest and most guaranteed method of getting resolution to your problem.

Online Resources

The Internet has more information than any one person could ever hope to consume in a lifetime, and these days it is easier and faster than ever to publish information online. However, unlike books and magazine articles, information that can be found on the Internet doesn't always go through a technical editing process, and it can't be trusted to be accurate without additional validation. Determining the accuracy and applicability of online information can be a difficult task at times. This section will help to point you to major sites that have more credibility in the community at large due to their readership.

Articles

A number of websites dedicated to SQL Server publish, on a daily or weekly basis, articles that are written by members of the community and popular authors. These sites are subject to intense community scrutiny, so incorrect information is quickly highlighted and corrected. Furthermore, the articles are generally subject to technical review and editing prior to publication, in order to reduce the likelihood of error. This book, for example, would be fraught with mistakes if it wasn't for technical editing and the combined knowledge and experience of the authors and editors, working together to provide the most accurate information possible. Even then, you have to be careful what you trust online because even the most experienced people make mistakes at times. Two of my favorite sites are:

- HTTP://WWW.SQLSERVERCENTRAL.COM/ARTICLES/

- HTTP://WWW.SIMPLE-TALK.COM/SQL/

Blogs

On the one hand, blogs are an excellent source of up-to-date troubleshooting knowledge, often provided by highly knowledgeable experts. Many of the members of the SQL Server development team maintain a blog, for example, as do many of the SQL Server MVPs. On the other hand, despite all this, the quality of blogs can be highly variable, and it is not uncommon for a MVP blog to contain technically incorrect information.

When reading a blog post, always validate the author's experience and the information presented against the other information that is available on the subject online. Some of the best blogs are found at:

- HTTP://SQLSKILLS.COM

- HTTP://WWW.SQLBLOG.COM/

- HTTP://BLOGS.MSDN.COM/

- HTTP://WWW.SQLBLOGCASTS.COM/

- HTTP://WWW.SQLSERVERCENTRAL.COM/BLOGS/

- HTTP://WEBLOGS.SQLTEAM.COM/

Forums

The Internet has a multitude of "free" public access forums for SQL Server that can be used to receive support for non-critical, non-production down-type problems (though critical, server down-type problems do crop up as well!). While it may be possible to get an answer to a critical production down problem on the forums, the Customer Support Services route is the recommended path to resolve production down problems as there are no guarantees of a response to a forums question within any period of time.

It is impossible to cover each specific SQL Server community forum, so this chapter will only cover a few of the busiest: Microsoft MSDN, SQL Server Central, and StackOverflow.

The answers provided in the busy forums attract a high level of scrutiny, and active members of these forums will generally quickly correct any misleading advice. Again, however, do not be surprised if you receive conflicting or bad information from a forum thread.

Microsoft MSDN forums

The Microsoft MSDN forums are categorized into product-specific groups of forums, each covering a particular problem area for a product. One of the benefits of the MSDN forums is the level of involvement by Microsoft product team members, who routinely respond to complex questions in conjunction with a number of MVPs.

However, with all the activity, this forum can also be very much like the Wild West, with new members firing answers at anything that pops up, in an attempt to gain points and medals on the site. In most cases, wayward answers are corrected by other forum members or moderators, but the sheer volume of posts on certain forums can mean that incorrect information is not spotted, and you need to use due diligence in testing and verifying any information provided.

SQL Server Central forums

SQL Server Central is a site that was primarily created by three members of the SQL Server Community, Brian Knight, Steve Jones, and Andy Warren, in March of 2001. The site is currently owned and operated by RedGate Software, and Steve Jones continues to be the site's editor at large. The site has a very busy set of forums that are categorized and subcategorized in an attempt to drive specific types of questions into areas of interest, where members of the community offer responses and advice.

The high level of community involvement on this site makes it a fairly credible resource for information. The articles and tips provided on this site have discussion sections associated with them that should be reviewed to determine the community response to the information that was published. In some cases, a better solution, or corrections to inaccuracies in the article, can be found in the discussion.

SQL Server Central also runs a separate site, Ask.SQLServerCentral.com, which operates using the StackOverflow model, but is dedicated solely to SQL Server questions.

StackOverFlow

StackOverflow is an interesting newcomer in the forums space, offering a new model for a community supported forum. The goal behind StackOverflow is to promote single-response answers to questions and to reward "good" responses through "up-votes" by members of the community, so building a solid platform of reliable responses to common problems.

However, the up-vote mechanism is a double-edged sword, and it's entirely possible and common for generally accepted, but *wrong* answers to get up-voted. An example of this would be some of the common responses to the "Transaction Log Full" problem (covered in *Chapter 8*), which promote solutions such as backing up the log using the `TRUNCATE_ONLY` option and then use `SHRINKFILE` to shrink the physical file on disk. While this may fix the temporary problem at hand, it doesn't actually address the problem that caused the log file to grow significantly in the first place, and can also cause new issues such as physical file fragmentation or broken SQL Server backup sets.

Hiring a Consultant

As part of the process of solving a critical SQL Server-related problem, it might be advisable to hire a consultant to come in and fill a particular knowledge void within the company. Hiring a consultant is a complicated task and your choice should be based on a number of factors.

Often, budget is a key factor in the selection process. However, focusing only on the hourly cost of a consulting agreement, rather than the level of experience of the consultant, can lead to higher costs in the long term since it's possible that a cheaper, less-experienced consultant will take two or three times longer to resolve the issue.

When dealing with consultants, make sure that you have a well-defined statement of work that covers the specifics of the work to be performed, the maximum number of hours, and cost per hour that will be covered for the work, and specific deliverables associated with the work to be done.

Index

Symbols

4 Gigabyte Tuning (4GT) 137. *See also* **Memory management: 32-bit VAS limits: VAS tuning**

-g startup parameter 140

-T834 startup parameter 149

A

Access control measures 334–342

Access Methods counters 35

Accidents waiting to happen 311–342

Address Windowing Extensions (AWE) 138–139, 162. *See also* **Memory management: 32-bit VAS limits**

ADO.NET SqlExceptions in .NET code 272

Application design

    chatty applications 234

    reading too much data 234

    user input within transactions 233

ASYNC_NETWORK_IO 27

AWE (Address Windowing Extensions) 132, 133

B

Benchmarking 69

BIOS power saving options 120–121

Blocked process report 221–225

    blocked process report event class 219

Blocking 195–238

    automatic detection and notification 219–229

        Sp_blocker_pss80 process 220

        SQL Trace 220–225. *See also* SQL Trace

    event notifications 225–227

    Extended Events 228–229

    monitoring blocking 206–219

        cumulative wait statistics 210

        DMVs 210–218

        PerfMon 218–219

        sysprocesses 207–210

    resolving blocking 230–234

        bad database design 231

        inappropriate isolation level 231–232

        missing indexes 233

        outdated hardware 234

        poor application design 233–234

        poorly written queries 232

        short-term measures 235–238

Bookmark lookup deadlock 262

Buffer Cache Hit Ratio counter 151

C

Change control process 332

Change Data Capture (CDC) 279

Code examples, download link 17

Common causes of high CPU usage 85–121

    ad hoc non-parameterized queries 103–107

        fixing the application 105

        forced parameterization 106

        optimize for ad hoc workloads 107

    configuration options in SQL Server 2008 120

    implicit conversions 93–95

    inappropriate parallelism 108–117

        diagnosing 115–116

    missing indexes 86–88

    non-SARGable predicates 89–92

    outdated statistics 88–89

    parameter sniffing 95–103

short-term fixes in SQL Server 2005 118–119

TokenAndPermUserStore 117–120

Concurrency and locks 196–205. *See also* **Locks and concurrency**

concurrency and transaction isolation levels 200–204

maximizing concurrency 204

optimistic concurrency 202–203

Cost threshold for parallelism 110

CPU issues

additional resources 122–125

CPU-intensive queries 83–85

CPU pressure 73. *See also* Dynamic Management Views (DMVs); *See also* Performance Monitor (PerfMon); *See also* SQL Trace

CPU-related wait statistics 78–82

high CPU usage, common causes 73–125, 85–121. *See also* Common causes of high CPU usage

investigating CPU pressure 74–85

scheduler queues 82–83

CPU-Z 121

CXPACKET 25

CXPACKET waits 81

D

Database Engine Tuning Advisor (DTA) 165, 174

workload analysis with 175–182

database roles, membership of 334

Data files, disk configuration for 56

Data loss. *See* **Preventing data loss;** *See also* **Recovering lost data**

find the culprit 327–329

default trace 327–329

DBCC SHRINKFILE 303

DBCC SQLPERF(waitstats) 210

DDL Events and Groups 340

Deadlocks 239–274

deadlock graphs 240–251

reading deadlock graphs 251–261

deadlock priority 240

controlling deadlock behavior 273–274

eliminating common types 261–269

accessing objects in different orders 268–269

bookmark lookup deadlock 262–264

cascading constraint deadlocks 266–267

intra-query parallelism deadlocks 267

range scans caused by SERIALIZABLE isolation 264–266

handling to prevent errors 269–273

ADO.NET SqlExceptions in .NET code 272–273

T-SQL TRY...CATCH blocks 270–271

interpreting Trace Flag 1204 output 251–256

interpreting Trace Flag 1222 output 256–259

interpreting XML deadlock graphs 259–261

Lock Monitor 240

Default trace 327

Denali. *See* **SQL Server Denali**

Denormalization 231

Direct Attached Storage (DAS) 60

DAS vs.SAN 60–64

Disk I/O configuration 41–71

common problems 64–70

capacity vs.performance 65–66

incorrect bandwidth using SAN configurations 69–70

incorrect partition alignment 67–68

incorrect workload isolation 66

diagnosing issues 64

disk size vs. disk throughput 43–44, 53–56

RAID levels 45–59

random versus sequential I/O 44–45

workload considerations 56–60

DML triggers 335

Dynamic Management Views (DMVs) 77–86

find active blocking with 210–218

missing index DMVs 175

E

Error 701 159

Error 9002, transaction log full 301

Event notifications 225–227

Extended Events 228–229, 248–251

F

FAILED_VIRTUAL_RESERVE 159

FILESTREAM attribute 172

Forced parameterization in SQL Server 106

Free List Stalls/sec counter 153

Free Pages counter 153

Further assistance 343–349

H

Hardware configuration 41–71

Hints

locking hints 235–238

isolation level hints 235

lock granularity hints 236

lock mode hints 236

Hiring a consultant 349

Hyper-threading and parallelism 113

I

Indexes 165–194. *See also* **Missing indexes**

identifying duplicate 193

identifying unused 191–192

included columns 171–174

index locking options 237

index rebuilds 283–285

index reorganisation 285

index width 174

key column order 167–171

reviewing recommendations 181–182

selection and design 166–174

further details 171

IO_COMPLETION 26

IOmeter 55

Isolation levels

READ COMMITTED 201

READ_COMMITTED_SNAPSHOT 203

READ UNCOMMITTED 201

REPEATABLE READ 202

SERIALIZABLE 202

SNAPSHOT 203

K

KEY locks 198

L

Large Page Allocations (LPA) 149

Latches 205. *See also* **Locks and concurrency**

    LATCH_* 27

    page I/O latch 205

    page latch 205

Lazy Writes/sec counter 153

Lock Escalation event class 219

Lock Monitor 239, 240

Lock Pages in Memory 145, 146–149, 157

    additional references 149

Locks and concurrency 196–205. *See also* **Concurrency and locks**

    latches and latch contention 205

    LCK_* 26

    lock escalation 199–200

    lock modes 196

        exclusive 197

        intent 197–198

        shared 197

        update 197

    lock types 198–199

Log file fragmentation 281

Log files, disk configuration for 57

Log management 307

Log recovery tools 325

Log Sequence Number (LSN) 314

Lost data. *See* **Data loss;** *See* **Recovering lost data;** *See* **Preventing data loss**

M

Managing archiving 293

Max degree of parallelism 111

Max server memory option 144

Memory Grants Outstanding counter 154

Memory Grants Pending counter 155

Memory management 127–163

    32-bit VAS limits 132–141

        AWE 138–139

        -g startup parameter 140–141

        VAS tuning 136–137

    64-bit VAS limits 141–143

        caching behaviour 143

        do not enable AWE 147

        memory configuration options 144–150

        memory pageable, not locked 142

    common problems 156–162

        App Domain marked for unload 158–159

        Error 701 159–160

        OS instability 157–158

        over-provisioned VM 160–161

        paging problems 156–157

        settings for multiple instances 161–162

        SQL Server memory leak myth 156

    memory allocation 128–150

        non-buffer pool allocations 135–136

    memory pressure, diagnosing 150–156

        basic types of 131–132

Memory Manager counter 36

Memory-related DMVs 155–156

MemToLeave (VAS reservation) 135, 140, 142

Methodology 19–40

    defining 20–22

Microsoft Customer Support 343

Min server memory option 144

Missing data, example 312

Missing indexes 165–194

    DMVs 183–187

information in XML showplans 187–190

missing index feature 182–190

on foreign keys 190–191

Multiple named instances 161

N

normalization 231

O

OBJECT locks 198

Ola Hallengren's scripts 287

OLTP system 167

Online index rebuilds 283

Online SQL Server resources 345–349

articles 346

blogs 346–347

forums 347–350

MSDN forums 347–350

SQL Server Central forums 348–350

StackOverFlow 348–349

Optimize for ad hoc workloads 107

OPTIMIZE FOR hint 101

P

PAGEIOLATCH_* 26

PAGELATCH_* 27

Page Life Expectancy counter 152

PAGE locks 198

Page Table Entries 137

Parallelism

cost threshold 110

diagnosing problems 115–116

hyper-threading and 113

max degree of 111

resolving issues 116–117

Performance Analysis of Logs (PAL) tool 31

Performance counters 30–37, 151–155

Performance Monitor (PerfMon) 64, 74–76, 218

PFS, GAM, and SGAM contention 59

Physical Address Extensions (PAE) 138

Plan Cache 38–39

Preventing data loss 329–341

Q

Query performance tuning 39

R

RAID (Redundant Array of Independent Disks) 45–59

RAID 0 47

RAID 1 48–49, 52–53

RAID 5 49–51

RAID 6 50–51

RAID 10 51–52

Random I/O 44

Range locks 264

ReadCommitted isolation level hint 235

ReadCommittedLock isolation level hint 235

ReadUncommitted/Nolock isolation level hint 235

Recompilation options 102

Recovering lost data 313–326

appropriate security model 333–334

change control process 332–333

planning for recovery 330–332

recovering from backup 313–323

restore to a marked transaction 314–321

restore to a point in time 321–323

recovering without a backup 323–326

log recovery tools 325

recovering data from a secondary/replica
database 326

recovering objects from source control 325

Reorganizing and rebuilding indexes 286

RepeatableRead isolation level hint 235

RID locks 198

Rollback cost 240

Rowset provider

impact on Profiler performance 177

Row versioning. *See* Concurrency and locks:
optimistic concurrency

S

security model 333

Sequential I/O 44

Serializable isolation level hint 235

Server Virtualization Validation Program (SVVP)
160

Service Broker 225, 245–247

Signal wait time 78

Snapshot Replication schema change 299

Solid state drives 44

SOS_SCHEDULER_YIELD 26, 81

Source control 325

sp_blocker_pss80 219, 220

SQLIO 55

SQLIOSim 55, 56

SQL Server:Buffer Manager object 36, 151

SQL Server Denali 228

changes to Extended Events 251

SQL Server:Memory Manager object 154–155

SQL Trace 76–77, 220

blocked process report 221–233

SSMS graphical deadlock graph 260

Storage Area Network (SAN) 61–64

and incorrect bandwidth 69–70

DAS vs.SAN 60–64

Stored procedures

database changes through 334

permissions through 335

Striping 47

Sysadmin server role 118

sys.dm_db_missing_index_columns 183

sys.dm_db_missing_index_details 183

sys.dm_db_missing_index_groups 184

sys.dm_db_missing_index_group_stats 184

sys.dm_exec_query_memory_grants 155

sys.dm_exec_requests 212

sys.dm_exec_sessions 212

sys.dm_os_memory_cache_counters 155

sys.dm_os_memory_clerks 155

sys.dm_os_sys_memory 155

sys.dm_os_waiting_tasks 214

sys.dm_os_wait_stats 217

sys.dm_tran_locks 215

T

Target Server Memory (KB) counter 154

tempdb 58–59

THREADPOOL 26

TokenAndPermUserStore 117–120

Total Server Memory (KB) counter 154

Trace Flags 119-125

information on 238

interpreting Trace Flag 1222 output 256-259

Trace Flag 1204 241-243, 251-256

Trace Flag 1205 248

Trace Flag 1211 237

Trace Flag 1222 243, 248

Trace Flag 1224 238

Trace Flag 4136 100

Trace workload

analyzing 179-181

Transaction isolation levels 200. *See also* **Isolation levels**

Transaction logs 275-310

controlling excessive logging 286-287

handling "Transaction Log Full" error 301-303

how they work 276-282

how SQL Server writes to them 278

log truncation 279-280

sizing and growing the log 280-282

lack of log space reuse 287-297

active transactions 289-297

FULL recovery model without log backups 288-289

identifying the active transaction 294-297

long-running transactions 290-297

uncommitted transactions 293-297

other possible causes of log growth 297-301

ACTIVE_BACKUP_OR_RESTORE 300

DATABASE_MIRRORING 300-301

replication 298-299

proper log management 307-308

uncontrolled growth of 282-301

index maintenance operations 283-287

what not to do 304-307

detach database, delete log file 304-305

force log file truncation 305-306

scheduled shrinking of the transaction log 306-307

Triggers 335-341

DDL triggers 340-341

DML triggers 335-340

Troubleshooting methodology 19-40

T-SQL TRY...CATCH blocks 270-271

V

Virtual Address Space (VAS). *See* **Memory management: 32-bit VAS limits**

User mode VAS allocation 134

VAS reservation. *See* MemToLeave (VAS reservation)

VAS tuning. *See* Memory management: 32-bit VAS limits

VirtualAlloc 134, 142

Virtual file statistics 28-30

Virtual log files (VLFs) 279

W

Wait statistics 23-28, 78-82

CMEMTHREAD waits 82

CXPACKET waits 81

Signal wait time 78

SOS_SCHEDULER_YIELD waits 81

Windows logins 334

WMI Provider for Server Events 247-248

Workload isolation 66

Workload trace 176

Write-Ahead Logging (WAL) 276

WRITELOG 26

X

XML Deadlock Graph event 240, 243–245

    interpreting XML deadlock graphs 259–261

XML showplans 175

SQL Server
and .NET Tools
from Red Gate Software

Pricing and information about Red Gate tools are correct at the time of

going to print. For the latest information and pricing on all Red Gate's

tools, visit www.red-gate.com

redgate®

ingeniously simple tools

SQL Compare® Pro $595

Compare and synchronize SQL Server database schemas

↗ Eliminate mistakes migrating database changes from dev, to test, to production

↗ Speed up the deployment of new databse schema updates

↗ Find and fix errors caused by differences between databases

↗ Compare and synchronize within SSMS

> **"Just purchased SQL Compare. With the productivity I'll get out of this tool, it's like buying time."**
> **Robert Sondles** Blueberry Island Media Ltd

SQL Data Compare Pro $595

Compares and synchronizes SQL Server database contents

↗ Save time by automatically comparing and synchronizing your data

↗ Copy lookup data from development databases to staging or production

↗ Quickly fix problems by restoring damaged or missing data to a single row

↗ Compare and synchronize data within SSMS

> **"We use SQL Data Compare daily and it has become an indispensable part of delivering our service to our customers. It has also streamlined our daily update process and cut back literally a good solid hour per day."**
> **George Pantela** GPAnalysis.com

Visit **www.red-gate.com** for a 14-day, free trial

SQL Prompt Pro $295

Write, edit, and explore SQL effortlessly

- ↗ Write SQL smoothly, with code-completion and SQL snippets
- ↗ Reformat SQL to a preferred style
- ↗ Keep databases tidy by finding invalid objects automatically
- ↗ Save time and effort with script summaries, smart object renaming and more

> **"SQL Prompt is hands-down one of the coolest applications I've used. Makes querying/developing so much easier and faster."**
>
> **Jorge Segarra** University Community Hospital

SQL Source Control $295

Connect your existing source control system to SQL Server

- ↗ Bring all the benefits of source control to your database
- ↗ Source control schemas and data within SSMS, not with offline scripts
- ↗ Connect your databases to TFS, SVN, SourceGear Vault, Vault Pro, Mercurial, Perforce, Git, Bazaar, and any source control system with a capable command line
- ↗ Work with shared development databases, or individual copies
- ↗ Track changes to follow who changed what, when, and why
- ↗ Keep teams in sync with easy access to the latest database version
- ↗ View database development history for easy retrieval of specific versions

> **"After using SQL Source Control for several months, I wondered how I got by before. Highly recommended, it has paid for itself several times over"**
>
> **Ben Ashley** Fast Floor

Visit **www.red-gate.com** for a 28-day, free trial

SQL Backup Pro $795

Compress, encrypt, and strengthen SQL Server backups

↗ Compress SQL Server database backups by up to 95% for
  faster, smaller backups

↗ Protect your data with up to 256-bit AES encryption

↗ Strengthen your backups with network resilience to enable
  a fault-tolerant transfer of backups across flaky networks

↗ Control your backup activities through an intuitive interface,
  with powerful job management and an interactive timeline

"SQL Backup is an amazing tool that lets
us manage and monitor our backups in real
time. Red Gate's SQL tools have saved us
so much time and work that I am afraid my
director will decide that we don't need a
DBA anymore!"

Mike Poole Database Administrator, Human Kinetics

Visit **www.red-gate.com** for a 14-day, free trial

SQL Monitor

SQL Server performance monitoring and alerting

↗ Intuitive overviews at global, cluster, machine, SQL Server,
  and database levels for up-to-the-minute performance data

↗ Use SQL Monitor's web UI to keep an eye on server performance
  in real time on desktop machines and mobile devices

↗ Intelligent SQL Server alerts via email and an alert inbox in the
  UI, so you know about problems first

↗ Comprehensive historical data, so you can go back in time to
  identify the source of a problem

↗ Generate reports via the UI or with Red Gate's free SSRS Reporting Pack

↗ View the top 10 expensive queries for an instance or database
  based on CPU usage, duration and reads and writes

↗ PagerDuty integration for phone and SMS alerting

↗ Fast, simple installation and administration

> "Being web based, SQL Monitor is readily
> available to you, wherever you may be on your
> network. You can check on your servers from
> almost any location, via most mobile devices
> that support a web browser."
>
> **Jonathan Allen** Senior DBA, Careers South West Ltd

Visit **www.red-gate.com** for a 14-day, free trial

SQL Virtual Restore $495

Rapidly mount live, fully functional databases direct from backups

↗   Virtually restoring a backup requires significantly less time and space than a regular physical restore

↗   Databases mounted with SQL Virtual Restore are fully functional and support both read/write operations

↗   SQL Virtual Restore is ACID compliant and gives you access to full, transactionally consistent data, with all objects visible and available

↗   Use SQL Virtual Restore to recover objects, verify your backups with DBCC CHECKDB, create a storage-efficient copy of your production database, and more.

> "We find occasions where someone has deleted data accidentally or dropped an index etc., and with SQL Virtual Restore we can mount last night's backup quickly and easily to get access to the data or the original schema. It even works with all our backups being encrypted. This takes any extra load off our production server. SQL Virtual Restore is a great product."
>
> **Brent McCraken** Senior Database Administrator/Architect, Kiwibank Limited

SQL Storage Compress $1,595

Silent data compression to optimize SQL Server storage

↗   Reduce the storage footprint of live SQL Server databases by up to 90% to save on space and hardware costs

↗   Databases compressed with SQL Storage Compress are fully functional

↗   Prevent unauthorized access to your live databases with 256-bit AES encryption

↗   Integrates seamlessly with SQL Server and does not require any configuration changes

Visit **www.red-gate.com** for a 14-day, free trial

SQL Toolbelt $1,995

The essential SQL Server tools for database professionals

You can buy our acclaimed SQL Server tools individually or bundled. Our most popular deal is the SQL Toolbelt: fourteen of our SQL Server tools in a single installer, with **a combined value of $5,930 but an actual price of $1,995**, a saving of 66%.

Fully compatible with SQL Server 2000, 2005, and 2008.

SQL Toolbelt contains:

↗ **SQL Compare Pro**

↗ **SQL Data Compare Pro**

↗ **SQL Source Control**

↗ **SQL Backup Pro**

↗ **SQL Monitor**

↗ **SQL Prompt Pro**

↗ **SQL Data Generator**

↗ **SQL Doc**

↗ **SQL Dependency Tracker**

↗ **SQL Packager**

↗ **SQL Multi Script Unlimited**

↗ **SQL Search**

↗ **SQL Comparison SDK**

↗ **SQL Object Level Recovery Native**

"The SQL Toolbelt provides tools that database developers, as well as DBAs, should not live without."

William Van Orden Senior Database Developer, Lockheed Martin

Visit **www.red-gate.com** for a 14-day, free trial

ANTS Memory Profiler $495

Find memory leaks and optimize memory usage

↗ Find memory leaks within minutes

↗ Jump straight to the heart of the problem with intelligent summary information, filtering options and visualizations

↗ Optimize the memory usage of your C# and VB.NET code

"Freaking sweet! We have a known memory leak that took me about four hours to find using our current tool, so I fired up ANTS Memory Profiler and went at it like I didn't know the leak existed. Not only did I come to the conclusion much faster, but I found another one!"

Aaron Smith IT Manager, R.C. Systems Inc.

ANTS Performance Profiler from $395

Profile your .NET code and boost the performance of your application

↗ Identify performance bottlenecks within minutes

↗ Drill down to slow lines of code thanks to line-level code timings

↗ Boost the performance of your .NET code

↗ Get the most complete picture of your application's performance with integrated SQL and File I/O profiling

"ANTS Performance Profiler took us straight to the specific areas of our code which were the cause of our performance issues."

Terry Phillips Sr Developer, Harley-Davidson Dealer Systems

"Thanks to ANTS Performance Profiler, we were able to discover a performance hit in our serialization of XML that was fixed for a 10x performance increase."

Garret Spargo Product Manager, AFHCAN

Visit **www.red-gate.com** for a 14-day, free trial

.NET Reflector ®   From $35

Browse, compile, analyze and decompile .NET code

↗ View, navigate and search through the class hierarchies of .NET assemblies,
  even if you don't have access to the source code for them

↗ Decompile and analyze .NET assemblies in C#, Visual Basic and IL

↗ Step into decompiled assemblies whilst debugging in Visual Studio,
  with all the debugging techniques you would use on your own code

"One of the most useful, practical debugging tools that I have ever worked with in .NET! It provides complete browsing and debugging features for .NET assemblies, and has clean integration with Visual Studio."
Tom Baker Consultant Software Engineer, EMC Corporation

SmartAssembly ®   from $795

.NET obfuscator and automated error reporting

↗ Obfuscate your .NET code and protect your IP

↗ Let your end-users report errors in your software with one click

↗ Receive a comprehensive report containing a stack trace and values of all the local variables

↗ Identify the most recurrent bugs and prioritize fixing those first

↗ Gather feature usage data to understand how your software is being used
  and make better product development decisions

"I've deployed Automated Error Reporting now for one release and I'm already seeing the benefits. I can fix bugs which might never have got my attention before. I really like it a lot!"
Stefal Koell MVP

Visit **www.red-gate.com** for a 14-day, free trial

Performance Tuning with SQL Server Dynamic Management Views
Louis Davidson and Tim Ford

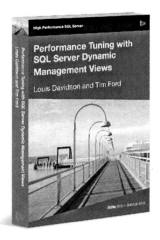

This is the book that will de-mystify the process of using Dynamic Management Views to collect the information you need to troubleshoot SQL Server problems. It will highlight the core techniques and "patterns" that you need to master, and will provide a core set of scripts that you can use and adapt for your own requirements.

ISBN: 978-1-906434-47-2
Published: October 2010

Defensive Database Programming
Alex Kuznetsov

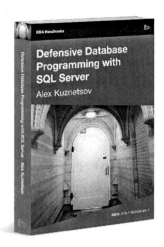

Inside this book, you will find dozens of practical, defensive programming techniques that will improve the quality of your T-SQL code and increase its resilience and robustness.

ISBN: 978-1-906434-49-6
Published: June 2010

Brad's Sure Guide to
SQL Server Maintenance Plans
Brad McGehee

Brad's Sure Guide to Maintenance Plans shows you how to use the Maintenance Plan Wizard and Designer to configure and schedule eleven core database maintenance tasks, ranging from integrity checks, to database backups, to index reorganizations and rebuilds.

ISBN: 78-1-906434-34-2

Published: December 2009

The Red Gate Guide to SQL Server
Team-based Development
Phil Factor, Grant Fritchey, Alex Kuznetsov,
and Mladen Prajdić

This book shows how to use of mixture of home-grown scripts, native SQL Server tools, and tools from the Red Gate SQL Toolbelt, to successfully develop database applications in a team environment, and make database development as similar as possible to "normal" development.

ISBN: 978-1-906434-59-5

Published: November 2010

CPSIA information can be obtained at www.ICGtesting.com
Printed in the USA
BVOW080307201011
274124BV00002B/16/P